POISON PENMANSHIP
The Gentle Art of Muckraking

JESSICA MITFORD

Preface by
JANE SMILEY

NEW YORK REVIEW BOOKS

New York

THIS IS A NEW YORK REVIEW BOOK
PUBLISHED BY THE NEW YORK REVIEW OF BOOKS
435 Hudson Street, New York, NY 10014
www.nyrb.com

Library of Congress Cataloging-in-Publication Data
Mitford, Jessica, 1917–1996.
 Poison penmanship : the gentle art of muckraking / by Jessica Mitford ; preface by Jane Smiley.
    p. cm.
ISBN 978-1-59017-355-8 (alk. paper)
1. Journalism. I. Title.
PN4726.M55 2010
070.92—dc22

                        2009050089

ISBN 978-1-59017-355-8

Printed in the United States of America on acid-free paper.
10 9 8 7 6 5 4 3 2 1

CONTENTS

PREFACE

If there is a more forthright, good-natured, and witty American investigative journalist than Jessica Mitford, I don't know who it would be. In the course of a career that spanned almost forty years, Mitford wrote eleven books (including a volume of letters collected after her death). Carl Bernstein, in an afterword to an earlier edition of *Poison Penmanship*, calls her "an amateur," but she was hardly inexperienced as either a reader or a writer, as her many hilarious and insightful letters show. In fact, she was self-educated, like the great majority of women writers once were (including Jane Austen and Virginia Woolf)—haphazardly but effectively.

Poison Penmanship is conceived not only as a collection of occasional pieces but, since Mitford enjoyed the teaching posts she held once she had established herself as a journalist, also as a how-to book for aspiring muckrakers. The lengthy introduction describes how she got started writing and gives tips—how to gather background information, how to interview (meaning how to get antagonistic interviewees to betray themselves), how to find information not available to the general public, how to recognize a blind alley, and how to organize and write the article. She also discusses potential consequences of a career in muck-raking. In the section labeled "Libel," she writes, "I have often been asked whether I have been sued for libel in the course of my writing career. The answer is no, alas." Mitford was careful to check her facts.

Mitford unabashedly wrote for money, and part of her charm in this volume is in the afterword to each piece, in which she describes how she came to the subject and what the challenges were—the challenges of writing about a silly upscale spa seem to have been greater than the challenges of writing about a surge in the rate of syphilis infection among teenagers of the 1960s and the refusal of NBC to air two fairly anodyne but explicit episodes of popular programs on the subject, even though the government begged the network to do so ("Not in the best interests of the viewing public," said the network). Mitford's specific argument evolves into a condemnation of the bland commerciality of network TV. One wonders what she would have made of *Jon and Kate Plus Eight* or *Fear Factor*.

Above all things, Mitford liked a worthy opponent, and her weapons of choice were factual accuracy and a tone of amazement. Perhaps the best piece in here is "Let Us Now Praise Famous Writers," in which she reveals the anatomy of the scam that was the Famous Writers School, a correspondence course that was advertised through magazines then sold through coercive follow-up visits by "representatives." The advertising materials promised personal attention to a student's manuscripts by such literary luminaries as the head of Random House, Bennett Cerf, as well as popular writers, all of whom lent their names to the advertising campaign and invested in the school, although none engaged with the "students." In this piece, Miss Mitford is a bit less amused, and the result was suitable embarrassment all around.

With her customary honesty, Mitford raises the question of whether muckraking journalism is effective or not at changing the world for the better. She mentions Lincoln Steffens (who eventually decided that it wasn't) and Ralph Nader (who is still at it), as well as Robert Scheer (then young, who is also still at it). She is honest about the immediate results of her own exposés—some worked better than others. From our vantage point in a time when muck is being raked (and flung) vehemently and constantly twenty-four hours a day, the question of effectiveness is overwhelmed by the question of whether any person in America with access to the media remains shockable or persuadable. In this regard, Mitford was a toiler in the muck who cared about facts and believed in the idea that her fellow citizens were generally honest and expected the same of business and government. She might have been daunted by the way that lies and spin have taken over our public discourse. But given her habit, in *Poison Penmanship*, of being thrilled by a good fight, I doubt it.

—JANE SMILEY

POISON PENMANSHIP

To
Rita Wiggins and Marge Frantz
with deep gratitude
for their inestimable help

INTRODUCTION

In his essay "Stop the Press, I Want to Get On," Nicholas Toma-lin, a talented and versatile English journalist, wrote: "The only qualities essential for real success in journalism are ratlike cunning, a plausible manner, and a little literary ability." He added, "The capacity to steal other people's ideas and phrases—that one about ratlike cunning was invented by my colleague Murray Sayre —is also invaluable."

In this collection I have tried to reconstruct my own efforts, over a twenty-year period, to acquire these qualities and to demonstrate, through one person's experience, the development of investigative techniques. In the comment accompanying each piece or group of pieces, I have sought to convey something of the story-behind-the-story: how I stumbled onto the particular subject; the joys and sorrows of research, the lucky breaks and mistakes, things overlooked through sheer ineptitude for which one could kick oneself; difficulties of getting published; and in some cases the afterglow of satisfaction (how the Famous Writers went bankrupt) or the aftermath of dissatisfaction (see comment on "My Short and Happy Life as a Distinguished Professor"). And now, thinking it all over, I would say there are two important omissions from Tomalin's otherwise excellent list of essential qualities: plodding determination, and an appetite for tracking and destroying the enemy.

As even muckrakers take an occasional day off for other pursuits, I have sneaked in some pieces that do not belong to this category because they illustrate some of the problems encountered in preparing articles for publication: "The Best of Frenemies," "Proceed with Caution," and "Egyptomania."

I first began to think of myself as a muckraker when *Time*, commenting in its press section on the Famous Writers School Fracas (see page 148), called me "Queen of the Muckrakers." I rushed to the dictionary to find out what I was queen of, and discovered that "muckraker" was originally a pejorative coined by President Theodore Roosevelt to describe journalists like Lincoln Steffens and Ida Tarbell, who in his view had gone too far in exposing corruption in government and corporate enterprise. Thus the *Oxford English Dictionary* says "muckrake . . . is often made to refer generally . . . to a depraved interest in what is morally 'unsavoury' or scandalous." (I fear that does rather describe me.) In the *OED* supplement of 1933, "muckraker" has come up in the world a little bit and is now defined as "one who seeks out and publishes scandals and the like about prominent people." And by 1950 additional respectability is conferred by *Webster's New International Dictionary*, defining "muckrake" as "To seek for, expose, or charge, esp. habitually, corruption, real or alleged, on the part of public men and corporations."

As a consequence of my *Time*-bestowed sovereignty, I was invited to teach a course in muckraking at San Jose State University, and later at Yale. These were workshop sessions in which my students undertook actual investigations of "corruption real or alleged" in their college or community. Together we explored techniques of research, how to conduct interviews, how to put the results together in readable form. Some of our findings:

———————————

CHOICE OF SUBJECT is of cardinal importance, as one does by far one's best work when besotted by and absorbed in the matter at hand. After the publication of *The American Way of Death* (a study of the funeral industry), I got hundreds of letters suggesting other infamous rackets that should be investigated and exposed. I discerned a pattern to these letters—all from rightly disgruntled victims—and began to file them by categories. Surprisingly, complaints about hearing aids led the field. These cheaply mass produced, inefficient little gadgets, sold at extortionate prices to desperate people, are doubtless a source of unconscionable profits to a predatory industry and of hardship to countless buyers; but somehow, although there may well be need for such an exposé, I could not warm up to hearing aids as a subject for the kind of thorough, intensive, long-range research that would be needed to do an effective job.

In my Yale class, each student (or group of students if they preferred to work in teams) chose his or her own subject to investigate. Those who tackled hot issues on campus, such as violations of academic freedom, or failure to implement affirmative-action hiring policies, turned in some excellent work; but the lad who decided to investigate "waste in the Yale dining halls" was predictably unable to make much of this trivial topic.

GATHERING BACKGROUND INFORMATION. The goal is to know, if possible, *more* about your subject than the target of the investigation does. To this end, I soak up books and articles on the subject, type out relevant passages, and accumulate a store of knowledge before seeking an interview with said target.

Obvious reference sources are the *Readers' Guide to Periodical Literature, The New York Times Index,* and back copies of news weeklies, all easily available in any library. Harder to come by are small provincial newspapers which may be a prime source for the light they shed on local issues not covered by wire services or major metropolitan dailies. These can often be had on microfilm through the inter-library loan system. I learned about this invalu-

able service from a library school student who was helping with
the research for *A Fine Old Conflict,* memoirs of my subversive
life during the McCarthy era. I was writing a chapter about the
case of Willie McGee, a black man falsely accused of rape in
Mississippi, which had received only perfunctory attention in *The
New York Times* and the news weeklies. The student procured the
Jackson, Mississippi, *Daily News* for a three-month period in
1951, the only charge a fee for postage. This newspaper, its blood-
thirsty coverage of McGee's execution, its virulent editorials
echoing the authentic voice of the Ku Klux Klan, re-created as
nothing else could the violent and pervasive racism in the deep
South of those days.

PICKING OTHER PEOPLE'S BRAINS is an art worth
cultivating. Frequently an investigation will lead you into some
specialized field with which you are unfamiliar. This is the
time to consult an expert, assuming you can find one who is
sufficiently interested in you or your subject to give advice
gratis. Rather than trying to unravel some tricky point of law
yourself, ask a lawyer. If you need to understand corporate
records, get an accountant to help. Technical literature in most
fields is written (no doubt deliberately) so as to be unintell-
igible to the layman, and there is grave danger that in trying to
decipher it without expert help you will make some ghastly mistakes upon which the professionals will gleefully leap once your
piece is published.

I have found experts to be amazingly generous with their time
—they actually seem to like the chance to expound their knowledge to us ignorami, although I recall one rather disappointing
experience: wanting to know what 6 percent of a million is, I
called the Department of Higher Mathematics at the University of
California. The person who answered said, "Oh, it's six hundred.
No, it's six thousand . . . no, wait a minute, I think it's sixty
thousand. Could you call back after lunch?" I have long since
forgotten the definitive, post-lunch answer. But thereafter I relied

on a thirteen-year-old friend in junior high school, who knows such things off the top of his head.

Medical jargon is particularly confusing. I remember a horrifying moment in my doctor's office when the doctor was called out of the room and I took a surreptitious peek at my file. "Head: Negative," he had written. When he returned I confronted him with this unkind diagnosis. He said stiffly that it was not as bad as I supposed and that in the future I should refrain from reading my file which was confidential and for his use only.*

For a chapter in *Kind and Usual Punishment: The Prison Business*, I was exploring the use of convict populations by the giant drug companies as subjects for experimental research, and happened upon a copy of the *California Department of Corrections' Annual Research Review* in which some thirty medical experiments are summarized in brief paragraphs. To me, these read like pure gibberish, so I sought out Dr. Sheldon Margen, chairman of the Department of Nutritional Sciences at the University of California. He proved to be not only a good translator but excellent copy, exploding with fury as he examined the *Review:* "God, that kills me!" "Wow!"

A sample Margen translation: the study of "Cleocin HFC levels," for which "10 healthy normal volunteers" were selected, to "determine antibiotic levels in various tissues and/or fluids." Each subject gets "150 mg. of Cleocin q.i.d." following which he will be relieved of "sebum, 2–4 ml.; sweat, 4–5 ml.; semen, amount of normal ejaculation; and muscle tissue, 1 gm. . . ." As Dr. Margen put it: "Here's what happens to these ten guys. First they make them masturbate to collect semen. Then they cut into the arm or go through the flesh to get the gram of muscle tissue. That's the horrific part; this procedure is cockeyed, it would never be approved for student-subjects." Had I tried to puzzle this out myself, with the aid of a medical dictionary and scholarly articles on the

---

* He was wrong, of course; under California law medical records are the property of the patient, and if you have the written consent of the patient, medical and hospital files must be made available for copying.

subject, it might have taken me weeks and I should never have had the benefit of Dr. Margen's graphic comments.

TRADE MAGAZINES. I cannot overemphasize the pleasure and profit to be derived from reading trade journals and house organs in the field of your investigation. It is important, however, to distinguish between publications intended for public consumption and those that are "eyes only," privately circulated to the trade. For example, the *Journal of the American Medical Association* (*JAMA*) and the *American Bar Association Journal* are well-reputed, widely known organs of their respective professions, their contents often the basis of press releases and news stories about medical advances or new legal breakthroughs. There is little muck to be raked in these journals, as they serve essentially a public relations purpose for their sponsors, projecting them as conscientious, upright professionals whose only concern is patient/client welfare.

If you were going after doctors, a more rewarding starting point would be *Medical Economics,* a publication that most laymen have never heard of but that is delivered free to every member of the A.M.A. In its glossy pages you will find many a crass and wonderfully quotable appeal to the avarice of the practitioners of the healing arts. Lawyers? Try such in-house publications as the *American Trial Lawyers Association Journal,* in which the nation's top ambulance chasers exchange tips on how it is done. If you are, like most of us, a patient or a client, you will get many a bitter laugh out of these, as the whole point of the articles and editorials is how to diddle you out of more money.

The public posture of undertakers can readily be ascertained by reading their ads in the metropolitan dailies, generally on the obituary page, stressing dignity, refinement, professional competence, sincerity. Ah, but their private face! When preparing *The American Way of Death,* I first began to appreciate the enormous value of trade publications. "Without whom this book could never have been written," as authors are wont to say in dedications, is certainly true of *Casket & Sunnyside, Mortuary Management*, and —my favorite title—*Concept: The Journal of Creative Ideas for Cemeteries.* Here were undertakers and "cemeterians" talking to *each other*, in the secure belief that no prying outsider would ever have access to their inner councils.

But how to lay hands on such magazines? They are not to be found in public or university libraries, and must be obtained by subscription. Although a simple request, accompanied by a check, may bring results (for these publishers are, like others, interested in expanding their circulation), you cannot always count on it. Paranoia tends to reign in some of these circles, a pervasive fear of the word getting out via a nosy journalist. You may have to spend much time and effort cajoling fringe types—backsliders in your field of investigation who are sympathetic to your viewpoint—to supply the coveted publications.

An example: When researching *Kind and Usual Punishment*, I kept thinking that lurking somewhere in this wide land must be an equivalent for the prison administrators of *Casket & Sunnyside*—a frank and explicit interchange of views and news by and for prison wardens. Finally I found a clue to the existence of such a publication, contained in a stuffy, almost unreadable sociological magazine called *American Journal of Correction*, official journal of prisondom and counterpart for the Correction crowd of *JAMA* or the *ABA Journal*. Leafing through this, I came across a sort of gossip column headed "News from the Affiliated Organizations." Seeing my own name in there, I read more closely:

WARDENS TALK ABOUT HOSTILE NEWS REPORTING

G. Norton Jameson, editor of *The Grapevine*, mimeographed monthly of the American Association of Wardens and Superintendents, in its November 29 issue wrote about an interesting contrast between words spoken by Warden Lash of the Indiana State Penitentiary and Jessica Mitford. . . .

The article went on to say, "Miss Mitford is noted for her caustic pen. Her kind of reporter is one of the realities of life in these troubled times. . . ."

The Grapevine, I felt sure, was the publication I was looking for. At the time, an undergraduate named Kathy Mill was helping me with research, and together we pondered how to find out the address of *The Grapevine,* and how to get a year's back issues. I telephoned around the country to my undercover collaborators, disaffected workers in various Departments of Correction, and eventually one of these mailed me a copy of *The Grapevine.* Step one was completed; we now had the address, a box number in Sioux Falls. I suggested to Kathy that she concoct a letter to the editor saying she was a graduate student in the Criminology School at the University of California (then under severe attack by the law-and-order people for being too radical), that she was unhappy with the content of the instruction, and she wanted to get the viewpoint of the wardens as set forth in *The Grapevine.* She should sign a man's name, I said, as Corrections is by and large a man's world. She produced the letter, signed "Karl Mill." I thought it masterly for the purpose, but fearing that "Karl" had a slightly subversive ring, I changed that to "Kenneth" and sent it off.

In the course of time twelve mint copies of *The Grapevine* appeared on Kathy's doorstep. They proved to be just what I had hoped for, a gold mine of material affording rare glimpses into the Correctional mind: exchanges of opinion on how to circumvent court rulings favorable to prisoners' rights without getting caught, how to starve out convict sit-down strikers, how to avoid investigation of prison conditions by the state legislature: "Warden Frank A. Eyman of Arizona State Prison revealed that he had refused three black legislators admittance beyond his office to meet with black prisoners last year. They stormed out of his office in a rage, he said. . . . 'I'll make Attica look like a picnic,' the warden said today."

I spent the afternoon underlining passages for quotation in the book. On the last page of the final issue, I came across this:

The following letter may be helpful in dispelling the idea that not much can be learned at the college level concerning the operation of prisons. Real intelligence is where you find it. Here is a young man who sees much farther than many and questions the soundness of the college courses. Now he just could be right and some day he might make a "top notch" prison administrator.

Dear Mr. Jameson,

As a graduate student in criminology at the University of California at Berkeley I was very impressed with a copy of your publication, "The Grapevine," which I ran across here at school. I have long felt that my education here has been jammed into a liberal mold of propaganda. I see your publication as a credible news source of our profession undistorted by the rampant irresponsible and unrealistic biases of the media and campus liberals. Your publication offers the *real* current news. After all, as prison staff members you are the people who know what is really going on in our prisons. I am tired of reading the sentimental phantasies of reporters.

Our library does not receive your publication. How can I obtain the issues of the past year? I would be delighted to subscribe and to pay for a year's back issues if available. Also, perhaps there is a local organization here that would have your newsletter on file. I look forward to hearing from you. Thank you for your work.

Sincerely,
Kenneth Mill

I N T E R V I E W I N G is where the fun really begins, and where you may uncover information that is accessible in no other way. There may be some delightful surprises in store as you pursue your quarry. Over the years, I have found through trial and sometimes painful error that the following methods are useful.

The individuals to be interviewed will generally fall into two categories: Friendly Witnesses, those who are sympathetic to your point of view, such as the victim of a racket you are investigating, or an expert who is clarifying for you technical matters within his field of knowledge; and Unfriendlies, whose interests may be threatened by your investigation and who therefore will be prone to conceal rather than reveal the information you are seeking.

While your approach to each of these will differ, some general rules hold good for *all* interviews. Prepare your approach as a lawyer would for an important cross-examination. Take time to think through exactly what it is that you want to learn from the interview; I write out and number in order the questions I intend to ask. That way I can number the answer, keyed to the number of the question, without interrupting the flow of conversation, and if the sequence is disturbed (which it probably will be, in the course of the interchange), I have no problem reconstructing the Q. and A. as they occurred. Naturally other questions may arise that I had not foreseen, but I will still have my own outline as a guide to the absolute essentials.

Immediately after the interview, I type up the Q.s and A.s before my notes get cold. If, in the course of doing this, I discover that I have missed something, or another question occurs to me, I call up the person immediately while the subject is still freshly in mind.

In the case of the Friendly Witness, it often helps to send him a typescript of the interview for correction or elaboration. I did this to good effect after interviews with defense lawyers from whom I was seeking information about the conspiracy law for *The Trial of Dr. Spock*, and with Dr. Margen and other physicians who revealed the nature of drug experiments on prisoners for *Kind and Usual Punishment*. In each case the expert whom I had consulted not only saved me from egregious error but in correcting my transcription of the interview enriched and strengthened the points to be made.

For Unfriendly Witnesses—which in my experience have included undertakers, prosecutors, prison administrators, Famous Writers—I list the questions in graduated form from Kind to

Cruel. Kind questions are designed to lull your quarry into a conversational mood: "How did you first get interested in funeral directing as a career?" "Could you suggest any reading material that might help me to understand more about problems of Corrections?" and so on. By the time you get to the Cruel questions— "What is the wholesale cost of your casket retailing for three thousand dollars?" "How do you justify censoring a prisoner's correspondence with his lawyer in violation of the California law?"—your interlocutor will find it hard to duck and may blurt out a quotable nugget.

While some potentially Unfriendly Witnesses are more or less bound to grant interviews because they are public officials, or industry spokesmen, there are others—corporate executives, presidents of television networks, prosecutors—who will refuse, and routinely refer the inquiring reporter to their public relations departments. Occasionally it may be possible to break through this reticence. When I was doing research for *The Trial of Dr. Spock,* I chanced upon a most enlightening exchange with just such a witness.

Having interviewed most of the Friendly Witnesses (defense lawyers and defendants) and learned from them the circumstances leading up to the indictment of Spock and four others on charges of "conspiring to aid, counsel and abet" draft resisters, I was anxious to confront the prosecutors and hear their version. But my legal friends assured me that this would be impossible— "The prosecutors won't talk to you, why should they? They'll say they can't comment on a pending case." Nevertheless I called up the Justice Department whose press chief, Cliff Sessions, told me substantially the same thing: "We can mail you copies of our briefs and press handouts," he said, "but you won't be able to talk to the prosecutors while the case is in court." I was going to be in Washington anyway, I said, so I would drop round to his office to pick up the material.

I arrived in Washington on the day Martin Luther King, Jr., was assassinated, and that night the town went up in flames. There

were burning buildings a block from the house where I was staying with friends. In the morning I picked my way through the
rubble to the Justice Department where I inquired for Cliff Sessions. His secretary told me he had flown to Memphis at 6 a.m.
with the Attorney General. "Oh—well, he said *something* about
me being able to see the Spock trial prosecutors," I said (which
was, after all, perfectly true). She answered that the prosecutors
were there, and phoned down to John Van de Kamp, chief of the
special unit set up to prosecute draft law violators. He readily
agreed to see me—in fact seemed glad of the opportunity to chat.
I gathered he was feeling a bit bored and neglected; the eyes of the
nation were on the King tragedy, his colleagues were off investigating the ghetto uprisings, nobody was interested in draft prose-
cutions that day.

We talked about some of his earlier experiences in prosecutorial
work—at one point, in Los Angeles, he had been involved in the
prosecution of some undertakers for antitrust violations and in
this connection had found *The American Way of Death* a useful
source of information. "How lovely! You're a fan, then." Yes,
indeed. We were soon on thoroughly cozy terms and I steered
cautiously into the matter at hand. Had he read Dr. Spock's famous baby book? Yes, and thought it was very good. Was he a
Spock-raised baby? No, he was born a few years too soon.

Now to the point: "Who ordered the prosecution, and why?
Did L.B.J. initiate it?" Van de Kamp explained: There had been a
recent altercation between the Justice Department and General
Hershey (then head of Selective Service), who had just been
publicly rebuked by the Department for overstepping his authority
in sending an injudicious letter to the 4,081 local draft boards.
"The prosecution of these five came about as a result of our flap
with Hershey. It was thought to be a good way out—it was done
to provide a graceful way out for General Hershey." "What made
you pick out Dr. Spock and his four co-defendants from the tens
of thousands protesting the draft?" I asked. "Because of their
names and personalities," answered Van de Kamp. "We managed

to subpoena a large amount of television newsreel footage of their activities. We wouldn't have indicted them except for the fact there was so much evidence available on film. They made no great secret of what they were doing."

So that was it: Dr. Spock and the others were offered up in unabashed response to political pressure, as a sacrificial offering to placate an irascible old man who had become an embarrassment to the Administration. And the sole evidence of their "conspiracy" was contained in newsreels of press conferences and protest rallies that took place in a blaze of television publicity. The defense had suspected such grubby machinations, but confirmation from the chief prosecutor was an unexpected bonanza.

A good example of how *not* to conduct an interview was furnished by one of my Yale students, a seventeen-year-old freshman. He was investigating a publication called *Who's Who in American High Schools,* sold to proud parents of the listed high-school seniors for $16.95 a copy. The volume looks something like a telephone directory and the purchaser may need a magnifying glass to find the distinguished scholar's name, followed by a reference to the accomplishment that merited his or her inclusion as: "Smith, Susan, chr. ldr." My student had done an assiduous and imaginative job of preliminary research: he had consulted reference librarians who attested to the book's worthlessness; he had turned up several dissatisfied purchasers of *Who's Who in American High Schools.*

He had arrived at the stage in his investigation where he was ready to call the publisher, who lived in Illinois, and attempt to interview him by telephone. I suggested that he should start off with some general questions about reference books: their usefulness to researchers, the number of libraries that carry *Who's Who in American High Schools.*

We listed half a dozen Kind questions along these lines before proceeding to the Cruels: "Have you ever been sued by the Marquis people for breach of their trademark of the title *'Who's Who'*?" "How much profit do you realize from each sale to a high-school senior?" "Do you make many multiple sales for the same honoree—one for Auntie, one for Grandma?"

But somehow when my student had the publisher on the line he got flustered and, skipping over the first series of questions, waded precipitately into the Cruel ones. "Well, I don't think I want to discuss these matters on the telephone," the publisher said mildly. "Oh, so you won't talk?" said the student belligerently, to which the publisher replied, "That's right, I'm hanging up the phone." Which he did, leaving my poor student bristling with impotent indignation.

There came a time when I regretted having imparted this particular secret of my trade. When *A Fine Old Conflict* was published, Knopf sent me on a publicity tour of various cities including Boston, where one of my favorite Yale students, now graduated, had a job on the *Globe*. He managed to wangle an assignment to interview me for the "Living" section, and came up to meet me in my room in the Ritz-Carlton hotel. I was delighted to see him all grown up and a working journalist; there was much gossip and giggling over the old days at Yale—only a year before, but it seemed to him like a lifetime.

"Actually, knowing you as well as I do, I could write up this interview without even talking to you," he said. "But I suppose I should ask a few questions." He pulled out his notebook. How are you enjoying the tour? he asked. Which cities have you visited so far? How is the book selling? And then: "Oh, by the way, somebody once told me that one should list one's questions in order from Kind to Cruel, so here comes the Cruel one: How does a person of your alleged radical persuasion square her conscience living it up in this super-posh hotel?" Covered with confusion, I hedged and glugged, finally managing to get out the lame response "Well, my publisher is paying for it."

L U C K. In my experience luck has always figured large, so often have I accidentally chanced upon invaluable slivers of information volunteered by informants who happened to know something about my subject.

This was especially true while I was writing *The American Way of Death*; it seemed that countless people wanted to get into this strange act with their own horror stories. One such shocker: a friend told me about making arrangements for her brother-in-law's funeral. She had steadfastly insisted on the cheapest redwood coffin available, but the undertaker said the brother-in-law was too tall to fit into it, she would have to take a more expensive one. When she objected, he said, "Oh, all right, we'll use the redwood, but we'll have to cut off his feet." This grisly little anecdote, which came my way just as the book was going to press, was eventually seized on by reviewers as one of the more telling examples of funeral salesmanship.

Another incident that illustrates the luck factor: I was curious to know what happens about funeral arrangements in the event of mass disaster, such as plane crashes in remote mountain areas. Do competing undertakers from nearby communities converge upon the scene in a wild scramble for the business? What would typical costs be, and who pays—the airline or the next of kin? Questions like these, I thought, could best be answered by a lawyer who, like the undertaker, makes his living out of such tragedies: one who specializes in personal injury cases. I called up Melvin Belli, San Francisco's best-known practitioner in this line (nicknamed by the press "King of Torts"), and explained in detail what I was after.

Belli, never averse to publicity, readily gave me an appointment. I arrived promptly—and sat for five hours in his reception room while a parade of the lame, halt, and blind, some on crutches, some in wheelchairs, wearing surgical collars or plaster casts, filed past me into his inner office. By the time Belli came out, I was steaming with rage at being kept waiting for all that time, the more so when he admitted he actually had no information on the subject of my visit. Perhaps to mollify me, he said he did have an old trial transcript that might be of interest, and he sprinted up a huge ceiling-high ladder to fetch it down from a top shelf. The transcript (which had nothing whatsoever to do with plane crashes) proved to be a gem of rare fascination: a lawsuit brought against an undertaker charging negligence and fraud for his failure to properly embalm the plaintiff's ninety-nine-year-old mother. The Q. and A. examination of the plaintiff by Mr. Belli made for one of the most bizarre, and successful, passages in *The American Way of Death:* although in the excitement of this discovery I forgot all about the plane crash possibilities and never did follow through on this.

BLIND ALLEYS. The converse of luck is blind alleys. Lest it appear from the comments in this collection that efficient investigation follows a straight and easily traversed path, that normally everything comes clattering neatly into place, I should say that I have come to expect blind alleys as a major natural hazard of investigating. Looking over old notebooks, full of "Possible Sources," and lists of "Things to Do," I see that I could fill a volume with accounts of endless days laboriously spent pursuing false leads—which would be depressing to write about and tedious to read. I have found, however, that tenacity does usually pay off in the end, and that frequently an apparent *cul de sac* will magically open up into a broad highway that makes the excursion all worthwhile.

ORGANIZATION—all-important; here is where the article does or does not come together. You now have a thick notebook full of interviews, plus your typed versions; a flock of papers with details of other research, manuals, financial reports, newspaper clippings overflowing your desk, or kitchen table, or both. How to put it all together in readable fashion?

One technique I have found useful in the early stages of an inquiry is to write letters to friends about what I am doing. In that way I perforce start editing the material for fear my correspondent's eyes will glaze over with boredom if I put in everything I have learned. Also, one's style is bound to be more relaxed than it will be at the dread moment when one writes "page 1" on a manuscript for an editor.

When preparing *Kind and Usual Punishment*, I went to a five-day conference of the American Correctional Association in Miami and filled up several notebooks during the many sessions I attended. Each night I wrote to a friend in California, drawing on my notes to give what I saw as the highlights of the meetings. These letters became the basis for that chapter in the book. Similarly, during the Spock trial I attended court for four weeks, took down what amounted to a longhand transcript of the proceedings, dashed back to the hotel, and wrote a seven- or eight-page single-spaced letter to my husband telling what had happened that day. Eventually I boiled these down to about 110 pages in my book about the trial.

Having reached this point, one is, of course, only at the beginning of one's troubles; you have the letters (or carbon copies, if you remembered to insert the carbon paper) and all the other research paraphernalia, but you still have the problem of where and how to start and finish, plus what goes in the middle and in what order. With luck, the subject will suggest the form (see comments on "You-All and Non-You-All" and "Checks and Balances at the Sign of the Dove").

Sometimes it helps to draft in haphazard order the most striking, and hence the easiest, sections of the work in progress. At least this is fairly pleasurable; you can juggle these fragments around later, determine the best sequence, string them together with other material, rewrite them as needed. In the course of this a good beginning paragraph may occur to you; good endings are in my opinion far harder, and your editor will not be pleased if you give up the struggle and simply write (as I have done on occasion) THE END, hoping he will not notice your failure to construct an elegant conclusion and a chic final sentence—what a journalist friend of mine calls a "socko ending." Nor will he welcome a dreary summation of what went before. I can offer no useful guidelines here, as each piece of work will present its own unique problem. One can only hope the solution will occur in a sudden blinding flash of insight.

S T Y L E. Most textbooks on writing skirt around this knotty problem and caution against reaching to achieve "style"—be yourself, be natural, they seem to say. In a way I see what they are driving at, yet I am not totally convinced; I should have welcomed a splash of style (and did welcome it, when it occurred) in the student papers I read at San Jose and Yale. Many an important message in book or article is lost, founders on *lack* of style; unreadable, nobody has read it. Thus a conscious effort to foster style may not be amiss.

Of the many texts on the writer's craft, I recommend the following as pleasurable and amusing reading from which I, for one, have learned a great deal about the cultivation of style:

The Art of Writing, by Sir Arthur Quiller-Couch, the anthologist who compiled the *Oxford Book of English Verse. The Art of Writing* is a collection of his lectures delivered at Cambridge in 1913–14—in itself a poignant thought; how many of his adoring and gifted students (as I imagine them) perished shortly thereafter in the First World War, never to put into practice his cogent teachings? The lectures, as Sir Arthur makes clear in his "Inaugural," were a complete departure from the dry dronings-on of pedagogues, standard fare served up to students in those days. I detect that Sir Arthur had deliberately set out to be something of an iconoclast who would disrupt the calm and even flow of traditional academic instruction. He combines erudition and informality, depth and humor, in the most entertaining fashion. To cite just one sample passage that struck home to me: "Whenever you feel an impulse to perpetrate a piece of exceptionally fine writing, obey it—whole-heartedly—and delete it before sending your manuscript to press. *Murder your darlings.*" A marvelous piece of advice; thanks to Sir A. Q.-C., my wastepaper basket is a veritable

Herod's graveyard of slaughtered innocents. (Editor: Please delete last sentence.)

The Elements of Style, by William Strunk, Jr., and E. B. White, which first appeared in 1959, is now a standard high-school text; hence older readers may think it beneath their dignity to consult it. If so, they will be missing a rare treat and much valuable instruction. I only wish I had had access to this book when I first started writing; I could have avoided many a stylistic blunder (see comment on "Trial by Headline"). The last chapter, "An Approach to Style," is particularly rewarding.

On Writing Well, by William Zinsser. This book, which grew out of a course that Mr. Zinsser teaches at Yale, also appears at first glance to be rather elementary. Yet it is full of excellent advice that any writer, whether beginner or professional, would do well to absorb; see, for example, Zinsser's chapters on "The Lead" and "The Ending," and his delightful comments on humor as the secret weapon of the nonfiction writer.

In addition to these texts there are a few reference books that I use as crutches or mind-jolters, consulting them constantly when struggling with some particularly difficult and elusive passage: *Roget's International Thesaurus*, Fowler's *Modern English Usage*, and *Bartlett's Familiar Quotations*. The last two can also be great time-wasters, as one can easily get sidetracked into reading all sorts of interesting passages having nothing to do with the work at hand; but wasting time is also part of the writer's lot, since nobody can be expected to grind out word after word, sentence after sentence, without a bit of relief.

E D I T I N G. There are two stages: (1) your own editing, a continuous process until you are finally satisfied that you have organized, revised, pruned, polished your work to the limit of your ability and are ready to consign it to the uncertain mercies of book or magazine publisher; (2) professional editing by the latter.

In the first stage, I rely heavily on the advice and criticism of friends who are good enough to read what I am doing and who give opinions on everything, ranging from the general thrust of the piece to faults of grammar and syntax. These amateur editors include my family, students, neighbors, the thirteen-year-old junior-high math wiz. Seldom has any one of them failed to come up with some valuable suggestion. On one occasion, when *Kind and Usual Punishment* was in galleys and had been proofread by me and half a dozen highly literate pals, I offered the thirteen-year-old a dollar for every mistake he could find; I wound up owing him eighteen dollars.

I also make it a practice to consult with people who have first-hand knowledge of the subject matter. When writing *Kind and Usual Punishment*, I circulated the draft to members of the San Francisco Prisoners Union, all ex-convicts, who supplied many vivid details from their own prison experience. However, this method may not appeal to everyone. Most writers I know would shudder at the thought of passing around drafts of their work to miscellaneous friends. I can only say it works very well for me, in fact I could hardly survive without it.

The final step in preparing a manuscript for submission is meticulous proofreading. This may seem too obvious and elementary to mention, yet at both San Jose State and Yale I was continually amazed at the number of jarring and annoying typographical and spelling mistakes, sloppy constructions, confusing inserts in otherwise excellent papers turned in by students. I urged them to consider that failure to proofread is like preparing a magnificent dinner and forgetting to set the table, so that the wretched guests have to scramble for the food as best they can.

As to the second stage, professional editing, whether your piece will be helped or harmed depends on the individual editor. I recall a very nasty moment when, having been given a contract for *The American Way of Death* by both an English and an American publisher, I sent them each a draft of the chapter on embalming. It was met with instantaneous and thunderous disapproval from the editors on both sides of the Atlantic; this chapter is too revolting, it must go, they said. I could, of course, have acceded to their wishes and excised the offending passages. After much agonizing, I decided not to do so even though it meant losing the contracts—and I was sustained in this decision by my circle of amateur editors.

After this disheartening setback the book was eventually accepted by Robert Gottlieb of Simon & Schuster, who loved the embalming chapter and whose sympathetic editing vastly improved the text as a whole. A year after publication, those self-same embalming passages were chosen for inclusion in a college textbook on writing. Well! Of course I felt vindicated. The obvious moral is that although *some* editors can *sometimes* perform wonders in improving your work, in the last analysis your own judgment must prevail.

While book publishers rarely alter a manuscript without the author's approval, magazine editors, with their space limitations and frantic deadlines, are apt to take all sorts of liberties. The first time I wrote a piece for *Life*—and was ecstatic over its acceptance —the editor assured me that it would be published as submitted "except for word changes." It was only after I saw the piece in print that it dawned on me that the only changes that can be made in a written text are word changes. In this collection I have generally used my own unedited manuscript, and will discuss some of the differences between my text and the published version in the comments on these pieces.

JOURNALISTIC ETHICS. My students at San Jose and Yale often brought up this subject and questioned me closely about what is/isn't "ethical" when in pursuit of a hot lead. Unfortunately ethics is not one of my strong points, so I am not sure my answers were satisfactory. In general, I think that if you have promised anonymity to the person you are interviewing, or if it is agreed in advance that he is speaking "off the record," such agreement should be respected. Better, however, to steer him away from such untoward thoughts, which can often be done by fast and

dexterous talk about the matter at hand, so that the problem does
not arise. I shall have more to say about this in the comment on
"Let Us Now Appraise Famous Writers."

On a level with "ethics," and likewise a subject of great interest
to my students, is "objectivity." Some ventured to suggest that I
lack this quality. If to be objective means having no point of view,
or giving equal weight to all information that comes one's way, I
plead guilty—although *accuracy* is essential, not only to the integrity of your work but to avoid actionable defamation. It can be
ruinous to try to tailor the evidence to fit your preconceptions, or
to let your point of view impede the search for facts.

But I do try to cultivate the *appearance* of objectivity, mainly
through the technique of understatement, avoidance where possible of editorial comment, above all letting the undertakers, or
the Spock prosecutors, or the prison administrators pillory themselves through their own pronouncements. "When are you going
to get *angry?*" a friend asked after reading a draft of my article
about the Famous Writers. Never, I answered; it is not in my
sweet nature to lose my temper, especially in print.

L I B E L. Many of my students lived in perpetual dread of com-
mitting the murky crime of libel, and were forever anxiously asking whether some statement or characterization in a paper was
"libelous." I begged them not to worry their pretty heads over this,
because should one of their efforts be accepted for publication the
author would be subjected to the dubious benefit of counsel from
the publisher's libel lawyers.

To the extent that I have had dealings with this curious subspe-
cies of the genus lawyer, which breeds and proliferates mainly in
the swamplands of Eastern publishing centers, I have concluded
that their main function is best summed up by the title of a recent
best-seller: *Looking Out for Number One.* Like the prison psy-
chiatrist who habitually overpredicts "violent behavior" by
inmates in his care—fearing for his own skin should a violent

crime be committed by a prisoner he has cleared as safe to release —the libel lawyer will go to wonderful lengths to identify passages in a manuscript that he asserts might give rise to a lawsuit. Thus in one effortless operation he protects himself and garners a fat fee for doing so.

To illustrate: After my manuscript of *The Trial of Dr. Spock* was submitted, I received a six-page single-spaced letter from Knopf's libel lawyers listing thirty-four potentially libelous statements, beginning with "Page 1, para 1: it is alleged that Mitchell Goodman, Michael Ferber and Marcus Raskin were co-defendants with Dr. Spock and Rev. Coffin, which would be libelous if untrue. . . ." Some other gems from this bizarre document: "The statement that Rev. Coffin spent time in Southern jails is libelous and should be deleted unless it can be verified from court records." "The statement that Bertrand Russell was prosecuted is libelous and should be deleted unless it can be proven true from court records." "The statement that Dwight Macdonald said he was ashamed to be an American, as used in the context of this passage, may be libelous as charging a federal crime." And my favorite, from a passage in which I was describing a particularly boring moment in the trial: "It is alleged that Mitchell Goodman's lawyer 'perhaps was dozing off.' Since he was supposedly defending Goodman at the trial, this is libelous and should be deleted."

"But what am I supposed to DO with this pile of junk?" I wailed to my editor at Knopf. Shrieking with laughter, he said I would have to go over it with the lawyer, which I did, patiently elucidating as I went: "Page 1, para 1—that's from the indictment, which lists the co-defendants. . . . All the newspapers carried stories about Coffin's imprisonment in Southern jails—of which he was immensely proud. . . . Bertrand Russell describes his prosecution in his autobiography. . . ." And so on. "Oh, then that's all right, that can stand," the lawyer would respond to each of my explanations. The upshot was that not a single change was made in my manuscript as a consequence of the lawyer's labors. How much would he have charged for this memo? I asked a lawyer friend. He took it in his hands and weighed it thoughtfully; upward of a thousand dollars, he would guess, maybe two thousand.

I am often asked if I have ever been sued for libel in the course of my writing career; the answer is no, alas. I have been threatened with suit a few times—after *The American Way of Death* came out, executives of Forest Lawn Memorial Park announced they were preparing suit "against the authoress and her publishers," but regrettably no such suits have thus far been brought; I should have enjoyed defending against them. I cannot, however, lay the failure of these libel suits to materialize at the door of the publisher's libel lawyers. I take the blame upon myself for being quite careful to check facts—tedious yet necessary, if one's work is to have any standing and value for the reader.

R E S U L T S ? Finally we should explore the question, Does muckraking really accomplish anything, or does it at best lead to reforms that merely gloss over the basic flaws of society? Lincoln Steffens, originator of the genre and author of the pioneering *Shame of the Cities*, eventually came to take a dim view. "He was now certain that muckraking in itself had run its course and led to no solutions," writes Justin Kaplan, Steffens's biographer. "Muckraking, it seemed, had only been a way of shouting at society, and this was pointless, especially now that one had to shout louder and louder to get people to listen, much less to do something."

What of today's muckrakers? Ralph Nader is probably the leader in exposing misdeeds of the giant corporations. At least his loud shouts have succeeded in creating a nationwide awareness of consumer fraud, ranging from unsafe cars to dangerous and overpriced prescription drugs, thus educating a whole generation of consumers as to their rights, and to the possibilities of organizing and fighting back through the courts and legislatures.

My own efforts have been (with the possible exception of *The Trial of Dr. Spock* and *Kind and Usual Punishment*) on a far less consequential scale. The undertakers are, after all, hardly on a par with such formidable Nader adversaries as General Motors or the puissant drug industry. Most of the subjects of investigation in this collection are odd pockets of American enterprise that happened to strike my fancy (or, as the OED would say, appealed to my "depraved interest in what is morally unsavoury or scandalous"): Elizabeth Arden's retreat for rich fat women; the Famous Writers' correspondence school; the Sign of the Dove, a high-priced New York tourist trap. I wish I could point to some overriding social purpose in these articles; the sad truth is that the best I can say for them is that I got pleasure from mocking these enterprises and the individuals who profit from them.

On the political front, it seems clear that over the last decade young and energetic muckrakers succeeded in laying the groundwork for the toppling of two presidents. Robert Scheer's early pamphlet *"How We Got Involved in Vietnam,"* originally published in an obscure journal, became the text for innumerable teach-ins and source material for scores of subsequent books and articles. These in turn were immensely influential in fanning the anti-Vietnam War protest which led to the downfall of L.B.J. Similarly the Woodward-Bernstein exposures initiated the chain of events that brought down Nixon. In each case the written word lit the fire and fed the flames.

But then (you will groan) we had Ford and now Carter, there have been no fundamental changes or improvements in any aspect of American life. Which merely points up the need for a new generation of muckrakers who will hone and perfect the craft, and will shout long and loud enough to get people not only to listen but to do something.

TRIAL
BY HEADLINE

NATION / *October 26, 1957*

Our fathers claimed, by obvious madness moved,
Man's innocent until his guilt is proved.
They would have known, had they not been confused,
He's innocent until he is accused.

> Ogden Nash,
> *You Can't Get There From Here*

In varying type sizes, San Francisco's four daily newspapers for July 25th and 26th carried identical if slightly ungrammatical headlines: " 'THAT'S HIM!' "

"Girl Victim Identifies 'Fang' Suspect", continued the *News* (7/25/57). Directly under the headline, a picture of the person thus identified bore the caption:

"Baring his teeth in response to a reporter's half-whimsical suggestion, Allan Messinger* shows his buck teeth that made him a suspect in the 'Fang' case".

---

* Not his real name. I've changed it to a fictitious name in order to protect his privacy.

Thus the news was broken that, after five days of intensive police search, one Allan Messinger had turned up as a likely suspect in the latest sensational sex crime, and had been identified by the victim.

From first commission of the crime on July 20, the papers had evidently decided here was an event of unusual public interest. Even in the absence of any new developments it was seldom off the front pages.

The heat was on the police department to produce the culprit.

Briefly, the facts as related by the victims were these: At about 10.30 p.m. of a Saturday night, a pretty young nurse and her escort, a Mr. James Lonergan, were approached by a stranger as they stopped their car in Golden Gate Park. At knife's point, the stranger bound Lonergan with cord and gagged him with adhesive tape, manacled the girl with leg irons, cut off her hair with a pair of scissors, burned her with a cigarette, raped her twice, and before leaving pricked her and Mr. Lonergan with his knife. To top all, he had stolen Mr. Lonergan's wristwatch.

The San Francisco *News* (7/23/57) had reported that, according to the victim, the most outstanding feature of the assailant was his "canine teeth, which protruded fanglike over his lower lip. They were more than twice normal size . . ."

The *News* thereupon had become the first newspaper to use the descriptive and alliterative nickname, "FANG FIEND".

The rest of the published description was unexceptional, although it was to have some bearing on later developments: a white man, 20 to 25, 5' 9" tall, 150 to 160 lbs., dark complexion, big nose, light horn rimmed glasses.

The young girl's identification of Messinger as the culprit drove most other news off the front pages. First reports variously described him as "insular, suspicious and withdrawn", (*Chronicle*, 7/26/57) "evasive", (*News*, 7/25/57) a "schizoid personality with an incipient hysterical psychosis" (*Examiner*, 7/26/57) "querulous" (*Call-Bulletin*, 7/25/57)

To San Francisco newspaper readers, this treatment of a sus-

pect in a notorious crime revived uneasy memories of another
recent big sensation—the arrest, trial and subsequent execution of
Burton W. Abbott, for the kidnap-murder of a Berkeley school-
girl.

Newspaper handling of the Abbott case had resulted in a flood
of protest in the letters columns. While many readers had complained that the newspapers had shown "bad taste" in the undue
publicizing of gruesome details of the case, others had raised a
more fundamental question: Was it possible for Abbott to have
received a fair trial, in view of the unending flood of adverse
publicity he had received, both during the trial and for months
beforehand?

Could the jury have been truly unbiased, coming as it did from
a community saturated by so thorough a press bombardment—all
pointing to Abbott's guilt?

Does the traditional American concept of freedom of the press
extend to the trial of such a case in the newspapers before the
defendant has been brought into court?

An English judge, holding a newspaper in contempt for commenting on a case before the trial, once said: "It is possible very
effectually to poison the fountain of justice before it begins to
flow." (Wills J., Rex. v. Parke)

Had the fountain of justice been poisoned for Abbott? And was
it now being poisoned for Messinger?

The newspapers themselves were quick to notice the parallel
between the two cases.

Under the headline, "MESSINGER TALE RECALLS THAT OF AB-
BOTT", the afternoon *News* (7/26/57) was first to draw attention
to the physical resemblance between the two men, running pictures
of them taken in identical poses.

Messinger's very protestations of innocence became sinisterly
Abbott-like:

" 'I hope someone saw me. I sure hope so. Because I didn't do it' . . .
"To newsmen his words sounded strangely like those spoken a year

ago by Burton W. Abbott . . . and his cry of 'frame-up' is the same as
that put forth by Abbott and his attorneys . . ."

Pointing out that under California's Little Lindburgh Law
Messinger could also get the death penalty, the *News* continues
with this apparent non-sequiter: "Stephanie was 14 when Abbott
killed her. The student nurse Messinger is charged with attacking
is 19".

The *Call-Bulletin* for the same afternoon played it from a
slightly different angle, featuring an exclusive interview with
Messinger in which he expressed fear he might "become another
Abbott".

The morning papers quickly followed suit: ". . . like Abbott, he
was calm and detached in expressing himself" (*Examiner*,
7/27/57). "Messinger's appearance and mien have been compared to that of Abbott" (*Chronicle*, 7/30/57).

In the days that followed, news coverage of the case might be
compared with the rising strains of a huge orchestra, swelling from
crescendo to crescendo, through which, however, occasional
dissonant notes could be heard implying doubt of Messinger's
guilt.

Often, it would have required a very thorough newspaper
reader to discern these notes of dissonance. Thus, the *News,
Examiner* and *Chronicle* built up Messinger in headlines as having
a "police record of sex crimes".

The *Chronicle* (8/2/57) noted "three sex crimes on his police
record". The *Examiner* (7/26/57) reported "Parolee Served
Time in Quentin for Assault". Only those who read to the end of
the news stories learned that the sole jail sentence served by Messinger had been for forgery, and that the only sex offense for
which he had ever been convicted (and for which he was given
probation) was that of *statutory* rape, at the age of 17.

Under California law, statutory rape is an act of intercourse
with a girl under 18 years old, with her consent. By definition it
does not imply violence, and is not an assault. Probation is

granted when authorities deem the offense to be technical in nature, and in the absence of aggravating circumstances.

"Queer" and "sinister" aspects of Messinger's personality received major attention. An *Examiner* interviewer (7/28/57) asked, " 'What about girls he had dated?' Would any of them come to his aid now?' For a few minutes he became tense, almost agitated. 'I don't want to drag any girl into this case' . . ."

His living quarters were reported to be "amazingly clean, and without the usual small items a man would have around". (*Examiner*, 7/26/57) Here was evidently the very opposite of the all-American boy, the lovable bachelor living in a glorious mess among his untidy masculine belongings!

The suspect's repeated declarations of innocence, his efforts to establish an alibi, even his expressed desire to take a lie detector test quickly earned him the label in newspapers of "con-wise".

His protestations that he in no way fitted the published description of the assailant—he was too short (5′ 6″), had straight teeth and a pale complexion—got scant notice.

The real "personality angle" came after police invited reporters to listen to some taped recordings which figure in Messinger's alibi. Messinger claimed he was at home making the recordings, consisting of poetry and philosophical essays, at the time the crime was committed.

The *News* (7/29/57) voiced the opinion that the "philosophical discourse made it clear that he considers himself above the law . . ." and as proof, quoted from Messinger's essay: " 'The only law is the law of self respect. Observe that.' "

Going one better, the *Examiner* (7/30/57) headlined "Messinger's Poetic Rambling Indicates He's Sexual Psychopath, Inspector Says".

"(The recording) turned out to be a one-hour pot pourri of poetry by Kahlil Gibran, author of 'The Prophet'; various works by Messinger himself . . . and an Anarchistic essay in which the ex-convict suspect said 'it is half-witted living when we allow our way to be blocked by some silly inhibition'.

"This last effort generated far more interest among police than anything else. It said in part,

" 'If a thing is worth desiring, planning for, and reaching out for, why is it denied us because of some small voice in our traitorous inhibited character or consciousness?' . . .

"In conclusion, he said: 'If a man does not fail himself—if he lives up to his own rules—he can do no wrong. Let him fail to live up to his own due respect and he will earn the destruction or injury which will surely come to him . . .

"Inspector Frank Gibeau, while conceding he was no literary critic, said yesterday the 'alibi' tape recording made by Allan Messinger 'clearly indicates he is a sexual psychopath and sadist'.

"And he said he believed Messinger, whose voice rose to a vibrating emotional pitch toward the end of the tape, may have become so excited while recording that he left home and immediately set out for trouble".

A contrasting estimate of the poems was also reported. A University of California extension course instructor had jotted on the margin of a typed copy of one of the poems: "Excellent and beautiful. Technical control and emotional restraint make this a real poem. You have real ability. Keep writing!"

The *Chronicle* (7/30/57) reported "An essay on justice struck police inspectors as revealing. It said in part that the 'Golden Rule allows more leeway than any law that has been written since' . . . Police were sure they spotted a Freudian slip in one of the strange stories. The central character is a man named Cabot and after the story had rambled on for a while, Messinger mispronounced the name, 'Abbott' ".

Police were quoted as saying Messinger should be in jail for the poems alone, to which he retorted that if Edgar Allen Poe were alive today, Inspector Gibeau would no doubt have him behind bars!

These excerpts represent only a very tiny sampling of press coverage of this part of the case. Most papers devoted an entire page to the poems and to interpretations derived therefrom of Messinger's personality.

Again, an alert reader might have remembered, amid the thunderous chorus that accompanied release of the poems, a note of contradiction heard a few days previously.

Walter Stone, Chief of the State Division of Adult Paroles, had said that frequent and intensive psychiatric examination of Messinger had revealed "some personality problems, but no evidence whatsoever of any sadistic drive. It just wasn't there . . ." (*Chronicle*, 7/27/57)

Police were less inclined to let the press in on their progress in cracking Messinger's alibi for the night of the crime. However they reported that Messinger admitted lying in accounting for part of that night. His statement that he had been alone in his room had been contradicted by an ex-convict who claimed to have been with him before 8 p.m. and after 1 a.m.

Actually at this point the police had a very thin case. No physical evidence linking Messinger with the crime had been found. No manacles. No adhesive tape. No wristwatch. Police criminologists, subjecting Messinger's clothing and sweepings from his room to microscopic examination, had turned up nothing.

True, a knife had been found in Messinger's room, which "officers inferred belonged to Messinger and . . . was the one used in Golden Gate Park". (*Chronicle*, 7/27/57) True, FAILURE to find any scissors in his room was "considered significant" by police, who commented "they may have been thrown away". (*Examiner*, 7/26/57)

True, a quantity of Venetian blind cord "of the type that was used to bind the victim" turned up in the basement of Messinger's rooming house, and among his effects were "a crumpled pair of suntan pants and a tan sports shirt with what could be blood on the collar . . ." Meagre though they were, these clues got front page treatment from all papers.

In the absence of more impressive copy from police sources, at least two newsmen turned detective and sought to dig up evidence themselves.

Ed Montgomery of the *Examiner* found a bit of Venetian blind cord with hair adhering to it in the flower bed near where Messinger parked his car. The color of the hair was "similar to that of the girl", and Montgomery, in true amateur sleuth fashion, was reported to have "carefully avoided touching it until police arrived". (*Examiner*, 7/27/57)

Once again, the dissonant theme—that pointing to innocence—was almost drowned out. But it was there, for the observant reader, at the end of the story: ". . . the cord was considered to be of secondary importance, since the landlord at Messinger's rooming house is in the Venetian blind business". Thus vanished the spine-chilling significance of the blind cord!

From time to time the dissonant theme would crop up in unobtrusively placed paragraphs:

"The D.A.'s office indicated the possibility that the inquiry might be running into a wall by saying 'we are not prepared to take the case to the Grand Jury at this time'" (*Examiner*, 7/31/57) or, "Inspectors still had no physical evidence to link Messinger with the attack and preliminary reports from the Oakland crime laboratory showed 'only possibilities, nothing obvious'". (*Chronicle*, 7/29/57)

Only once did an authoritative voice, bluntly expressing dissatisfaction with the turn of events, take precedence in headlines and news space over the "chase" aspects of the case. Public Defender Abraham Dresow was prominently featured in all newspapers (8/1/57) as saying, after an interview with Messinger, "The police are holding the wrong guy".

However, a new development swiftly banished Dresow's statement from the front pages.

The second of the *Examiner* sleuths, Larry Cahn, had been

working on a store-by-store check of the city looking for the person who sold Messinger the manacles used to chain the victim's legs.

On August 3rd, the *Examiner* reported success: "Mrs. Jenelle St. James, former surplus store clerk, positively identified Allan Messinger as the man to whom she sold a set of manacles about 2 months ago".

She was quoted as saying, "I am sure that is the man . . . I am certain of it . . ."

This was, by any standards, new evidence of real importance in the case against Messinger. A second positive eyewitness identification linking him with the crime had now been added to that of the victim. Chief of Inspectors Daniel McKlem was prominently quoted in all papers as being "firmly convinced he is the man".

Just a week earlier, Mrs. St. James had told the Examiner she had seen Messinger in the store but "was unable to recall whether he had bought the manacles". What could have happened in the intervening time to refresh her recollection?

The disturbing question was never answered. For within hours on that busy Saturday an *Examiner* extra had hit the streets with the headline,

"NEW SUSPECT ADMITS TORTURE; MESSINGER ELIMINATED".

By afternoon the whole story was out.

Three days earlier, two narcotics agents following up a routine tip, had picked up a tiny, 5-foot drug addict, Melvin Bakkerud, former inmate of an insane asylum. The arrest had not even merited one line in any newspaper. Bakkerud was held for investigation of peddling dope in San Francisco's South of Market area.

A search of his room turned up, among other things, a gold wristwatch with distinctive markings. A police inspector "remembered reading in the Chronicle" Lonergan's description of his stolen watch. He checked the description with the watch found in Bakkerud's room. It tallied. Confronted with the watch, Bakkerud readily confessed to the assault in Golden Gate Park. He led police to the hidden "torture kit", containing tape, cord, scissors, knife. The police criminologist found within ten minutes microscopic evidence that fibres taken from Bakkerud's belongings matched those from the victims' clothing.

And the manacles? Bakkerud had stolen them from the glove compartment of a San Francisco police car on the night of the crime. Apparently the theft had never been noticed or reported, much less linked with the assault.

A badly shaken press and police department set about picking up the pieces—and assigning the blame.

"San Francisco police had worked up a case strong enough to send an innocent man to San Quentin for life", said the *Chronicle* (8/6/57)

"The cops were out for a conviction more than they were out for the truth. They think a case is solved when they get a suspect", said Public Defender Dresow. (*Examiner*, 8/4/57)

"I never said positively that I was sure he was the one," said the victim (*Examiner*, 8/4/57)

"(Chief of Inspectors) McKlem denied having been 'certain' Messinger was the man," reported the *Examiner* (8/4/57)

"The description furnished by the victim was way off", said the *Chronicle* (8/6/57), pointing out that in every essential the published description, that of Messinger and that of Bakkerud were totally at variance.

"Above all, Messinger lied", editorialized the *News* (8/6/57). "Had it not been for his falsehoods, police would never have been able to build up a case against him".

There was little comment by the newspapers on their own part in the case. The *News* (8/6/57) was the only one to tackle this aspect of the post mortem. It editorially extolled the "spotlight of public interest which said in effect, 'you must be certain; you must prove your case' . . . Our kind of society demands facts. Spurred on by public interest, the police produced the facts—and cleared him".

In a subsequent television program, *News* editor Albert Colgrove explained newspaper use of the word "FANG". He pointed out that it made for easier headline treatment than SUSPECT because it contains fewer letters.

Questioned about the relationship between crime news and circulation, he answered that there is indeed a most important relationship. He cited the fact that the day of Abbott's execution had been the second biggest circulation day of San Francisco's history, exceeded only by the day of the recent earthquake.

He pointed out that, in the absence of crime news, there would be many fewer newspaper readers, and thus many would be denied the opportunity to read about such worthy activities as those of the United Crusade.

A New Zealand judge had taken a different view of the matter. Commenting on pre-trial discussion of sensational cases by the press, Mr. Justice Blair said: "It is idle for such newspapers to claim they adopt such practices in the public interest. Their motive is the sordid one of increasing their profits, unmindful of the result to the unfortunate wretch who may ultimately have to stand trial . . ."

The Messinger case disappeared speedily from the pages of the city's newspapers, but it had thrown into sharp relief some disquieting questions.

How reliable is eyewitness identification? The girl's positive accusation, to which was added that of the manacles saleslady, was the heart of the case against Messinger. Yet the young victim, it turned out, had not the slightest idea of what her attacker looked like.

Should police be permitted, prior to indictment and trial, to feed the press step-by-step details of their work?

Should the scramble for headlines, in turn, be permitted to build up such pressure on police to "produce" that careful, dispassionate, scientific investigation of the facts becomes a near impossibility?

Should U.S. courts be given power of contempt over the press such as exists in England where all pre-trial comment on evidence is forbidden? English law is very clear and extremely severe on this subject. "To speak of an accused person as a rogue . . . is wrongful, and is certain to be followed by a fine . . ." (Harvard Law Review, Vol. 48). Presumably, the same penalty could be expected to apply in England with even greater force to one who spoke of an accused person as a "fang fiend".

Americans, traditionally zealous in defense of freedom of the press, may be reluctant to accept such drastic curbs.

But there is a growing awareness of the menace of trial by headline.

What happened to Messinger could have happened anywhere in the U.S.

Indeed, two cases—those of Abbott and Dr. Sam Sheppard in Cleveland, Ohio—already had stirred consideration of the problem in the ranks of the legal profession.

Joseph A. Ball, President of the California Bar, writing in the State Bar Journal (May-June, 1957) comments:

"The controversy between free press and fair trial continues . . . It is an undeniable fact that freedom of the press or the freedom of lawyers to discuss pending trials in newspapers has resulted in trial on the front page rather than in the courtroom.

"The disgraceful episode in Cleveland during the trial of Dr. Sheppard received the criticism of bench, bar and the conservative press.

"Said the Toledo *Blade:*

'The press never left any doubt of the verdict it expected, which was not surprising in view of its having plunged so deep into the processes of administering justice by its own rules.'

"Then followed the Burton Abbott case in Oakland, California, where the news stories outdid the prosecution in prejudging the result . . ."

He proposes "a code of civilized restraints which would insure a fair trial for all accused of crime" as an objective of both lawyers and press.

He states in conclusion, "No freedom is more important than that of personal freedom, and no right more sacred than that of due process of law. Unfair trial is a social evil. Practices which threaten the fairness of a trial must be curbed . . ."

The story of the Messinger case illuminates the urgent need for the press to take strong action to police itself.

Short of some pretty drastic measures on the part of news editors to end the evil of trial by headline, it seems not unlikely that courts and public may demand legal sanctions like those used in England to end the prejudging of cases in the newspapers.

end

COMMENT

To put this in context: in 1957, when this article was taken by the *Nation*, I was plugging away at my autobiography, *Daughters and Rebels*, various drafts of which had already been turned down by at least a dozen distinguished American publishers. This freezing reception discouraged me, so I put the book aside; it was anyway a bit late, I thought, at the ripe age of forty to embark on a writing career. However the Messinger story, for several days an ongoing newspaper drama, caught my eye and I thought I would try my hand at writing an article about it.

At the time this now musty old piece was published, I was inordinately proud of it: my first article ever to be accepted by a national magazine. I loved writing it and I adored seeing it in print. As my firstborn, I still feel some maternal affection for it; but rereading it, I detect all sorts of lapses of style and content. For that reason I reproduce here the original typescript, just as it was submitted, so that the reader can pick it to pieces as an exercise in editing.

Why those oddly short paragraphs, having nothing to do with change of subject, which I have since learned is the whole point of paragraphs? Because at the time my chief mentor and volunteer editor was a newspaper reporter, the only professional writer I knew; he loathed long paragraphs as anathema to daily news writing, and was forever cutting mine into minuscule (and, as I now see, illogical) bits. Also, I regret those exclamation marks, which strike me as a form of unnecessary emphasis.

Why did I not seek to interview the principals in the story—police, prosecutor, Messinger, the victim, and above all those culpable newspaper editors whose comments would doubtless have made excellent copy? I suppose I assumed they would rebuff me and refuse to answer questions. I now know better. It is the rare and exceptional individual, in almost any line of work, who will decline the opportunity to expound his views to a reporter.

Despite these shortcomings, the story itself was, I think, of intrinsic interest at the time; in any event, the *Nation* liked it enough to accept it from an unknown writer.

The *Nation*'s editors fixed it up considerably, beginning with the first sentence; they struck out that silly phrase "if slightly ungrammatical" (after all, who but some hoary grammarian would exclaim "That is he!" when identifying the person who assaulted her?), they brought order and logic into the paragraphing, they improved many a laboriously constructed sentence, they deleted all those boring dates of newspapers which I had put in as evidence of my meticulous research, and corrected the misspelling of "nonsequitur."

But also, to my annoyance, they left out the whole conclusion, presumably because they did not agree with my point about the need for judicial restraints on the press. As the main purpose of the exposé type of article is to generate corrective action—in this case, to alert courts, legislatures, and the general public to the evil of trial by headline—excision of these proposals robbed the piece of much of its intended thrust. Thereafter I have tried (not always successfully, as we shall see in the comments on some of the other pieces in this collection) to extract an agreement ahead of time from magazine editors that *no* changes will be made without consultation.

Looking back, I realize that publication of this slim effort was for me a turning point. It gave me encouragement to continue struggling with my book despite rebuffs—it made me, for the first time, begin to think of myself as a "writer."

ST. PETER,
DON'T YOU
CALL ME

FRONTIER / *November, 1958*

The American Way of Death, though not extolled in song, story, and news articles to the same extent as its more popular counterpart, the American Way of Life, has nevertheless come in for a fair share of attention in recent years. Sometimes it is the subject of an uneasy kind of humor. Thus, San Francisco *Chronicle* columnist Herb Caen suggests a slogan for mortuaries who desire to compete with the auto industry's recent anti-recession campaign: "You Auto Die Now." *The New Yorker* ran a cartoon of a mortuary decorated with signs announcing, "We Give Green Stamps." Evelyn Waugh based his best-selling novel *The Loved One* on the romance between the head cosmetician of an ornate Los Angeles mortuary and an employee of a pet cemetery.

In a more serious vein, Hugo Gernsback, writing for the *American Funeral Director*, points the way to the funeral of the future: "The loved one will be quick-frozen, encased in a light metal casket, and placed aboard a space ship, which will take off for Outer Space. When the gravitational pull decreases, the casket will be ejected from a tube, in direct polarity from the sun. The casket will disappear in a few seconds to fly for eternity and a day, in perfect preservation, in the infinite void." Presumably, arrangements could also be made for the quick-frozen loved one to orbit, Sputnik fashion, thus allowing the bereaved to catch an occasional glimpse of Uncle Ned as he flashes by on course in the heavens.

However, if the conversation of ordinary citizens chances to drift to the subject of funerals, a tone of bitterness is likely to creep in. At best, complaints will be voiced about the high cost of dying; at worst, there will be a chorus of horror stories about fleecings at the hands of unscrupulous undertakers.

Perhaps it is not surprising that dissension has begun to spread in the ranks of the living. There are growing up in dozens of communities, scattered throughout the United States and Canada, consumer cooperative groups dedicated to the principle of "dignified funerals for a reasonable cost." Their philosophy may be summed up in the blunt preamble to the Chico, California, Burial Society's by-laws: "Every funeral is a pagan funeral when based on show only money can buy. The costliest of caskets decays with the body, and cannot make a home for the soul." According to literature issued by the Memorial Association of Seattle, the funeral cooperatives have declared war on "materialistic display, showing of the corpse which necessitates embalming, the sending of expensive floral pieces."

The Battle of the Bodies has been joined. A clue to some of the practices opposed by the funeral co-op movement may be found in the pages of funeral trade magazines. For instances, *Mortuary Management*, a flossy, glossy funeral industry publication located (appropriately) in Los Angeles, announces this revealing offer from the National Casket Company: "$5 each for experiences, stories or anecdotes that illustrate where a $50–100 better sale was made because the casket had qualities, features or demonstrable values that made it a better buy than the offering at the lower price."

As in a table-d'hôte restaurant, where the price of the entrée determines the price of the dinner ($2.25 for halibut, $7.50 for filet mignon), so in the burial business the price of the casket usually determines the cost of the funeral. According to Warren J. Ringen, past president of the Funeral Directors of San Francisco, "In keeping with our high standard of living, there should be an equally high standard of dying. The cost of a funeral varies according to individual taste and the niceties of living the family has been accustomed to" (quoted from the San Francisco *News*, September 20, 1955). A bewildering assortment of the niceties of dying is described in *Mortuary Management:* "Solid copper—a quality casket which offers superb value to the client seeking long-lasting protection," "Hand Grained Artistic Designs for the Discriminating Purchaser," "The Colonial Classic Beauty—18-Gauge Lead Coated Steel, Seamless Top, Lap-Join Welded Body Construction . . ." In addition to the casket, which is the *pièce de résistance,* innumerable other frills are offered. The Cheney casket-lining people provide "magnificent and unique masterpieces—more than 60 color matched shades—you'll find that the extra pennies mean more profitable dollars." Chrisette will supply "Handmade Original Fashions—Styles from the Best in Life for the Last Memory—Dresses, Men's Suits, Negligees, Accessories," while Hydrol Chemical Company offers "Nature Glo—the ultimate in cosmetic embalming."

THERE'LL ALWAYS BE AN AD MAN

Honors for a truly imaginative approach to their lugubrious wares must go to the vault men. An advertisement in the 1957 souvenir edition of *Mortuary Management* reads:

Deep sea fishing off Mexico can't be beat! When you feel that old tug on your pole and that line goes whistling into the deep, that's it brother! And, there is nothing quite like the way I feel about Wilbert burial vaults either. The combination of a ⅜" pre-cast asphalt inner liner plus extra-thick, reinforced concrete provides the essential qualities for proper burial. My advice to you is, don't get into "deep water" with burial vaults made of the new lightweight synthetic substitutes.

Just keep "reeling in" extra profits by continuing to recommend WIL-BERT burial vaults. . . .

A two-page spread in a recent issue of the same magazine presents the reader with this startling thought: "DISINTERMENTS—RARE BUT REWARDING. It needn't be a problem. *It can lead to repeat business.* . . . Prove your wisdom in recommending the trusted protection of a Clark Metal Grave Vault."

Is a new folklore being created—a specifically twentieth-century American form of funeral rite which may seem as outlandish to the rest of the world as the strange burial customs of the past revealed by anthropological studies?

QUAINT CUSTOMS OF OTHER PEOPLE

Babylonians were embalmed in honey; Indians required self-immolation of the widow on her husband's funeral pyre; Vikings were buried with their ships. Are these customs any weirder or more inappropriate than those described in the American funeral industry's house organ? Etruscans buried the deceased's treasure at his side—a practice hardly likely to win the approval of the modern funeral director, who generally manages to arrange for a different disposition of the deceased's treasure. Indeed, many mortuaries provide a form with disarmingly direct emphasis on such questions as, "Location of Safe Deposit Boxes; My Banks Are; Savings Accounts; Location of Insurance Policies."

Perhaps some of the frankest testimony ever uttered on the subject of funeral costs was that given by W. W. Chambers, million-dollar operator of four large mortuaries in Washington, D.C., at a 1947 Senate committee hearing:

"An undertaker never protects anybody but himself. The first thing he asks is, 'How much insurance have you got, and how much of it can I get?' . . . In dealing with anything you buy, you have the refusal of it, but if your mother dies and you get in the hands of an undertaker, he just soft-soaps you along. You do not oppose him much as to the price. . . . A $30 casket is generally sold today for $150." Explaining why he left his job in a livery stable to become an undertaker, Mr. Chambers continues: "What appealed to me mostly was when I saw one of them [undertakers] buy a casket for $17 and sell it to a poor broken widow for $265. I said, 'This is awful sweet, I can't let this go.' "

The U.S. Coal Mines Administration, investigating funeral charges demanded of the 111 Centralia mine disaster victims, found the average funeral cost was $732.78; the highest, $1,178.50 (*The New York Times,* August 3, 1947). To add insult to injury, when Centralia's businessmen were asked to contribute to an emergency relief fund for widows and orphans the funeral directors made their contribution in the form of a discount on funeral charges—the discounts ranging from $11.85 off a $567 funeral to $22.50 off a $937.50 funeral!

Not only the survivors of sweeping community disaster feel the financial blows inflicted by the cost of modern funerals. A recent study of twenty-two Probate Court cases taken at random in the San Francisco Bay Area disclosed that the cost of funerals ranged from $344 to $3,027. The average of the twenty-two was $952. A similar study in St. Louis showed average funeral costs were $900.

It would be wrong to assume from these facts that morticians are a special, evil breed. It should be borne in mind that the funeral industry faces a unique economic situation in that its market is fixed, or inelastic. There are only a certain number of deaths each year and the funeral directors must compete with each other to obtain their share of the business. The television industry touts the advantages of a TV set in every room; auto salesmen advocate several cars to each family; cigarette manufacturers urge "a carton for the home and one for the office"—but in the funeral business it's strictly "one to a customer," and the number of customers is limited by circumstances beyond the control of the industry. Very likely many a funeral director has echoed with heartfelt sincerity the patriotic sentiments of Nathan Hale: "My only regret is that I have but one life to lose for my country."

Some morticians handle as few as twelve funerals a year, and the national average is under sixty a year. From these few funerals enough cash must be realized to meet all the overhead and operating costs of the establishment for a full year. Little wonder that the funeral industry has tended to become one of the most predatory and competitive in the country, that behind the decorous façade of the funeral home lurks some of the slickest salesmanship to be found this side of a Baghdad bazaar.

A network of legal realities and myths tends to keep funeral costs sky-high. For example, the California Health and Safety Code (Section 9625 *et seq.*) imposes fantastic requirements for the construction of mausoleums and columbariums. Unlike schools or homes, they must be earthquake-proof, fireproof, waterproof, and their exterior trim must be of "travertine, serpentine marble or Grade A exterior type marble only." There is an almost universal belief in California, carefully nurtured by the undertakers, that the law requires embalming and the use of a casket in all cases of death. Three Oakland morticians, selected at random from the phone book, assured me that cremation without a casket is illegal. One added, with some truth, "The average person has neither the facilities nor the inclination to haul dead bodies around." However, a quick check with the State Board of Health revealed that there are no such legal requirements, and that in fact indigents are frequently cremated "as is," without benefit of casket or embalming.

Legal skirmishes are frequently part of the guerrilla warfare waged by the burial cooperatives against entrenched morticians, and many of the co-ops have had their "day in court." The Cooperative League of the U.S.A., while stressing the necessity for competent legal advice in organizing a funeral cooperative, nevertheless points out that "the legal battles with the private undertakers over the organization of the co-op can be used to great advantage, if handled correctly. One co-op association greatly increased its membership as a result of widespread newspaper publicity over a court case" (*Cooperative Funeral Associations,*

James Myers, Jr., published by Cooperative League of the U.S.A.). The Chico Burial Society, prosecuted at the behest of local morticians for engaging in an insurance business without a license, grew in the course of the trial to an amazing 2,000 membership in this tiny California community of 12,000.

Existing co-ops have been organized in a variety of ways. Some function as a trade union service, as the Union Co-op Burial Service of United Auto Workers in Detroit; others, like the Cleveland Memorial Society, were formed by church groups. Some of the co-ops maintain their own burial facilities while others have negotiated contracts with one or more morticians who, guaranteed a large volume of assured business from co-op members, are willing to buck the disapproval of their colleagues. From time to time, a rare—*very* rare—soul will be found in the funeral business who has become disgusted with some of the financial practices of the profession and who welcomes the formation of a cooperative funeral society.

SIMPLICITY IS THE OBJECTIVE

The East Bay, California, Memorial Association, which grew out of an existing co-op center in Berkeley, is typical of this small but growing movement. Its literature stresses community education for simplicity in disposal of the human dead, and provides detailed information on how to go about willing one's body to a medical school or hospital for research purposes. The Association offers what it is pleased to call a "lifetime membership" covering an entire family for a single payment of ten dollars. It is interracial and requires that its contracting funeral directors follow a policy of nondiscrimination. Nonsectarian, it provides for religious services or memorials of any denomination desired. Although, like most of the co-ops, the Association holds cremation to be preferable to burial, this matter is left to the discretion of the family. The cost of funerals arranged by the Association runs between $100 and $200—for service which would cost nonmembers $450 to $1,000. "We don't operate as a bargain basement or a discount house," a board member emphasized. "We are able to reduce the cost to our members through the simple method of collective bargaining—but the funerals we arrange are in every way identical to those which would normally cost four times the amount."

For the average, rational person who even in these days of "do it yourself" would balk at setting up a Monsieur Verdoux home crematorium in the backyard, and who would like to avoid such refinements as a quick-frozen trip to outer space, it would seem that the co-op funeral movement offers a most reasonable solution to the final return of dust to dust.

COMMENT

The title comes from a popular song of the 1950s: "Sixteen tons and what do you get?/Another day older and deeper in debt./St. Peter, don't you call me 'cause I can't go/I owe my soul to the company store." The idea for the piece came from my husband, Bob Treuhaft. Among the clients of his law office were a number of trade unions, and from time to time it fell to him to deal with the estates of union members who had died. He began to notice, to his great irritation, that whenever the breadwinner of a family died, the hard-fought-for union death benefit, intended for the widow, would mysteriously end up in the pocket of an undertaker: whether the benefit was $1,000, or $1,200, or $1,500, that would be the exact sum charged for the funeral. This prompted him to suggest to the directors of the Berkeley Cooperative Society that they organize a funeral cooperative, patterned after one in Seattle which had flourished since the 1930s.

Bob became absolutely immersed in this curious project; as

president of the newly formed Bay Area Memorial Association, he devoted his every waking hour to thinking up ways of spreading the message and expanding the membership. He pursued the few writers of our acquaintance, local journalists and English teachers, and tried to persuade them to do a magazine piece on the funeral industry and the emergent funeral cooperatives; nobody was interested. I was still mired in my book *Daughters and Rebels*, for which there was no publisher in sight. Why don't *you* do the article? he urged. It would provide me with some comic relief and a needed break from the book, and could be useful to the funeral societies as part of their information kit. Reluctantly at first, but with growing enthusiasm as I began to see the fascination of the subject, I set to work.

By now I had an agent who was assiduously, though unsuccessfully, trying to place *Daughters and Rebels*. He offered "St. Peter" to half a dozen nationally known magazines, including the *Saturday Evening Post*, *Coronet*, the *Atlantic*, the *Nation*, all of which turned it down on the ground that the subject matter was too gruesome. It finally found a home in *Frontier*, a Los Angeles-based liberal Democratic monthly with a circulation of two thousand, for a fee of forty dollars.

Rereading this, my second published piece, together with the earlier "Trial by Headline," I detect some improvement: it seems to flow along better, and the paragraphing makes more sense. But this piece, too, could have been vastly improved by interviews with some of the principals: undertakers, vault men, funeral society leaders. However, the quotations from the funeral press and the testimony of W. W. Chambers brighten it up somewhat.

When three years later I started writing *The American Way of Death*, "St. Peter" proved to be virtually an outline for the book; in fact, I recycled some of the material in the piece for use in the book, a form of self-plagiarism that I recommend, as one does not want to waste one's better bits on the readership of one magazine, especially if that readership is as tiny as *Frontier*'s. Ironically, to

my extreme pleasure after the book was published the same editors who had rejected "St. Peter" were after me to write follow-up
articles on the very subject they had found so distasteful (see
comment on three funeral pieces, page 103). Is there a moral here
for the aspirant writer? The old bromide "If at first you don't
succeed, try, try again" would seem to apply nicely.

PROCEED
WITH CAUTION

LIFE / *June, 1961*

There are various reasons why visitors to America do it. Some yearn to see enormous things like the Grand Canyon and Yellowstone National Park, and are in general devotees of scenic routes more easily attained by car than by jet or train. Others long to linger at the site of Abe Lincoln's log cabin, the battlefields of the Civil War, the final resting place of the late President Millard Fillmore.

"Did you have fun on your trip?" I asked an eight-year-old, just returned from a long journey with his history-minded parents. "No!" he said disgustedly. "We had to stop at all the darn old hysterical monuments."

I sympathize with him. There are many other disadvantages to the long and grueling transcontinental auto trip, or the drive from California to New Orleans. It is, however, far and away the cheapest and most practically adventurous way to go.

Nothing in your previous experience will have prepared you for the turnpikes, freeways, thruways, skyways you will encounter in America—particularly if you are, as I was, a Londoner. The actual sensation of highway driving in America is that of traffic whizzing slowly. This contradiction is achieved by getting up to the legal speed limit (50, 70, or 80, depending on the state) and staying there—which is precisely what every other car is doing. For hours and hours you drive at this speed, with no necessity for slowing, accelerating, or changing gear—you are alone on your track, like Yuri Gagarin in his space capsule.

There are sinister portents, however. From time to time your nervous eye will rest momentarily on recurrent signs along the way, proclaiming starkly, "NO STOPPING OR TURNING," and, more unnerving still, "CRIPPLED CARS TO THE RIGHT." If you are a person ridden by imagination, the question will inevitably occur to you, what then?

You visualize the scene: a dreadful and threatening sound develops in your motor, or that funny feeling in the steering wheel that means a flat tire. Your car is crippled. Obediently you draw up and stop at the right. Years later your skeleton is discovered. The image persists even though turnpike authorities assure you that a policeman will pick you up within a half-hour if you simply tie a handkerchief to your radio aerial.

Other American highway signs tend to be tautological ("SLIPPERY WHEN WET" is a great favorite), suggestive ("SOFT SHOULDERS"), or baffling because they are impossible to comply with ("BEWARE OF FALLING ROCKS" or "DEER CROSSING").

Here and there one encounters "POINT OF INTEREST AHEAD." These signs are strategically placed a quarter of a mile or so before the point of interest to enable the driver to slow or stop as the extent of his interest may dictate. If there are children in the car, they will start jumping up and down, shouting, "Point of Interest! Point of Interest!" at the top of their lungs. Once, acceding to those screams in the back seat, I actually did stop. It was somewhere in the Middle West, and we saw a tree growing out of a rock, which really was rather extraordinary. Small thanks I got, however. To this day, the children complain in heavy tones of censure, ". . . And the *only thing* we saw on the entire trip was a crummy old tree growing out of a rock."

One must rest, naturally, between such lively points of interest.

Places to stay along the way in America range from luxury run wild, at corresponding prices, to the most heavenly camping in the world.

The really expensive motels ($16 to $25 a night), found on the West and East coasts but not much in between, reach heights of fantasy hard to believe. They are usually called Magnolia Court, no doubt after a person named Magnolia. They may be Tudor, Queen Anne, Colonial, Knotty Pine, Ranch Style, or Futuristic in décor, and are invariably built around a heated swimming pool of immense proportions (a Tudor swimming pool?).

Inside, you are in a sort of Eliza Doolittle dream world; and you, grimy from hours on the road, with your battered little overnight kit, are Eliza. Your dusty old sandals or tennis shoes sink into two-inch-thick wall-to-wall carpeting; your eye lights on yards of built-in Mr. and Mrs. drawer space into which you will unpack your one clean blouse (for you have been cautioned to travel light). The soft, adjustable, concealed lighting reveals rich satin brocade bedspreads and matching curtains. An entire paneled wall may slide back at the touch of a button to reveal a giant clothes wardrobe; on one of its myriad hangers will go your rumpled mackintosh. Various discreetly placed knobs will reproduce for you at will the climate of the equator, the North Pole, or any point between. Even the huge color TV set fades into insignificance before all this glory.

To your amazement, these truly extraordinary surroundings seem to be taken for granted by the other patrons; there may even be an occasional shrill complaint: "What's the matter with this joint? No tissues in the dispenser!" Are they, then, millionaires who live this way normally? In a word, no. They are middle-income tourists like yourself. The point is whereas in most parts of the world overnight stays are a necessary evil, normally attended by discomfort not endured at home, in America the situation is exactly reversed. The motel patron has come to expect and demand a standard that boggles the imagination—and that must transcend in all ways his daily mode of life.

As for camping, one dollar a night will get you a private camp-site in a state park under towering pines or redwoods. Here again, at the other end of the scale, the American genius for comfort under all conditions will astonish you—if you have been accustomed really to roughing it. Each campsite is usually supplied with rustic table and benches, barbecue pit, tap with spring water, a cupboard fastened to a tree where your provisions will be safe from bears. The facilities in the more frequented camps usually include communal W.C.s.

But when it comes to dining along the American highway, the connoisseur of descriptive writing is likely to fare better than the gourmet. Standard menu offerings are often phrased in whole paragraphs of lyrical prose—a pleasure to read if not to eat: "Juicy young farm-raised milk-fed broad-breasted baby roast tom turkey, served with golden tender-sweet oven-baked yams, garden-fresh tiny peas, home-style hot Southern biscuits, crisp mixed-green chef's salad . . ." Sorting fact from fancy, it may occur to you that whereas a turkey is almost by definition "farm raised," you cannot visualize one actually *eating milk:* that how else could one bake yams except in an oven? You will soon learn that "garden fresh" too often is synonymous with "canned" (first cousin to "frozen fresh") and that the adjectives "young," "hot," "juicy," "crisp," and even "chef's" are apt to be in the realm of poetic license.

One final observation may be useful to the foreign visitor. Because of the great distances, keeping in touch with friends or family in America can become extremely expensive as the miles stretch on and the telephone charges mount. There appear to be two techniques for overcoming this difficulty—both of which can be effective. The standard gambit is to put through a person-to-person call for yourself. Your friends or family need merely report to the operator that you are not at home; thus you save the expense of a telephone call and your loved ones know at least that you are still alive.

But some elaborative travelers I know use a more esoteric

approach. Thus if the operator announces, "Person-to-person call, collect, for Minnie S. Oder," it is clear to the husband who answers that his wife has arrived in Minnesota. Sometimes a further stage of reasoning is required to get the message: Homer V. Hickles—Home of Vehicles—conveys Detroit, where cars are manufactured. Wishing to know whether any important letters have arrived, the wife may ask for "Esther Annie Mehl?" On one occasion the wife, having just reached Mexico, asked for Mary Atborder. She clearly heard her husband tell the operator: "No, Mrs. Atborder's not here at the moment—but she can be reached in a small town called Checkbookunderseatindesotopleasesend." It did sound like an odd name for a town, even in America; but the husband's checkbook, which he needed desperately, was on its way to him in the next morning's mail.

COMMENT

I include this piece not because it has any intrinsic merit—in fact it has many of the built-in defects of a written-to-order article—but because of how it came about, and some unforeseen consequences of its publication that brightened my life at the time.

By the time "Proceed with Caution" was commissioned, I had reached a plateau in the long upward climb to become what is known in the trade as "an established writer." *Daughters and Rebels* had at last been accepted, and had been published the year before by Houghton Mifflin. It had even made a brief appearance on *The New York Times* best-seller list, albeit at the bottom. I gradually began to notice that doors to magazine publishing, formerly closed to me, were magically opening up. (Not that my difficulties were over, far from it; they are not over to this day. On several occasions I have written articles on assignment that for one or another reason proved when submitted to be unacceptable to the magazines that commissioned them. In this case, one must make do with a "kill fee," a singularly brutal phrase meaning some fraction, generally one-third to one-half, of the agreed-on payment, and try one's luck with the piece elsewhere.)

In the spring of 1961 I went to a cocktail party in New York and there met a young woman who was doing research for a special "Come to the U.S." issue of *Life International*, beamed to Europeans. I happened to mention that I'd just driven nonstop from California with a couple of friends, and that we had made it in three and a half days. True to life, so to speak, she immediately expressed interest; she would send a teletype to Mr. Whipple, overseas *Life* editor, to see if he might want a piece on this subject. To my absolute amazement, she telephoned the next day to say the piece was commissioned, it was to be fifteen hundred words, the fee would be five hundred dollars. This news was thrilling yet horribly overwhelming, because (a) how could fifteen hundred words possibly be worth five hundred dollars, and (b) how could one make that dull trip sound interesting? The deadline for the article, she said, was Wednesday. It was now Monday. I was cast into a sort of euphoric despair: my first major commercial magazine breakthrough—until then I had aspired no higher than the *Nation*, which paid seventy-five dollars—but how on earth to pull it off?

I spent the next two days holed up in a friend's apartment, a soul in agony because the writing was such uphill work, but I got it done. By the time I learned that the piece was actually accepted, I even felt rather pleased with it—after all, what was my opinion against that of the *Life* editors? Furthermore, they told me, it would run not only in the international edition but also as a "Special Report" in domestic *Life*, for which they would pay yet another five hundred dollars.

What followed was even more pleasurable. The only part I had rather enjoyed writing was the last paragraph explaining our telephone gambit. This had been developed and refined over the years by our family and a few friends since the 1957 earthquake in

Mexico City, when my sixteen-year-old daughter, who was staying there, had called person-to-person for Alice Okie—her way of assuring us, without paying for the call, that All is O.K.

I never really expected *Life* to run that paragraph—surely these giant corporations stick together against the slingshots of us little Davids—so I was mildly surprised to see it in both the overseas and the domestic editions. However, there were swift and terrible reprisals. A friend who worked at *Life* told me all about it: "The telephone company was fit to be tied; they called all the brass at *Life* on the carpet and ordered them to show cause why the phone company should pour millions of dollars into advertising in *Life* only to be knifed in the back like this." What happened? I asked. "Well, first we fired Murphy." Murphy, my friend explained, is a fictitious *Life* editor who is always fired whenever some high-up in politics or business complains of being maligned in an article. To further assuage the phone company's injured feelings, my friend continued, *Life* arranged to produce a special eight-page color spread on the company's contribution to the space program.

In such small ways do we influence the portentous decisions of Captains of Industry; but this was not all. A few months after "Proceed with Caution" appeared, an article clearly inspired by the telephone company ran in the *Wall Street Journal* and other newspapers around the country, describing various kinds of thievery suffered by the company necessitating (they claimed) an increase in rates. Rip-offs reported in the article were for the most part rather crude, such as teen-agers breaking into pay phones and stealing the money; but one example given was that of a traveling salesman in Detroit who, wishing to let his wife know his whereabouts, calls his home number person-to-person for Homer V. Hickles. I, of course, was dying to sue the telephone company for plagiarism; but as usual, wiser heads prevailed.

YOU-ALL
AND NON-YOU-ALL:
A SOUTHERN
POTPOURRI

ESQUIRE / *May, 1962*

TRIP NOTES

All the advice you get when you're going on a trip. This time, it's mostly advice not to go at all. "You'll probably come back and write a do-gooder's tract," they say. Or, "I've got a good title for you: Live Oaks and Dead People." Or, heavily sarcastic, "Have *fun*." I can't get anyone to go with me. They all say, "We'd go if you were going somewhere sensible like New York."

The prejudice Northerners feel towards Southerners is roughly parallel to that felt by English people towards Americans, and is compounded of many of the same ingredients—a thoroughgoing dislike of their public policies, contempt for their level of education and culture, and a sort of instinctive recoil at the sound of the accent—larded in both cases, it must be said, with a thick layer of that particular form of snobbishness that sneers at the provincial. It is distasteful to the Northerner that a human being should have the given name of Lady Bird; it grates on the Northern ear to hear an educated person say "sumpn" and "prolly," or speak of a "mess of fried chicken" pronounced "maiss of frad chickn."

The photographs that appear so regularly in the newspapers of white faces caught in the act of hate outside some school or drug-store fill the Northerner with uneasiness and almost incredulity; for when the Northerner segregates and discriminates, he does it on the whole slyly rather than overtly, and without passion.

Thus the white South comes to be pictured in the Northern mind as an undifferentiated, arid wasteland of the human intellect and spirit, a hopeless mess of a place, cluttered with irrationality and ignorance, incongruously smeared over with a sticky coating of sugary politeness and sentimentality.

All the same, there are hints that changes may be on the way: a high-school student's appeal for reason in Little Rock; a white minister leading his child past hostile mobs to school in New Orleans; white college kids extending the hand of friendship to three black classmates at Georgia Tech.

My point in going to the South was, as a certain kind of tourist will often put it, "to see how the people really live." I was not too interested in the usual interviews with V.I.P.s on both sides of the integration question. To slide into the daily lives of people, to soak up their ordinary conversation, to savor their manner and manners, to achieve an oblique rather than a direct look was my plan. Slightly easier said than done, I found; people are always shoving you off to talk to community leaders or to meetings where The Problem is under discussion.

Also, although I deliberately chose a time when things seemed tranquil—the sit-in operation largely over in the communities I visited, the aims of the Montgomery bus boycott long since achieved—violence followed me, and unwittingly I found myself in the middle of it. However, I thought when it was all over, the mobs and the violence and the meetings to discuss ways of preventing violence *are* really part of the daily lives of ordinary people in the South.

TRIP NOTES

On the train, through Kentucky. There's already a marked change of atmosphere. The women on the train seem to travel in Sears catalogue dreamy date dresses. One is wearing a beige silk sheath, spangled semi-transparent top, high-heeled simulated glass slippers. She's a great kidder. The conductor, checking on reservations, just asked her, "Are you Mrs. Jennie Lee Kelley?" She answered, "Can't you see I am, by my browbeaten look?" Shrieks of laughter from all, especially her fat husband. . . . Lovely pale green, lush country outside . . . In a Louisville hotel: already the punctuation and spelling are breaking down. A brochure in my room says, "Derby Lounge. Stall's are named and portray famous derby winners . . ." and also, "YE-OLE KENTUCKIE BREAKFEASTE." Why the hyphen? Borrowed from you-all?

Louisville, a town on the turn, is a mass of contradictions. There is one major department store that not only refuses service to blacks in the cafeteria, but denies them the right to try on or return clothes. There is another, equally substantial, that not only serves blacks in the cafeteria—but has complained that not enough of them eat there! The manager points out that the transition to acceptance will be smoother in the long run if the whites become accustomed as a daily matter of course to seeing blacks served.

A black newspaper editor told me, "In these border communities it's not popular to believe in segregation. Most whites will tell you they have 'colored friends,' even though they generally mean their maids. But although there's abstract agreement about the inevitability of desegregation, there's no agreement about implementation—the when and how."

The editor asked me if I'd like to meet some women who were going to do "the Testing." He explained: In the wake of a successful sit-in movement by students the year before, some ninety eating places had agreed to desegregate, and now their good faith was being tested. The Testers, a group of well-dressed black women, gathered at the black Y.W.C.A. for instructions and assignments. There were the usual asides so familiar to anyone who has worked in P.-T.A., Girl Scouts, the usual civic organizations: "Can't work beyond two o'clock, my Jimmy gets back from school then." "Sorry I couldn't come Tuesday, Miz Brown, but my kids all came down with the flu." Efficient-looking mimeographed forms were handed out, with spaces for "Place Tested," "Time Tested," "Environment (check one): Low, Medium, High," "Attitude of Waitress or Manager (check one): Poor, Fair, Good."

"The trouble is, you have to drink so much coffee before the day's over," confided one woman—a complaint I had further occasion to hear in the course of my travels. The chairman, a pleasant-looking middle-aged schoolteacher, issued a few last-minute reminders: "Don't get in any arguments. Don't forget to bring the completed form next week." The Testers received their assignments and drifted off in pairs for the day's work. It was all very matter-of-fact, a chore that had to be done, a little reminiscent of a League of Women Voters survey of some community facility.

For another view of Louisville, I accepted an invitation to dinner at the country club. This was, for me, a little like being shown around a steel factory behind the Iron Curtain; never having seen the inside of one at home, I had no basis for comparison. Nevertheless, a certain amount of Southern life revolves around these country clubs, and I thought it would be a good thing to have a look.

We were a party of five, two couples and myself. Rather to my surprise, conversation centered for a time on the Servant Problem. I have, of course, heard and read of such discussions, but had never before been actually present at one. The subject was first broached by one of the guests, a middle-aged man whom I shall call Mr. Mitchell. He related the sad story of his experience with *Life* magazine, which had recently run a series of articles on domestic servants. A *Life* editor had called Mr. Mitchell about his old Uncle Mo, who has been with the Mitchell family for thirty-five years; then, just when Mr. Mitchell figured the story was all set, *Life* dropped him and Uncle Mo, and picked some upstart who had only been with *his* white folks for eighteen years. "With *Life*, many are called but few are chosen," I murmured, but the other couple now chimed in along these lines: "Why, Wilfred, you-all certainly have it easy! Why, our Chorine, she's simple terrible, I mean she's just awful, simply ruined the best silver by pouring bleach all over it, we've rechristened her 'Chlorine.' " . . .

Just as I was being overcome with prickly embarrassment, Mrs. Mitchell came to my rescue and turned the conversation to books. Mrs. Mitchell jerst lerves to read. In fact, the local branch of the public library simply can't keep up with her; she just *gobbles* up books, five or six of 'em a week. Why, books are just bread and meat to her. . . . Mr. Mitchell demurred. He never reads anything unless it has first been digested by the *Reader's Digest;* he's a ve'y ve'y slow reader, always has been, can't git through these long, long books of three-four hundred pages, that's asking too much of a man. He means, he *likes* reading, but why drag it out so? Mmm, you've got a point, I said.

I felt that time was staggering on and we were somehow missing the crux of life in the South today, and now undertook to change the subject myself. "What do you think of the sit-ins?" I asked of the general assemblage. Mr. Mitchell undertook to propound the position for the group. He explained that it was like this. In'egra-tion may be inevitable, but it's gotta be fought, because just as sure as night and day it will lead eventually to the Mongrelization of the Race. Using bits of tableware, he illustrated: "Here you've got a race horse," producing a fork. "And here's a cart horse," marshaling a sugar bowl that did look a little bit like a fat, plod-ding old nag. "Mix 'em, and what have you got?" Since, reader, you have heard this one before, I will cut it short: You've got sumpn that ain't fit for running and ain't fit for hauling—a cross-breed, a misfit. "And what, oh what, have you got if you breed a slow reader with a fast reader?" I asked anxiously; but answer came there none.

Fortunately there are other viewpoints to be found among Louisville whites. Louisville is the home of Barry Bingham, pub-lisher and owner of the liberal *Courier-Journal*. Bingham im-pressed me as one who would be more at home in London or Paris than in this provincial setting, a cosmopolitan in outlook and by preference; yet he works conscientiously with the locals for liberalization of racial attitudes in his home town. It is also the home of Carl and Anne Braden, who some years ago faced ostracism and criminal prosecution because they helped a black veteran buy a home in an all-white tract. Carl Braden is now in prison, serving his year for contempt of the House Committee on Un-American Activities. His wife keeps house for their three children and works full-time for the interracial Southern Conference Educational Fund. She is a pale, determined young woman who speaks in the accents of her native Alabama. She has great confidence in her fellow-Southern-whites: "Once people down in these parts start to shake loose from their prejudices, it'll be a landslide. It's beginning already among the young folks, college and high-school age. There's really an awful lot going on that you never read about in the newspapers."

TRIP NOTES

Last day in Louisville. No fair using taxi drivers for copy, but this one's an exception. She's a rugged, strong-looking woman, build of Marie Dressler. I ask her what she thinks of the sit-ins. "All for them!" she calls out gaily. Goes on to tell me about her son's elementary school picnic last year. There were about sixty white people, kids and parents, and one black boy. The park custodian refused to admit the black child—upon which the whites, by common agreement, decided to chuck the whole thing. Surprising, because I'm not at all sure this would necessarily have been the outcome had a parallel incident happened at home in California. . . . On to Nashville. I'm told it is known by its inhabitants as "the Athens of the South." Leads one to speculate for a fanciful moment on whether Athenians ever think of their city as "the Nashville of Greece."

In Nashville, I drove to a shady road on the outskirts of town, one of those roads bathed in the luminous green that is the hallmark of a Southern spring; you feel almost as though you were swimming through the weeds of a sunny, overgrown pond, so exuberant is the vegetation. The large, tidy house at the end of the circular drive was of the vintage of its inhabitants, perhaps a little older, and furnished in the style of their youth with lots of leather, varnished maps, flowery chintz, and fringed lamps.

Several ladies were gathered for tea, which was shortly served by a prim black maid. The sweet, soft voices twittered away: "I declare, Francie-Lou, these brownies are just mouth-watering." "And I never did get my ramblers to bloom just right last spring, but then the weather was downright unseasonable." Touches of lace rose and fell on dimity bosoms, old fingers groped in purses for photographs of grandchildren. One might have stumbled into a scene from a Mary Petty cartoon. Soon enough, as often happens in a gathering of the leisured elderly, the conversation turned to Good Works. The particular form of Good Works practiced by these ladies for the past several months was being Observers at the black sit-ins.

The role of an Observer, they explained to me, was merely to sit at the lunch counter or in the theatre where blacks were seeking accommodation, and in silence to lend moral support to the effort. There was no contact between Observer and sit-in demonstrator, and no words were ever exchanged; nevertheless, "by some sort of mental telepathy," as one expressed it, the friendly intent of the Observer was usually somehow transmitted to the black group. Looking round at these particular Observers, I felt it wouldn't require much detective work to divine that a Woolworth's lunch counter was not their customary eating place, nor *Son of Tarzan* their preferred form of entertainment. "I don't think Miz' Beardsley ever set foot in a Woolworth's before in all her born days," confided one, "because she turned to me real surprised, and said, 'Why, who'd have thought they serve coffee in these places?'" Mrs. Beardsley had good cause to find out that they not only serve coffee, but ply the customers with free refills; for after two hours, during which because of a temporary breakdown of organization no blacks showed up, she was heard to complain in an agonized stage whisper, "Where in the world are they? I simply *can't* drink any more coffee—and I *must* find the ladies' room." Coffee drinking seems to loom large in this struggle.

With a hundred or more white Observers involved, mostly women with free daytime hours to devote, a few minor hitches were bound to develop. One lady sailed angrily up to an ac- quaintance who had merely stopped at a lunch counter for a bite to eat after a hot afternoon's shopping, and snapped, "What are *you* doing here? This place is reserved for the Unitarians."

Integration of the movie theatres presented yet another prob- lem. Informal agreement was finally reached with some of the theatre managers that blacks would be admitted, but to smooth the initial stages of the change, they would be expected to walk directly to their seats and not to stand in the lobby, patronize the candy stand, or use the restrooms. A white lady Observer, seeing a black patron in front of her move as though to rise from his seat, reached forward and grabbed him, saying loudly, "You're not sup- posed to go to the restroom!"

What early experience or sudden turn in life had prompted the missionary zeal of the Observers? This was hard to discover. "I guess I've always felt this way, ever since I was a child," said one. "It's just that there was never any opportunity to *do* anything about it until the sit-ins started." I was to get the same sort of answer from many another Southern white.

I asked my hostess what sort of reaction her activities evoked among her friends and relations. "They never discuss it," she answered stiffly. I thought I could see why: she was in truth intimi- datingly ladylike, not the sort with whom one would seek a rough- and-tumble argument. Furthermore, it seems to be a characteristic of polite Southern society to avoid subjects which may lead to unpleasant controversy, or which start a train of thought at the end of which lies change and unrest. I had further occasion to remark this in Nashville. I spent an afternoon with an elderly intellectual, one of those rare women whose entire life is spent in the realm of scholarly endeavor. She was a leading authority on Boswell and Johnson, a translator of eighteenth-century French poetry, a student of modern thought from Freud to Sartre—and an alert, interesting conversationalist. At one point, I asked her what she thought the outcome of the segregation problem would be. She became exceedingly ruffled, and answered quite crossly, "To tell you the truth, I never give it a thought." Evidently, to think about this particular problem would be disturbing, and in an area in which she had no wish to be disturbed.

If one stayed long enough in the company of people like the Observer ladies, it might be possible to get the wrong impression. It would not be difficult to travel through the South entirely in such company, for today they exist to one extent or another in every state—even in the deep South—and, like all minority thinkers, they tend to hang together. They are for the most part a deeply dedicated lot. In the North, there are countless numbers of white people who contribute occasionally to CORE or NAACP, go once in a while to a meeting or lecture on race problems, and vote for a local black candidate; but these activities are on the periphery of their lives. Among the Southerners I met who have taken a stand for integration, it seems to have swallowed them whole, and to occupy their every waking moment.

Once you start out with the integrationists, they are likely to pass you from hand to hand and from town to town without giving you much chance to peer at the other side. I mentioned this to a young attorney, originally from Jackson, whom I met in Nashville. He laughed and said, "You should tra meetin' Kissin' Jim Folsom. *That'd* open yo' ass." For a moment, I was frozen with astonishment—until I realized he was saying *"eyes."*

TRIP NOTES

Atlanta. So far, everywhere I've been (Louisville, Nashville, and now Atlanta) people keep saying, "This isn't the *real* South," or, "It's more of a border city." Yet they look like Southerners, they talk like Southerners, they act like Southerners. I gather what they really mean is that Atlanta, Nashville, and Louisville have better newspapers, better col-

leges, more enlightened leadership, and consequently better race relations than other Southern communities. Therefore to say they are not
the *real* South seems vaguely unfair.

I met a couple of Southern belles, 1961 models. The first was a
senior at a women's college on the outskirts of Atlanta ("academically, the best school in the South," she told me). She had the
delicate look of a spring flower—yet a certain bounciness of
manner—and that special softness and highness of voice often
encountered in Southern women. "What made me join the sit-ins?
I don't know. I always wanted to do something about discrimination. When I saw them there, I felt I had no choice but to join in,"
she said. She had not known any of the Negro participants. One
day she was downtown shopping and came across a Negro picket
line. "I just started picketing with them, but the tears were rolling
down my cheeks." She distributed CORE literature all over
campus, and eventually about six of her fellow-students took part
in the picketing. She regards herself as "neither a leader nor a
follower—just an individual," yet she conveys the impression of
one who will make her mark on history.

The second Southern belle, conventionally honey-haired and
blue-eyed, was introduced to me by her mother who said, "I want
you to meet my li'l ole jailbird daughter. She's just been in and out
of those jails since the sit-ins started—haven't you, lamb chop?—
and now she's on her way to Jackson with the Freedom Riders."
Lamb chop, an honor student at a New Orleans women's college,
is jeopardizing a coveted Junior Year Abroad by making the
dangerous journey to Jackson; but with her, as with a growing
number of her generation, the "mewve-ment" (as they all pro-
nounce it) must come first.

The little old jailbird's attractive and delightful mother took me
to some meetings where I met the men and women of good will
who were busily organizing for D-day—that day in September
when the schools would be desegregated for the first time. ("Don't
ever say *integration,* we like to call it *desegregation*—it sounds so

much more palatable, somehow.") A network of committees and subcommittees with their cleverly contrived names—HOPE for Help Our Public Education, OASIS for Organizations Assisting Schools in September—were meeting almost daily, often to the background whir of a mimeograph machine grinding out the latest mailing. From the top-level planners, including Y leaders, churchmen, school board people, to the neighborhood groups and youth committees, hundreds were involved in this huge humanitarian enterprise. I heard the superintendent of schools tell a gathering that police protection for the entering students would be as carefully planned as the invasion of Japan. It was all thrilling, and heartwarming, and inspiring—with one tragicomic aspect: this great outpouring of best-intentioned energy was directed to the very modest end that nine black children (out of three hundred applicants) should be allowed peacefully to take their rightful places at school in September. These nine had survived every conceivable test known to educators. Academically, they had to be above the 50th percentile of the school to which they sought transfer, their behavior record had to be blameless, their personalities had to be declared outstanding. No such tests were required, of course, of their white classmates, which leads one to speculate whether the old phrase "separate but equal" is being supplanted for the blacks by the concept "together but vastly superior."

TRIP NOTES

Montgomery. At last people have stopped saying, "This isn't the *real* South." My favorite sort of houses everywhere, white frame, two or more stories, most with nineteenth-century gingerbread trim. Even in the better suburbs, none of this split-level streamlined modern that gets so tiresome in wealthy California . . . everything half-hidden by the rampaging vegetation, a Corot-Monet-Manet land . . . the frescoes round the walls of the cupola in the State Capitol, incredibly like the worst examples of Soviet art, depicting scenes of Montgomery history . . . one, titled "The Golden Years," shows a group of happy slaves toting bales of something, each with delighted smile on face. No postcards of this available, to my sorrow, as I should have liked to tease my friends at home with them . . . the Elite Café, Fine Food (pronounced "Eelight Cafe, Fan Fude"). . . . Weeds pushing up all over the tennis courts in the immense public park; a couple of years ago blacks won a court decision granting them use of the park, so the city authorities closed it up for everybody . . . noses and faces being respectively cut off and spited all over . . . they disbanded the zoo, too, and now if you want to take the kids to the zoo you have to go all the way to Birmingham—where the zoo is integrated!

Social gatherings in Montgomery are full of echoes of the past. The food in private houses tends to be in the shape of things—ice-cream boats or hearts, fish-shaped aspic salads—and almost everything is creamed, not only creamed but served with cream sauce. The fare is as mild and gentle as the ladies themselves, no bitter or pungent taste to offset the bland, no crisp consistency to contrast with the soft. The very form of conversation seems more nine-teenth century than contemporary. At ladies' lunches the talk proceeds like a croquet game, with three standard opening moves: (1) the weather: "Well, is it hot enough for you?" (2) the food, about which someone is bound to declare pretty near the beginning that Rosie-Belle's whatever-it-is is just simply out of this world, (3) the frontal-assault type of compliment where somebody declares that my you get younger-looking every day and how in the world do you manage it, and goes on to bet your husband doesn't like to let you out of his sight for one single minute. (This sort of remark may as well be delivered to a matron of fifty as to the latest bride, and trips off the tongue as readily.) Exaggeration as a way of life may confuse the auslander. My hostess answers the telephone and is heard to say, "Why Janie, that's just about the nicest thing I ever heard in my whole life"; upon being asked later what the call was about, it turns out that Janie has invited us over for a drink. No use to comment that my hostess must have had a rather thin time if that was really just about the *nicest* thing she *ever* heard in her *whole* life; she merely stares uncomprehendingly.

As conversation warms up—which of course it does, eventually —the sense of the past is intensified, for so much of it deals with endless ramifications of family history and gossip about old times. One thing leading to another, the long-ago romances of Aunts Willie-Jo and Sarah-Marie, Cousins Robbie-Lou and Marigold, are brought out for examination and speculation. Anecdotes often end, "And the thing of it was he simply up and took a shotgun and blew his brains out." "And of course she was found in the river. We all felt so bad and no one ever did exactly get the right of what happened." "The poor feller just actually took to the bottle (well you *know* he did, and of course it's in the family, his father died an alcoholic) and well anyway I declare one day they found him in the garage hanging from a belt. . . ." "Of course nothing was ever proved about it, but they do say her death was *not* accidental." Few seem to have died in their beds. All this, in surprising contrast to the peachy-creamy surface of life in Montgomery.

The Montgomery country club is much like the one in Louisville —spacious, old-fashioned, French windows giving on to a long outdoor terrace, presumably for Gone With the Windish occasions. As in Louisville, good whiskey and terrible food are served by old-family-retainer types of blacks in white coats. There were a lot of young people in the crowd, girls in diaphanous evening dresses, boys in white dinner jackets. Their talk was all but incomprehensible, their "y'alls" rang out like Rebel Yells. I found myself talking to a middle-aged man, introduced to me as a member of the school board; so we discussed education—in its noncontroversial aspects, for I was a guest and on my best behavior. The topic was the difficult situation of the unusually bright child, whether he should be "skipped" or handled otherwise. It is a safe and well-plotted subject, with enough "on the one hands" and "on the other hands" to keep one going for a while. My interlocutor explained that in his district, the problem is being tackled by grouping the children within each grade according to ability. I rejoined that the same system obtains in Oakland—and could not help adding that in our grammar school, there is a fifth-grade group of six children with I.Q.s of over 150—two whites, two Orientals, and two blacks. With genuine forehead-wrinkling puzzlement (and no apparent rancor) the school board member drawled, "Is that so? It don't seem possible no Nigra could have an I.Q. of 150, do it, now?" I started to say, "To me it do . . ." when our hostess hurriedly bore me off to talk to someone else. (A friend of mine in California, herself a transplanted Southerner, insists I have exaggerated this story, that educated Southerners do not talk like this. But I heard what I heard, and what's more I've caught her talking in the same vernacular when she gets around her own folks from down home. To forestall a probable further criticism— that I have represented the whites but not the blacks as speaking in dialect—I can only say that educated Southern blacks are indeed far more particular about their diction than are their white counterparts.)

For a breath of fresh air, I went to the mass meeting in the black community where Reverend Martin Luther King, Jr., was to speak with the Freedom Riders. Actually the air was disturbingly filled with tear gas at one point, and no one quite knew if we'd get out of there alive. The hostile white crowd outside, which had been gathering for some time before the meeting, was suitably attired, I noted with approval, in the latest thing in mob wear. In faded cotton frocks revealing insect-bitten bare legs, or dirty shirts and jeans, they might have been movie extras assembled by a rather unimaginative director to do a corny mob scene. A well-read lot, they appeared to be, too—versed in the literature of their region. Surely that half-beaten-down half-savage look, that casual yet brutal slouch, that mean glitter in the eye could only be achieved by one with at least a passing acquaintance with the works of Faulkner, Tennessee Williams, and Eudora Welty. There was no police protection, of course; just one or two very nervous-looking U.S. marshals. To achieve the church, I parked my borrowed car nearby and walked past the extras with all deliberate speed, as the Supreme Court would say—for, being hatted, gloved, and stockinged, I felt more than a little conspicuous.

Inside, the church was a loud, sweet-singing haven, warmly enveloping. It was filled far beyond its normal seating capacity with people of all ages: dark-suited men, women in best dresses and flowered hats, little girls in party shoes, little boys wriggling in their stiff collars.

As the evening wore on, its nightmare quality began to unfold. First there was the tear gas, an alien and threatening odor. Next, incredibly, Reverend King was telling us in matter-of-fact tones that the mob outside was completely out of control, they had injured some of the U.S. marshals and had overturned and burned a car. The implication was rather strong that the church might be next. More incredibly, the vast, packed audience was taking it in stride. There was not a sign of panic, not a shriek, not a fainting fit. Just murmurs of "Yes, Lord," "That's right," lots of singing, lots of patient confidence. It seemed to go on forever and ever. Later, it was announced by the General of the Alabama National Guard that no one could leave the church until morning because of the danger outside. The atmosphere became positively jolly—like an impromptu camping expedition, I thought, as we prepared to make ourselves as comfortable as possible for the long hours of confinement.

Searching that sea of calm, determined faces, I felt as though I'd stumbled on the very source of strength that would brace a young girl to exchange a year in Paris for a stretch in the Jackson prison, or a provincial gentlewoman to brave the scorn of her social set by publicly giving a hand to the black sit-ins.

Sometime after five o'clock in the morning, having learned that my borrowed car was the unlucky one that had been demolished earlier, I was driven home in an Alabama National Guard jeep. It was a morning of startling beauty—a soft, warm, breezy dawn in which the lovely little town looked its very best.

TRIP NOTES

Montgomery after the Freedom Riders. The Fire Marshal came round to see me about the burned-up car. I was rather hoping he might be interested in finding the vandals who had destroyed it but he only asked me whether I was connected with CORE or NAACP, whether I had made other stops in the South or had come directly to Montgomery from California, whether I had attended regular church that Sunday morning, whether I knew anyone else who was at the meeting, why I went, whether my friends had lent me the car "of their own free will." . . . An editorial in the Montgomery *Advertiser* deplores the view that mob violence will chase industry from Montgomery; it points out that Atlanta had the greatest race riot in history in 1906, six hundred blacks killed and carted off in trucks—and look at flourishing, industrial Atlanta today! . . . A twenty-two-year-old English student here is in trouble. She was quoted in a man-in-the-street interview as saying, "Negroes should be allowed to go any place they wish. I am for integration of the races 100 percent." Since when she has been dropped from, of all things, the English-Speaking Union! . . . The Country Clubbers have vanished from my life like summer snow since the car burning. One of them called me (sounding absolutely terrified) to say a rumor was spreading that she had accompanied me to the meeting, that her husband and in-laws are furious with her for even knowing me, that it wouldn't be safe for us to meet again. . . . Twenty-two students from Auburn University signed a letter which appeared in the *Advertiser*, first sane thing to appear locally. They've since been hanged in effigy on campus by counter-students. . . . A local white couple, Fred and Anna Gach, have been tried and convicted of disturbing the peace. They saw a black Freedom Rider being stomped by the mob, shouted to a policeman (who was standing with back to the scene, arms folded) to "do something." He did something—he arrested the Gaches. . . .

Just before I left, I was smuggled into one last drawing room for tea. By now there was virtually only one topic of conversation in Montgomery: the Freedom Riders, and for comic relief the case of the young English girl versus the English-Speaking Union. After the usual preliminary comments on the weather, the strawberry cream cake, and the youth and beauty of all present, our hostess patiently undertook to put me wise to the basic objection to the Freedom Riders; integration of the bus station facilities would surely lead to intermarriage. "But does one usually marry a person because one sits next to him at a bus stop?" She answered, with glint in eye and Scarlett O'Hara toss of head, "Honey, when *ah* sit next to a man—*any* man—ah jes' caint help thinkin' jest how he'd be, you know, to make love to. Ah might just as well come right out and say it—in baid. Now, you know yourself, *owl* women are lak that." Later, the ladies discussed a mutual acquaintance—somebody's aunt, I believe—who is currently in a nearby mental institution. "It's real, real nass out there," one of them said. "Ah declare! They have the loveliest grounds! It's all beautifully kept up, you should see the flowers at this time of year. The fude's fan, too, and she has such a pretty room." She added reflectively, "It *really* isn't so very different from the outside."

COMMENT

The South has always fascinated me. I have dipped into that strange territory many times over the years, principally to visit Clifford and Virginia Durr, a white lawyer and his wife, in Montgomery, Alabama. In the dangerous 1950s these two were among the tiny minority of white supporters of such black causes as the Montgomery bus boycott, and in consequence they suffered almost complete ostracism at the hands of the respectable white community. Observing their life and meeting their few staunch allies, I wanted to probe further into the curious mixture of nostalgia and guilt (and, in their case, courage) that permeates the white Southern psyche. I wanted to see how that psyche was faring in the aftermath of the victorious bus boycott of the late 1950s and the sit-ins of 1960–61, so I sent a proposal along these lines to the editor of *Esquire*, who agreed to commission the piece.

Armed with a sheaf of introductions, I spent about five weeks on the road visiting various Southern cities and filling up a dozen notebooks with my findings. It was a sometimes exhilarating, sometimes horrifying, and sometimes even amusing experience. But when I got home and started to write about it, loaded as I was with material, I found that by far the worst part was trying to devise some sort of organizational form for the piece. Clearly the most dramatic incident of my trip was the beleaguered church meeting for the Freedom Riders—which could have taken up the whole article. Yet that was not my intention; I had set out to record impressions of the contemporary white South.

Where to start and where to finish? I must have used up a ream of paper with false beginnings and endings. Finally I settled on a sort of travelogue format, a straight chronological account of the journey, the people I met, the episodes—which may seem the obvious way to do it, although it was far from obvious to me at the time. I also tumbled to the idea of "Trip Notes," to be set off in different type from the narrative, for transitions between the towns I visited. I put these down as actual jottings from my notebooks, wishing to spare the reader wearisome descriptions of train journeys, scenery, background information—and also hoping that since I single-spaced these in the typescript, the editors at *Esquire* would not notice that the article exceeded the agreed-on length by quite a bit.

Here, however, I may have outsmarted myself, for the editors cut, without consultation, the paragraph about Carl and Anne Braden, the only militantly left-wing characters in the piece. This was most annoying because the Bradens added a needed dimension to a discussion of white Southern supporters of the black cause: that of the politically conscious radical who is involved not only in the humanitarian issues, but who sees a whole reorganization of society as the only real solution. But Carl Braden was in prison at the time for refusing to testify before the House Committee on Un-American Activities. Were the *Esquire* editors still under the spell of fear cast by the then not so distant McCarthy era, hence reluctant to accord the Bradens favorable mention in the magazine? Another unauthorized change: my title, "You-All and Non-You-All," derived from my sister Nancy's book about U and Non-U usage, was changed to the meaningless "Whut They're Thanking Down There," which does not even catch the cadence of Southern vernacular.

In Montgomery I stayed with the Durrs—it was they who arranged through intermediaries for me to meet the Southern gentry, few of whom were on their own social list, and to be invited to the country club. It was their ancient car, worth no more than its value to a junk dealer, that was burned outside the mass meeting. Obviously I would have to reimburse them for this loss. When I got home, I called my insurance agent, whose sympathies were all with the Freedom Riders, and unfolded my plan for a claim: had it been my own car, whose blue-book value was $850, the insurance company would have had to pay up. Since it was just by chance that I was using somebody else's car, could I not collect this sum? Much to my surprise this rather specious reasoning paid off, enabling the Durrs, then living on the edge of poverty, to get a fairly decent replacement for the car.

The reaction of my Montgomery hostesses to the piece, as reported by Virginia Durr, was illuminating. She said they were not in the least disturbed by my remarks about their mindless bigotry —but were exceedingly offended by my description of the FOOD as being uniformly bland and creamy: "We didn't have cream sauce, we had roast lamb the night she came." "She never mentioned my lettuce-and-walnut salad."

AMERICANS DON'T WANT FANCY FUNERALS

SATURDAY EVENING POST / *November 23, 1963*

Has the twentieth-century American standard of dying evolved in response to public demand, as the funeral industry claims? Do people really desire that modern technology and "know-how" should be applied to the production of ever more elaborate funerary merchandise, gaudier caskets, finer burial negligées, bigger and more beautiful undertaking establishments with softer and thicker carpeting? Is there a clamor for newer and better embalming techniques for the purpose of achieving an ever more lifelike appearance in corpses? And are people only too willing and anxious to pay for all this, as the funeral merchants insist?

Judging by the response to my recent book criticizing American funeral practices the opposite is true, and there is in fact a revolution underway by the funeral customer—the American public at large—against the funeral industry and its bizarre product.

It would seem that this is one area of our affluent society in which a great many people yearn to see an end to proliferating "improvements" and "refinements," yearn for restraint and a return to rationality, and actively resent the fantastically high charges levied on bereaved families by the funeral trade.

The death industries—undertakers, cemetery men, florists, casket and vault manufacturers—are turning the deaf ear to rumblings of mutiny among their patrons. Nevertheless, they are in the grip of a nightmare: the deadly fear that their two-billion-dollar-a-year mortuary empire may be slipping from their grasp. At the moment, their spokesmen are rounding on "the Mitford menace" with fangs bared, refusing to see that their real trouble lies not with any one book or magazine article, nor with any one critic, but rather with large numbers of ordinary people in all walks of life who are becoming increasingly restive about the style and cost of the modern funeral.

The controversy that is taking place over my book seems to be shaping up not as a public debate in the usual sense of the term but rather as a battle between the funeral men on one side and the public on the other.

True, a small minority of undertakers are beginning to face the facts and to exhibit more flexibility in their approach to their customers, even to develop some understanding and respect for people who as a matter of principle do not want the full funerary treatment ordinarily prescribed by the industry. But the industry as a whole, and particularly the association leaders, are unable to come to grips with the situation that confronts them today because their whole operation rests on a myth: the assumption that they have the full and unqualified backing of the vast majority of the American people, that the costly and lavish funeral of today, with all its fabulous trimmings, is but a reflection of American insistence on "the best" in all things. It is particularly hard for them to grasp the idea that a person who has lived well or even luxuriously might *prefer* the plainest disposition after death.

The myopic assumption that all but a few crackpots and troublemakers approve and endorse the contemporary American funeral comes through strongly in the declarations of industry spokesmen. In the words of Mr. Wilber Krieger, Managing Director of National Selected Morticians: "Fortunately, there are tens of thousands of families in this country who, from experience, know this criticism is ill-founded. We leave it to them to judge the merits of the case put forward by Miss Mitford."

One might have supposed, then, that many readers would be offended by my book, by the suggestion that the typical American funeral of today with "cosmetized" corpse in elaborate casket is grotesque, inappropriate, and a ridiculous waste of financial resources. The behavior of a society toward its dead is, after all, an extremely sensitive subject and criticism in this area might be expected to arouse deep emotions. Is there (as the undertakers claim) a pent-up reservoir of good will for the trade and for the type of funeral it prefers to sell based on untold thousands of satisfied customers? Would these satisfied customers rise in their numbers to defend the undertakers and their practices, to protest the suggestion of restoring simplicity to our exit from this world?

The protest, when it came, proved to be one-sided indeed, and from one quarter alone: the funeral men themselves.

Of the avalanche of letters I have received about my book from all over the country, from all sorts of people, I have yet to hear from a satisfied customer. I find it rather surprising, in fact, that not one correspondent has so far come forward to praise or justify the typical contemporary funeral, to commend the embalmer's handiwork, or to say of a funeral in his own family, "It was worth every cent." On the contrary, I have been deluged with new complaints, new "horror stories" about the depletion of small estates by funeral charges, new expressions of revulsion against the style in which we bury our dead.

Typical of these was a letter from a schoolteacher in Chicago who had worked and sacrificed to provide adequate nursing and some comforts for her father during a terminal illness. When her father died, she refused to purchase the elaborate casket urged on her by the undertaker. She shocked him to his boots by insisting that even the "minimum-priced service" at $695 was too high; that if he would not supply a plain wood coffin for half that sum, as specified in her father's will, she would take the body elsewhere. This threat worked (as it often does) and the reluctant undertaker complied, but she learned later that he had confided to her relatives that "she must be a little off in the head."

There was the advertising executive who, while arranging for the funeral of his mother, was called on by the undertaker to choose between two materials for the casket lining. "What's the difference?" he asked. The undertaker explained that the more expensive material was pure silk and the cheaper was rayon: "We find rayon is a lot more irritating to the skin."

And then there was the report from a TV crew which recently filmed a program in the establishment of one of the largest and most "reputable" undertakers in California. The owner piously assured them that no hard selling was done in *his* place, the choice was entirely up to the family; in fact, they were encouraged to browse around among the caskets without a salesman even present. The TV men were impressed—until one of the sound crew spotted a hidden microphone in the casket selection room, placed there for the purpose of eavesdropping on the conversation of the bereaved family!

A further application of electronics to modern dying was revealed to me in a letter from a former embalmer. As soon as the undertaker, conferring with the family, ascertains the amount of insurance and other death benefits available, he signals by push button to an assistant in the casket sales room. The assistant's job is then to rush around changing the discreet little price tags on each casket so that the entire range of prices offered will be raised or lowered to fit the appropriate financial bracket.

Some of these revelations—and the extent and depth of resentment felt by people generally over funeral practices—came as a surprise to me. Not so the reactions of the funeral men, of which I had advance notice.

Long before *The American Way of Death* was published, the funeral industry became aware that it was in progress. Headlines began to appear in the undertakers' trade journals: "MITFORD DAY DRAWS CLOSER!" "JESSICA MITFORD PLANS ANTI-FUNERAL BOOK," and, on a more optimistic note, "WHO'S AFRAID OF THE

BIG, BAD BOOK?" On the eve of publication of my book, the *Director*, official organ of the influential National Funeral Directors Association, carried a front-page editorial on the subject, advising the nation's undertakers to "adapt to the situation calmly, to refuse to panic in either thought or action, remembering that the funeral is a custom long established by common consent." *Mortuary Management*, an undertakers' monthly voiced the same idea: "These are the days when you must hold steadfast even though you have every right to lash out against the unprovoked attacks with every weapon at your command."

Sound advice, perhaps, but not always easy to follow, as subsequent reactions showed. The very next week the *National Funeral Service Journal* was adapting far from calmly—was in fact lashing out with every weapon at its command: "A considerable amount of the current epidemic of funeral service criticism might properly be termed 'the Mitford syndrome,' evidences of which are vitriolic, vituperative and wholly unjustified attacks on American funeral customs and the dedicated people whose profession it is to bury the human dead with reverence and respect." And the bulletin of the Minnesota Funeral Directors Association delivered this bewildering judgment: "The Jessica Mitford book is probably the most damaging book of its kind ever written about the funeral profession. The author's approach is cunning, sly, at times intelligent, deceptive, often crude, completely biased, and sometimes truthful."

Mortuary Management said: "Actually, the danger to the equilibrium of funeral service is not in the book per se. It is in the residual use of Miss Mitford's material. . . . Newspapers, large and small, are reviewing the Mitford volume, passing and repassing its poisons among the citizenry."

The undertakers, long accustomed to operating behind discreetly closed doors, their business methods shrouded in secrecy, have traditionally done their best to avoid the spotlight. The focus of their fear is that the "citizenry" will become informed of facts hitherto concealed, facts about the repulsive and unnecessary procedure of embalming, the part this plays in "building up the sale," and, above all, facts about pricing of funerals. The undertakers are no doubt aware that public ignorance of these matters has long been the major factor in inducing the American public to accept the industry's funerary offerings without argument. They also know that the more people learn about these things, the greater the danger that they will seek some alternative and that the rebellion will spread.

My book describes a funeral reform movement, the funeral and memorial societies, first brought to national attention by the *Saturday Evening Post* two years ago in Roul Tunley's article "Can You Afford to Die?" These groups, led for the most part by the clergy, are organizing to guarantee freedom of choice in funerary matters. They help those who prefer simplicity to obtain dignified, inexpensive funerals—a return to the plain wood coffin at a reasonable price, usually between $100 and $200. Emphasis is on the spiritual aspects of death rather than on the beautified corpse in open casket. A memorial service honoring the memory of the deceased, and conducted by a clergyman of his faith, is generally held *after* burial or cremation—without benefit of the ubiquitous offices of the "Funeral Director."

An example of what one such society has accomplished for its members may explain the terror in the ranks of undertakers. In the San Francisco Bay Area, the minimum-priced funeral package (casket and undertaker's "services," including embalming and maquillage) offered in the great majority of establishments is in the range of $450 to $500. This, which covers *only* the undertaker's charges and does not include grave or burial vault, would be the rock-bottom price for the average individual—unless he could prove he was a charity case. The secretary of the Bay Area Funeral Society tells me that in the past year—June, 1962, to June, 1963—there were 250 funerals of Society members whose families had contracted for the simple funeral costing around $150. He estimates that each of these families saved *at least* $300, for an aggregate saving to the families of $75,000.

While the 250 funerals arranged for the Society members represent only a tiny fraction—a little over 1 percent—of the total deaths in the area, they are nevertheless regarded by the undertaker as a dread portent for the future. He is aware, too, that the influence exerted by the societies on funeral costs and customs extends far beyond the actual membership.

The methods by which the undertakers propose to silence criticism and hang on to their enormously lucrative traffic in the artifacts of death were blueprinted early this year by Mr. Frederick Llewellyn, Executive Vice-President of Forest Lawn Memorial Park. In a series of articles written for the *American Funeral Director* entitled, "Are Funeral Customs Going the Way of the Buggy Whip?" Mr. Llewellyn sets forth for his colleagues the major arguments to be used:

> There is a great tide sweeping over America today, washing away at the foundations of decent memorialization. . . . If the Communists can help undermine one of the most fundamental of religious rites, the way in which we care for our dead; if they can get more and more people asking, not "Is it right?" but "Is it practical?" they can undermine religion and along with it the laws of the land. Then, as Mr. Khrushchev said, "America will fall like a ripe plum!"

Elsewhere in the series he quotes the famous Khrushchev remark "We'll bury you!"—perhaps fearing that Khrushchev was actually intending to move in and give Forest Lawn competition in this respect.

The lesson was further driven home by Mr. Wilber Krieger, Managing Director of National Selected Morticians, who states in his press release about my book:

> A determined effort is being made today to strip the American funeral of all of its religious significance by the memorial society movement and substitute the funeral service, as we now know it in this country, with that practiced in communistic countries such as the Soviet Union.

The latest in this particular vein to come to my attention is an advertisement in an Oakland newspaper sponsored by the "Renowned Abbey Memorial Gardens" of Vallejo. A well-dressed father is pictured talking to his well-dressed little boy: the heads of both are bowed in sorrow. "My dear son," the father is saying. "I am so sorry you are going to have to live under Communism. It seemed to come so quickly. I didn't think their lies could win. . . ." Follows the punch line: "No nation has ever turned to Communism, Socialism or Fascism until the leaders have first been able to destroy MEMORIALIZATION. The dignity of man, the freedom of life and the worship of God—these principles on which our nation was founded—throughout all ages and in all lands have never been any greater than the MEMORIALIZATION shown in death. Many so-called 'memorial societies' are trying to destroy this MEMORIALIZATION. . . ."

Beyond these orbital flights of rhetoric, attempts on the part of industry leaders to refute the facts set forth in my book have been rather vague and obscure. For example, I estimate that the funerals of adults who died in 1961 cost an average of $1,450—including everything, undertaker's charges, burial vault, grave, marker, and so on. Howard C. Raether, Executive Secretary of the National Funeral Directors Association, says he thinks this estimate is high, but he does not attempt to supply one of his own; he says, "It is difficult if not impossible to estimate an average funeral, taking all expenses into consideration."

Discussing the memorial service of the type advocated by the funeral societies, held after the funeral with the body not present, he quotes a clergyman as saying: "It sets up a psychological detour around the reality of what has happened by encouraging a refusal to view the remains. . . . A memorial service does not furnish the surroundings that make it easy to express deep feelings, nor does it furnish the opportunity to give group support to the bereaved." This peculiar statement is not explained further. We are not told why a memorial service, which is generally held in a church or a home and is attended by friends and family of the deceased, fails to "furnish the surroundings that make it easy to express deep feelings," nor in what way it fails "to give group support to the bereaved."

Mr. Krieger of National Selected Morticians gets more specific. In refutation of my charge that in most communities it is impossible for the average person to buy a funeral for less than a fixed minimum of several hundred dollars, he says: "Families faced with the responsibility of arranging funeral services will find that every established and reputable funeral director can offer them a wide range of prices covering their services and the necessary merchandise beginning less than $200." This is the same Mr. Krieger who a few months before said in a speech to the members of his organization: "I am greatly disturbed at what I am seeing across the country. Where many funeral directors today are showing a minimum over $600, that is not defensible."

Is there such a thing as manipulation of the bereaved family to induce them to spend more than they might have intended? Of course not, says Mr. Krieger: "No reputable funeral director would attempt to influence the survivors on such a personal matter, or take advantage of their emotional state at such a time. It would be unthinkable." This is the same Mr. Krieger who developed an elaborate and clever scheme of casket arrangement in the Selection Room (where the customer is taken to make his purchase) designed to extract the maximum amount of cash from each sale. According to Mr. Krieger's plan, the higher-priced caskets should be placed in a nice, roomy part of the Selection Room which he calls the "Avenue of Approach" leading off to the *right* (because, he says, most people are right-handed and if lost they tend to turn to the right). The cheaper units can be crowded together off to the *left* in an aisle he calls "Resistance Lane." He warns his colleagues against displaying a "heavy concentration of units under $300, which makes it very easy for the client to buy in this area with complete satisfaction."

Unfortunately for the undertakers, it would seem that there is little popular support for the theory that a "fine funeral" is America's first line of defense and the highest expression of patriotism. "We should welcome a heavy concentration of units under three hundred dollars," the funeral customers seem to be saying. "We should even prefer to decide for ourselves whether we want to be transformed by the embalmer's art into Beautiful Memory Pictures, decked out for public exhibition in trappings we couldn't afford in life, or whether we should prefer to return quietly to dust after the fashion of our forefathers."

It may be that the emerging consumers' revolt against the Dismal Trade will restore meaning to the traditional (and poignant) epitaph, "Rest in Peace."

MY WAY OF LIFE
SINCE
THE AMERICAN
WAY OF DEATH

NOVA / *1964*

In England, the name Mitford is no doubt associated in most people's minds with my sister Nancy's novels and biographies. In America, like it or not (and I am not sure all the Mitfords *will* like it), our name has suddenly become synonymous with cheap funerals.

By way of illustration: At a New York cocktail party a woman related her conversation with the undertaker who was arranging her aunt's funeral. She said to him, "We want the plainest and least expensive funeral available," whereupon he replied, "Oh, you mean the Mitford style?" A Midwestern manufacturer sent me plans and specifications for a simple, low-cost coffin—which he proposes to market as the "Jessica Mitford Casket." A total stranger came up to me in a dress shop and ·with knowing wink asked, "Are you shopping for a shroud?"

The reception accorded my book and the nation-wide explosion over funerals that followed were so totally unexpected that I still have not recovered from the excitement of it all. I had assumed that a book on this somewhat unpleasant subject would have very limited appeal. *Mortuary Management,* an influential trade journal, agreed with this forecast in an editorial which appeared just before publication of *The American Way of Death*, entitled, "Who's Afraid of the Big, Bad Book?" The editor pointed out that books about "the funeral directing profession" (which is how all good American undertakers refer to their trade) are notoriously poor sellers. He knows this, he said, because his old Dad once wrote a book about the Profession; and although the Dad took an advertisement in the *Saturday Evening Post*, it only sold three hundred copies. With the sad example of the poor old Dad before me, I was utterly unprepared for what happened.

Not only were the sales gratifyingly huge, but newspapers all over the country took up the cudgels against the death industries. So did television and radio, in a number of coast-to-coast network programmes and in innumerable local programmes. So did the big, mass-circulation magazines—*Time, Life, Saturday Evening Post, Good Housekeeping*, and the like. So did the clergy; I have a bulging file of sermons preached on the subject, advocating a return to simpler funerals. All over America funerals suddenly became Topic A, a new subject for dinner-party small talk. There was a fictionalized episode about a wicked undertaker on the *Dr. Kildare* programme. *That Was the Week That Was*, newly imported to America from England, ran a skit in which the undertaker's assistant informs the bereaved widow, "I am your Grief Lady." On more than one occasion, our house in California was transformed into something like a Hollywood movie set (to the delight of the neighbours' children) by television crews filming interviews about the book.

I was inundated with letters, they poured in by every post. A young English friend living in California agreed to help me answer them. As I am not adept at dictating, she read the letters and composed the answers for me to sign. She only slipped up once, perhaps from the exuberance of youth. An earnest old soul in Kentucky had written, "I have thought the whole thing over and have decided to avoid a funeral altogether by bequeathing my body to a medical school." My English secretary wrote back, "What a smashing idea! I'm sure they'll be delighted to get it."

The reaction of the death industries to the curious national storm that is brewing over funerals in America has been fascinating. Of course they rounded on me in absolute fury. I still subscribe to their magazines with lyrical titles like *Mid-Continent Mortician, Casket & Sunnyside,* and *Concept: The Journal of Creative Ideas for Cemeteries.* In these journals I read month after month about "the Mitford bomb," "the Mitford war dance," "the Mitford missile," "Mitford blast," and "Mitford fury." They have condemned the movement for cheaper funerals as a Red Plot, and have found an ally in Congress: Congressman James B. Utt of California, who read a two-page statement about my subversive background into the *Congressional Record.* Of undertakers he said, "I would rather be buried by one of our fine, upstanding American morticians than to set foot on the soil of a Communist country," and of my book he added cryptically, "Better dead than read."

Has it all done any good, and have the grief-therapists (latest self-designation of American undertakers) been forced to mend their ways? It may be too early to tell. There are, however, some indications. The mortuary press report a decrease of 30 percent in the average funeral sale. A big New York trades union reports an average decrease of $134 in funeral bills of members. Casket manufacturers in New York State say there has been a "run on cheaper boxes." In four American states, official investigations of the entire funeral industry have been launched by the legislatures. Clergymen tell me their congregations are beginning to insist on funerary moderation.

There are people on both sides of the controversy who say the funeral furor may prove to be a short-lived flash in the pan, that when people get bored with the subject there will be a return to Funerals as Usual. Others think that profound changes in American funeral customs may result. I have no predictions. Yet, a remark made by the pastor of a wealthy suburban church in New York might seem to offer some hope for the Ultimate Consumer. He said, "I think funeral fashions are changing. The cognoscenti are beginning to think it's gauche to put on a big show because there's been so much ridicule lately of fancy, expensive funerals."

"SOMETHING TO OFFEND EVERYONE"

SHOW / *December, 1964*

In his preface to *The Loved One*, Evelyn Waugh described it as "a little nightmare produced by the unaccustomed high living of a brief visit to Hollywood." Under the tutelage of some freewheeling and original comic talents the little nightmare is growing into a monstrous incubus with new dimensions of satire, new and crazy turns of the screw.

A coalition ideally suited to this sort of skulduggery is masterminding the film, which is now being made in Hollywood: Christopher Isherwood, long a wry observer of the Los Angeles scene; Terry Southern, who did the script of *Dr. Strangelove;* Tony Richardson, fresh from his international success as director of *Tom Jones*. Haskell Wexler, cinematographer, and John Calley are co-producers.

I went down to Hollywood to watch them at work, feeling a little like an old salt watching a group of landlubbers struggle with the unfamiliar technical problems of a nautical movie. Having been immersed in mortuary lore myself for so long, I wondered how deeply the film company would succeed in penetrating the

inner workings and techniques of that world; and also how they
would resolve the problem of toning down the subject matter of
the book so it could be shown with propriety on film to mass
audiences. I found they are not concerned with propriety. Far
from toning down the material, they have made it wildly more
outrageous.

The Loved One, originally published in 1948, has been tossed
around Hollywood for many years as one of the hotter potatoes.
The story option has changed hands many times. Some film companies were afraid of this curiosity of literature, others cast lustful
looks but did not know quite how to approach it. Half a dozen
scripts were written and discarded over the years: Buñuel had a
crack at it, so did Elaine May. At one point Alec Guinness wanted
to play the male lead. More recently Elizabeth Taylor and Richard Burton wanted to do it, but that fell through.

Perhaps we should applaud these earlier hesitations and reservations. According to John Calley, the film as it is now shaping
up could not have been done two years ago. He thinks it has
become possible in 1964 because of the sudden popularity of
iconoclastic, strong satire of the *Dr. Strangelove* genre, and because of last year's wave of publicity about the excesses of the
funeral industry: "The subject is no longer taboo."

Waugh's novel describes the predicament of Aimée Thanatog-
enos, a young mortuary cosmetician at Whispering Glades
cemetery, who is unable to decide between two suitors: Mr. Joyboy, chief embalmer, and Dennis Barlow, a young English poet
who has found temporary employment at the Happier Hunting
Ground pet cemetery. In the background is the Dreamer, founder
and guiding genius of Whispering Glades. Aimée eventually
commits suicide by cyanide injection.

In embellishing this basic theme, Terry Southern & Co. have
stuck the knife into many other American institutions besides
mortuaries. The founder of Whispering Glades, now called the
Blessed Reverend, hits on a plan to "get rid of the stiffs" so he can

transform his cemetery into a more profitable Senior Citizens' Retirement City. With the help of General "Buck" Brinkman and other top-ranking space program chiefs, the loved ones are to be rocketed into outer space with the slogan "Resurrection Now!" There is a sex orgy, planned by the Blessed Reverend in his casket selection room, in which alluring mortuary hostesses tumble in and out of caskets with Air Force officers. Mr. Joyboy's Mom has become a food-crazed glutton who achieves orgasm by watching the food commercials on television. Aimée, having donned corpse maquillage, commits suicide by embalming herself alive.

As Liz Roberts, assistant to Tony Richardson, said dreamily, "There's something in the film to offend everybody."

Evelyn Waugh was one of the first to be offended. When he read in the papers that Tony Richardson was planning to update and expand the plot, he caused his agent to write a letter demanding that Richardson should be replaced as director. This curmudgeonly gesture of crabbed age has been ignored by the film company.

The City of Los Angeles is offended. An official of that township telephoned to John Calley to urge that the name "Los Angeles" not be used.

M-G-M's own legal department is worried stiff, and keeps peppering the filmmakers with anxious memoranda: "Goldwater Nut Flip [an ice-cream sundae in the commissary scene]: Delete. Our New York office advises that, while the mention of 'Goldwater Flip' was approved, the word 'nut' must *not* be used." Tony Richardson, a preoccupied young man whose mind is riveted to his work, appears to be paying not the slightest attention to these words of caution.

The Interment Association of California, an organization of cemeteries, reports nervously, "It looks as if they are getting closer and closer in producing a motion picture called 'The Loved One.' They now have a full sized billboard in the Beverly Hills area advertising the fact that the picture is being produced." The billboard in question reads, "MGM Presents THE LOVED ONE . . . For Those Who *Really* Care."

If the film has already, halfway through production, attracted an unusual amount of opprobrium, it has also engendered that special sort of excitement and enthusiasm that people feel for a masterwork in the making. The press, although excluded from the sets by Tony Richardson, is watching fascinated from the sidelines, and stories about the film have appeared in papers from *The New York Times* to the San Francisco *Chronicle*.

It seems that everyone wants to get into this odd act. Sir John Gielgud and Robert Morley flew out from England to take small parts. Liberace is in the mood to be cast as casket salesman. Jonathan Winters is the Blessed Reverend, Rod Steiger is Mr. Joyboy, Robert Morse is a super-caddish Dennis. An almost unknown twenty-three-year-old actress with the marvelous name of Anjanette Comer (her real name) has the lead role of Aimée.

All seem happy in their work. Liberace, with whom I discussed his part, sounded very sincere, like a casket salesman should. He once visited a funeral parlor and evidently felt at home there; he said the make-up and wardrobe departments were "just like in a studio." He advanced the really novel view that undertakers will be pleased with the film: "It will make everyone more cognizant of the Funeral Profession, which is one of the most prominent professions in the world." "*Prominent?*" "Well, I mean it's so *alive*," answered Liberace with a giggle. About his own funeral plans he said that, while he has not as yet decided on the details, he would want to "be as glamorous in death as in life, people would expect it of me, I expect I'll go all out."

Anjanette Comer, a lovely pale girl with dusky hair and huge green eyes, has embraced her role with alarming zeal. She thinks she is very much like Aimée in some ways; after all, Aimée was so in love with her work! Anjanette has read a number of books and manuals on embalming; indeed she seems, at this stage, "half in love with easeful death" herself. "In the suicide scene I'm like a woman going to meet her lover," she explained. "There's something very sexy about the whole embalming thing." Other members of the company to whom I repeated this raised their eyebrows and looked slightly worried.

Knowing something of the difficulties of getting firsthand information about the inner workings of the funeral industry (for if dead men don't talk, still less do their custodians), I was particularly interested in how Southern, Richardson, and their many assistants had gone about researching the subject. Judging by their descriptions of forays into cemeteries, casket rooms, and eventually into the forbidden territory of the embalming room, it must have been an extremely unsettling experience both for the film company and for the mortuary world.

Sometimes as many as ten or fifteen would invade a cemetery, deploying over the grounds with notebooks in hand to record every detail of statuary, grave markers, mausoleum crypts. This was easy, for cemeteries are open to the public and anyone can wander around in them at will. To gain access to the casket sales room, where normally only those strictly on business are admitted, they found it necessary to break up into small family-sized groups pretending interest in "pre-need" arrangements. Terry Southern, Tony Richardson, and Richardson's actress wife, Vanessa Redgrave, went on a pre-need shopping expedition in Los Angeles's best-known memorial park. They were bent on studying selling methods, casket styles, arrangement of merchandise. "For some reason, at the last minute Tony switched plans and insisted that Vanessa and I should pose as husband and wife," said Southern. "Well, of course Vanessa is an actress, and she got absolutely carried away by her role when we got up to the casket room— shed real tears, thinking of her poor old mother, who was supposed to be dying. I felt sorry for the poor salesman, she almost had him in tears, too."

A far more difficult problem was that of breaching the mortician's ultimate stronghold, the embalming room, and witnessing the embalming procedure. It is against the California state law for anyone save the next of kin to be present during an embalming.

This law, passed as a result of funeral lobby pressure, was presumably intended to shield the embalmer and his work from prying eyes, and particularly such irreverent eyes as those of Tony Richardson and his crew.

However, film folk generally manage to have their way. "There is a certain magic in the words 'Metro-Goldwyn-Mayer,' " said John Calley. Enough magic, it seems, to corrupt the morgue attendant in a community at some distance from Los Angeles, and to persuade him to become the company's technical adviser at a hundred dollars a day.

Initially, John Calley told me, there was quite a battle in the production department over how to handle the photography of corpses. Some favored the use of wax models and masks, but these would have been expensive and perhaps unsatisfactory. Nobody in the company had ever actually seen corpses on film; nobody knew how they would photograph. A screen test for corpses, who turned out not to be exactly easy on the eyes, was therefore the first essential. Calley called up his morgue man: "We want to see some dead bodies, and take moving pictures of them." "*Moving* pictures? But they don't move, you know," quipped the morgue man. "You'd better come over to the morgue and look around, we can have lunch here." Calley, though already strangely uninterested in lunch, concurred.

For some reason everybody wanted to be in on it, and a dozen members of the company repaired to the morgue. They took along one of the film extras, as a sort of control, to see if a live one posing as a cadaver would look any different from the real thing.

There were wild goings-on at the morgue that day. At one point Haskell Wexler, shooting from a stepladder, got corpse and live actor mixed up; when the latter opened his eyes for a moment, Wexler screamed and almost fell off the ladder.

The most shattering experience of all occurred when Tony Richardson, insatiably curious, opened a double door leading from the walk-in freezer where the "recent expirations" (as the morgue man called them) lay ranged on shelves. Behind the mysterious door were scores of bodies hung by their ears from what appeared to be huge ice tongs or hooks. "Tony was very upset, couldn't sleep for weeks," said John Calley. "I had weird dreams for ages afterwards. Haskell threw up and passed out." The morgue attendant, described by Calley as "a very eerie, spooky man," got into the spirit of things. He reached into a cupboard, pulled out five or six dried-up legs and arms, and waved them about like a handful of branches. He explained that they freeze the corpses as quickly as possible "to discourage people from playing grab-ass with them." "Tony's eyes lit up at this," said Calley. "Although none of us knew exactly what was meant."

So thoroughly have the screen writers done their homework that their ideas are beginning to echo those of *Casket & Sunnyside*. In the screenplay, a casket salesman displays the latest in shrouds, "a Texas-style embroidered cowboy windbreaker." Leafing through the current issue of *Casket & Sunnyside*, which I had brought along to Hollywood, I came across this: "An innovation in the burial industry is Western tailoring in burial garments designed in authentic ranch style." Great minds think alike. It is indeed hard to top the crazed inventiveness of the American funeral industry.

Tony Richardson hates studio sets on principle. Whenever possible, he prefers to film the real thing: airport scenes at the Los Angeles airport, a newspaper office at the *Times-Mirror* building. M-G-M's enormous facilities are only used briefly in *The Loved One*, for some scenes which are in fact a spoof on a movie company very much like M-G-M.

The production people combed Los Angeles for suitable locations which might be leased for the major action: Whispering Glades cemetery-cum-mortuary, the home of Mr. Joyboy and his revolting old Mom, the Happier Hunting Ground pet cemetery. As with everything connected with this film, luck was with them all the way.

The Joyboy home is a late-Victorian horror in a run-down section of Los Angeles. It was no trouble at all to persuade the large family who lived there to move into a motel for a few weeks at M-G-M's expense, while the prop men refurbished the house with monstrous art-nouveau lamps, tortured-looking carved chairs, and other Mom paraphernalia.

A perfect Whispering Glades has been created at Greystone, one of those bad-joke mansions that abound in Southern California. Teams of M-G-M gardeners have greened up its dying shrubbery and vast neglected lawns, which are now dotted with tons of frightful Forest Lawn-type statuary. A patio has become an "indoor-outdoor"-style mausoleum, its walls plastered with fake memorial plaques. The sizable recreation area of the house has been transformed into a mortuary. The erstwhile bowling alley is now the cosmeticians' room, divided into cubicles like a beauty parlor. The billiard room has become a "Gothic slumber room" decorated with medieval knights, heraldic flags, and other insignia of Merrie Olde England.

The immense kitchens are awash with embalming fluids and cavity solutions, for here Mr. Joyboy and his team of embalmers hold sway. Life-sized diagrams of human anatomy and circulatory systems decorate the wall. The observant filmgoer will catch glimpses of a variety of embalming aids procured by the diligent prop men from undertakers' supply houses. "Tony specially likes those big sticker things, what d'you call them?" said Haskell Wexler, who showed me round. "Trocars?" "Yes, trocars, he loves those." (A trocar is a murderous-looking giant hollow needle attached to a pump, used for extracting the fluid contents of chest and abdomen. Not everybody loves them. John Calley told me he thinks trocars are depressing.) There are also boxes of Trocar Perfect-Seal Buttons (shaped like thick, squat screws, for stopping up the hole made in the stomach by the trocar), K-T Hand Holders for Easy, Sure, Exact Positioning of Hands (glorified rubber bands), Cranial Caps, Perma Cosmetics, Infant Finishing Powder, and a gross of eye caps for fastening eyelids down.

Caskets have been rented from a local casket company which, for obvious reasons, prefers not to be listed in screen credits. Wexler is critical of their construction because they tend to fall apart when people get in and out of them: "They're definitely only intended for a one-time use."

The prop man told me he had been unable to obtain any ladies' burial dresses. A manufacturer of these garments, which cost from $100 to $275 wholesale, explained apologetically that her style is so well known that the designs would at once be recognized. Shades of Christian Dior!

Richardson's greatest coup of all was arranging to film at the premises of Pet Haven cemetery for a fee of two hundred dollars a day. It was at Pet Haven, where I spent several days watching the filming, that the validity of Richardson's stand against studio sets was borne in on me. The truth of Pet Haven is infinitely stranger than any fiction that could have been devised by the most imaginative of screen set designers.

Pet Haven is situated in one of those desolate, nondescript wastelands on the outskirts of Los Angeles. The acre or so of tightly packed animal graves is a riot of grubby artificial flowers. Statues of gods and dogs mingle indiscriminately, here a plaster Jesus, there a cuddly kitten, a blue-robed Virgin Mary cheek by jowl with a group of pottery poodles. Mr. Griffiths, founder and owner of the cemetery, told me there are 9,800 pets buried there, plus $20,000 worth of pre-need contracts. He delights in pointing out the resting places of the pets of stars: "Jerry Lewis has got four here, Edward G. Robinson's got three, and Mickey Cohen's dog is over there." The Cohen grave marker reads, "Mike—Always in Our Hearts, Mickey and Lavonne." Nearby is a memorial inscription, in Spanish, to "Diana, Cuba 1952—Los Angeles 1963, Political Refugee, Another Victim of Fidel."

Fact and fancy melt into each other in the most peculiar way at Pet Haven. Sometimes it is hard to tell whether the scene you are watching is part of the film or part of the routine business of the pet cemetery.

In a far corner of the grounds the film company is at work, equipment is scattered among the graves, and Dennis, in his seedy-looking nondenominational minister's garb, is saying a prayer

over the casket of a deceased mynah bird: "Bird born of egg . . ."
Seeking relief from the glaring sun, I drop into the cemetery office.
A weepy blonde, evidently a past patron of the cemetery, is discussing plans for the funeral of her boxer Donnie-Boy. She is
mildly grumbling between sobs: "I could've save thirty-nine dollars and fifty cents if I'd bought Donnie-Boy's grave pre-need
twelve years ago, when I buried Woofie." Mr. Griffiths suggests
she could still cut $7.50 from the price by omitting the white satin
casket lining. "No, I couldn't do that to my Donnie-Boy," she says
with a fresh burst of tears. "It's a funny thing: I knew he was gone
when I saw how his jaw had gone rigid. It was just the same when
my mother passed away, *her* jaw went rigid, just like that." After
she left, Mr. Griffiths remarked to his secretary, "She's real
touchy. Remember when her other dog passed she wouldn't even
let you fix his face?"

I left these extraordinary scenes and this unusual film company
with regret. I shall be curious to know how *The Loved One* is
received. Based on past experience in these matters, I have some
predictions:

The Loved One will be denounced as Communistic, Socialistic,
Atheistic, Anarchistic, Unaltruistic, Pessimistic, and a few other
istics by *Casket & Sunnyside, Mortuary Management, Concept:
The Journal of Creative Ideas for Cemeteries*, and a dozen or so
other funeral trade publications.

These denunciations will be echoed in meetings of the John
Birch Society, the American Legion, the D.A.R., and in the halls
of Congress by representatives from Cemetery Land—Southern
California.

Forest Lawn will loudly and publicly threaten to sue but will
think better of it.

Liberace will laugh all the way to his pre-need memorial estate.

Tony Richardson and his merry men will live happily ever after
—but they will never quite forget what they saw in the embalming
room.

Anjanette Comer will survive being Aimée and will star in many livelier roles in the future.

For my own part, I ain't gonna study Waugh no more—gonna study Terry Southern, Christopher Isherwood, and Tony Richardson instead.

COMMENT ON
THREE FUNERAL PIECES

After *The American Way of Death* was published in 1963, I found myself in the delightful position of being America's leading authority on funerals. This was not as difficult an accomplishment as it might seem; had I been writing about, say, the medical profession or public education, I should have been up against the competition of myriad experts in those fields. But precious little had been written about the American funeral; I was more or less the first that ever burst into that silent sea, so it was fairly easy to float up to the head of the class.

As a result, editors of a wide range of magazines—the *Nation*, *Saturday Evening Post, Good Housekeeping, Show, Atlantic*—asked me for articles. Needless to say, I milked the subject for all it was worth—and continue to do so; as recently as 1977, *Mc-Call's* commissioned an update on *The American Way of Death*—Death Warmed Over, so to speak, although that was not their title. (This piece is now permanently enshrined in a new paperback edition of *The American Way of Death*).

For a number of reasons I found those assignments highly enjoyable. In the first place, I was itching to make use of the stunning copy furnished by the funeral trade magazines in their denunciations of *The American Way of Death*—their branding as "atheistic Communism" my proposals for funerary simplicity, their incomparable prose style. I got deep pleasure out of once again crossing swords with such old adversaries as Howard C. Raether, Executive Secretary of the National Funeral Directors Association, who unwittingly supplied some of the best lines for *The American Way of Death*, including the epigraph: "Funerals are becoming more and more a part of the American way of life." Since much of *The American Way of Death* is a pastiche of their pronouncements, one might have thought the funeral industry spokesmen would have learned to keep their mouths shut, or at least to moderate their rhetoric; not a bit of it, their counterattack provided colorful material for any number of follow-up articles.

Secondly—all those clergymen flocking to my defense! Judging by their response to *The American Way of Death*, it seemed that for once in my life I was literally on the side of the angels, or at least their temporal representatives. I think that only those who have been, as I was, a target of the Truman-McCarthy-era assault on radicals can appreciate the feeling of decompression on having one's work accepted at its face value, no longer subject to the *ad hominem* (or should it be *feminem?*) attack that was such a depressing feature of those years.

Indeed, for the undertakers, their inability to shake clergy support for my position must have been a cruel blow; but cruelest of all was the publication of my articles in such Middle America magazines as *Good Housekeeping* and *Saturday Evening Post*—an enemy invasion of the undertakers' own turf, so to speak.

I, of course, went all out to consolidate my alliance with the clergy (and to exploit my new-found respectability) by lacing the articles with occasional references to "the spiritual aspects of death," a bit specious coming from me, as the undertakers may have divined, but there was nothing they could do about it.

The first two pieces included here, "Americans Don't Want Fancy Funerals," from the *Saturday Evening Post,* and "My Way of Life Since *The American Way of Death*," from *Nova,* illustrate my efforts to make maximum use of the funeral trade journals while not overdoing it—always a danger because there is such a plethora of marvelously comic material. My system in deciding what to include, in this or any other case where I am making extensive use of quotation, is to type out as fast as I can all the possibly useful passages, only a fraction of which will ultimately be used. That way I have the material before me in manageable form, and don't have to keep turning back to the magazine or other source in which it appeared. In the margins of the many pages of typescript thus assembled I scribble pencil notations of the subject matter, e.g.: "Mitford syndrome," "residual use of Mit. material—passing poisons among the citizenry," "Communism vs. memorialization," and so on.

The next trick was to see where these fit into the general scheme of the article, how best to pare them down for space reasons, and ruthlessly to sacrifice those passages that—hilarious though they may be—might appear to have been dragged in out of context. Then I tried to juxtapose the eminently sane, reasonable advice of the memorial societies ("led for the most part by the clergy," as I sanctimoniously put it) alongside the apoplectic outpourings of the funeral men. A few startling statistics don't hurt either (again, provided you don't overdo it) such as the aggregate savings in one year to 250 funeral society members of $75,000.

A word about style. Rereading the first two of these pieces, I note that I did somewhat tailor the writing to what I perceived as the readership. For the *Satevepost*, with its alleged circulation of ten million—always an inhibiting thought to me, those millions of faceless folks!—I see that I adopted a plonking one-two-three approach, setting the scene for the reader with a number of rather obvious rhetorical questions, and proceeding from there to my eminently logical (if self-serving) answers as furnished by the response of the American public to my book.

The piece for *Nova*, then a trendy English glossy mag, is a good bit more relaxed. The clergy have virtually disappeared to be replaced by cocktail party talk. The Nancy Mitford reference, the young English friend who answered my letters, the generally chatty and personal tone would hardly have struck the right note

for the *Satevepost*, whose readers would be looking for solid information rather than jokes and anecdotes. (I had written to tell
Nancy about the Jessica Mitford Casket. She replied that an
American friend of hers had just died and was expected to be
buried in a Mitford: "The *on dit* is that you get ten percent royalties." But her letter came too late to work it into the *Nova*
article.)

" 'Something to Offend Everyone' " was yet another spin-off
from *The American Way of Death*. Again I was called in as an
expert on mortuary practices, this time by *Show* magazine, who
wanted an article on the filming of *The Loved One*. The circumstances were idyllic: M-G-M put me up in the Beverly Hills
Hotel, height of Hollywood luxury, for ten days in which I trailed
around with the film company. I was to have an "exclusive"; all
other reporters (including, to her displeasure, Hedda Hopper)
were barred from the set. From time to time, I even fed the film
company lines; Liberace, cast as casket salesman, borrowed the
one in my *Saturday Evening Post* article about the undertaker
explaining the difference between casket linings: "We find rayon
is a lot more irritating to the skin." All this was most gratifying:
being in on the ground floor of a Hollywood production, a childhood dream come true. This time I had no inhibitions about the
potential readership of the piece; *Show* was a magazine of the
theatre and movie world, consequently I felt pleasantly free of
constraint in writing it—perhaps a trifle too free? For the editors
cut out one of my favorite passages, the morgue man's reference
to "playing grab-ass" with the corpses.

There is a footnote. After the *Show* article appeared, John
Calley phoned my husband's office. "M-G-M has decided to use
Jessica's title 'Something to Offend Everyone' as the sole advertising slogan for the film," he said. "We'd love to send her a
present—how is she off for watches?" "Oh, she's got a watch,"
said Bob, which was true; one of those good old-fashioned tick-
tocks, a stout timekeeper on a plain but serviceable band. Calley

sounded disappointed, and murmured that he'd been looking at some very nice diamond watches in Cartier.

"I could have bitten my tongue off," Bob told me later. "How could I face you with this awful lapse of judgment on my part?" But, making swift recovery, he had deftly replied to Calley ". . . but she is fresh out of brooches." Calley said that was a great idea, and what is her favorite color? "Blue-white," said Bob, now fully on top of the situation.

In the course of time a lovely little diamond brooch, shaped something like a funeral wreath, arrived from Tiffany—the only piece of real jewelry I possess, a valued (and valuable) memento of my brief sojourn in Filmland.

DON'T CALL IT
SYPHILIS

McCALL'S / *September, 1965*

Scene: *Blair General Hospital. Mr. Novak, teacher at Thomas Jeffer-son High School, enters an isolation room where Paul, a student, is recovering from a suicide attempt.*

MR. NOVAK: *Anything I can get you?*
PAUL: *Not a thing. What're you doing here?*
MR. NOVAK: *I had a feeling you might need a friend today.*
PAUL: *You know something, Mr. Novak? I've got syphilis.*

What is Mr. Novak doing in Dr. Kildare's hospital? Why have Novak and Kildare fans never seen this enacted on television?

"A hopeful view of relief from their dangerous malady might be more welcome to the half-million persons in the United States who acquire this disease each year than the veiled obscenity permitted by Columbia in the vaudeville acts of certain of their commercial programs."

These angry words which today, perhaps because of their forthrightness, have a slightly old-fashioned ring, were uttered in 1934 by Dr. Thomas Parran, Jr., then New York State Commissioner of Public Health. Because it contained the words "syphilis control," a radio talk he was to give on venereal disease had just been banned by the Columbia Broadcasting System. CBS explained the position: "In deciding what is proper for us to broadcast we must always bear in mind that broadcasting reaches persons of widely varying age levels and reaches them in family and social groups of almost every conceivable assortment. We do not believe that it is either wise or necessary to discuss and sometimes to mention some things. . . ."

Three years later Dr. Parran tried again, this time in the capacity of Surgeon General of the United States, to which office he had been appointed by Franklin D. Roosevelt. He prepared a speech on the rising incidence of syphilis, particularly among young people, to be given over the NBC radio network by General Hugh S. Johnson. Johnson arrived at the studio, script in hand; three minutes before broadcast time, NBC officials decided to ban the speech. NBC explained it this way: "While the broadcasting company is in sympathy with the objective of the war against V.D., it finds itself unable to contribute to this campaign without seriously embarrassing the family group." Which moved Dr. Parran to comment, "Nice people don't talk about syphilis, nice people don't have syphilis, and nice people shouldn't do anything about those who do have syphilis."

In 1964 history repeated itself. Meanwhile, both broadcasting and venereal disease had made enormous strides: two popular NBC television entertainment programs were reaching approximately sixty million viewers, most of them young people, and venereal infection had risen to the appalling figure of an estimated three thousand *new* cases each day, the steepest rise being among teen-agers. The Surgeon General's Office put these two facts together and proposed that a two-part fictional episode about the dangers of syphilis, designed to reach schoolchildren as well as their parents and teachers, should be given on the *Mr. Novak* and *Dr. Kildare* programs.

The M-G-M producers in Hollywood, who make the films for both programs, were enthusiastic about the idea; and so, at first, were the NBC officials in New York who have the final say about what goes over the air. The two-part script entitled "The Rich Who Are Poor" was written by E. Jack Neuman, a topflight TV writer who won the Peabody Award as executive producer of the *Mr. Novak* program. Then, just as production was about to start, NBC suddenly canceled the project.

This time NBC's official explanation was longer and murkier. Speaking for the network, Mr. Robert D. Kasmire told the newspapers, "All who took part in the decision recognize the seriousness of the problem of venereal disease, especially among young people. In addition, the subject was not held to be inappropriate for television. In support of both these points, I should like to point out that NBC personnel cooperated closely over many weeks with the producing organization with a view toward arriving at a treatment of the subject that would be consistent with the needs of an all-family audience. Out of this effort and, of course, the extraordinary talent of the writer came a skilled and sensitive treatment for our consideration. In the final determination, however, it was felt that passages within the story, considered by all concerned to be essential to development of plot and theme, made it inappropriate for such a program as *Mr. Novak*, and we decided not to proceed."

From which it is apparent that the gentle art of double-talk has also forged ahead mightily since the thirties.

Stunned and angry, the Surgeon General's Office and the National Education Association, whose experts had worked closely with the writer for many months to guarantee technical accuracy of the script, urged NBC to reconsider. When Val Adams broke the story in *The New York Times*, scores of medical groups, clergymen, and educators joined in the appeal. The network's only response was to reissue Kasmire's statement and to declare the matter was closed.

What brought on the sudden fit of nerves that led to cancellation of this patently worthwhile and constructive public service project? What sort of reasoning went into the decision? Was NBC really reflecting the wishes of the viewing public when it decided case to the health department. Dr. Kildare urges Paul to tell the names of girls from whom he might have caught syphilis—or to whom he might have given it—so that they in turn can be reached and treated. Paul admits to having had relations with two casual acquaintances and after much inner conflict tells Joyce ("a nice girl, not like those other girls") that he may have infected her. While there is no happy ending, we gather that Paul has learned much from his unfortunate experience.

The viewing audience also would have learned much. Within the familiar framework of the "family entertainment program" the writer has skillfully managed to weave in a great deal of basic information about syphilis. All of the important facts emerge in the development of the story: how the disease is transmitted, how it is cured; the consequences of untreated syphilis (it may lead to insanity and death); the inadequacy of present medical-school training in syphilology; the importance of questioning the patient as to possible sources of infection, and the dereliction of many private doctors in this regard; how public health departments work to break the chain of infection.

The merit of this approach to V.D. education seems self-evident: how much more palatable to tune in to *Dr. Kildare*, to hear that attractive and earnest young man explain these facts, than to read the same thing in a government pamphlet or even to hear it in a speech given by a health educator on the educational channel.

The conception (you'll excuse the expression), birth, development, and premature demise of the screenplay was poignantly described to me by the writer and the producers who had hopefully nurtured it over many months.

Apparently the suggestion for such a program came simultaneously from a number of public health centers. The Surgeon General's Office approached David Victor, producer of *Kildare,* suggesting an episode that would call attention to the epidemic of V.D. among fourteen- to twenty-year-olds. About the same time,

to abandon the two-part drama? And was the public interes
as Kasmire put it, "the needs of an all-family audience")
served? What were the "essential" yet "inappropriate" passag
the story? To find some answers, I read the banned script
talked with those most closely connected with the incident:
writer, his collaborators at M-G-M, public health workers,
NBC's Official Explainer.

The script of "The Rich Who Are Poor" is innocuous in
extreme, relying as it does on the tried-and-true formulas of
sort of television play. It is a simple moral tale involving ten
young romantic love, a lapse into transgression followed by
evitable retribution, a hint of happier days to come. The sto
characters are all there—the financially rich yet emotionally i
poverished parents (whence the title), the sensitive but confuse
teen-agers, the decent but worried teachers trying to muddl
through to some sort of understanding of the adolescent mind.

Briefly, the plot is this: Mr. Novak notices that one of his bes
students, eighteen-year-old Paul Stribling, seems out of sorts and
nervous. He questions Paul—has he been spending too much time
with his steady girl friend Joyce? Is he eating properly? Anything
wrong?—but gets nowhere. Meanwhile Paul's mother, who ha
also noticed that he seems unwell, has sent him for a checkup t
Dr. Quayle, the Stribling family physician. Dr. Quayle comes
see Paul at school and tells him he has syphilis. Quayle lectur
him: "I suggest you plan on behaving yourself. If you were r
boy, I'd take you to the woodshed," but assures him that "I
going to keep it strictly between us, Paul. I'm doing this out
respect for your father and mother." Paul, shocked and horrifi
tries to commit suicide. He is next seen being brought into
Kildare's hospital, where he is treated for an overdose of
biturates and where a routine blood test reveals his diseas
Kildare and Dr. Gillespie.

The doctors explain to Paul that while syphilis is extre
dangerous it can easily be cured if treated early enough
Gillespie gives Quayle a dressing-down for failing to report

the New York Department of Public Health wrote to E. Jack Neuman with a similar proposal for the *Novak* show.

"I began fishing around, and visited several high-school principals and some of the Los Angeles Health Department workers," said Neuman. "To a man, they told me what a frightful thing this is, what a devastating effect it is having emotionally and academically on uncounted numbers of teen-agers. They began plying me with facts and material—exciting, dramatic material."

Neuman discussed his findings with the executive personnel of the two shows, Norman Felton and David Victor of *Kildare*, and Leonard Freeman of *Novak*. Like the vast majority of people who are otherwise well informed and knowledgeable about current affairs, Neuman and his colleagues at M-G-M had absolutely no idea of the magnitude of the V.D. epidemic. They had assumed, as most people do, that the discovery of the penicillin cure in 1943 had pretty much eradicated these diseases.

They learned that following a steep drop in the incidence of V.D. during the middle fifties, it staged a comeback and is today a far more devastating killer than respectable, well-publicized diseases like smallpox and polio. That over the last six years infectious syphilis has tripled in the fifteen- to nineteen-year age group; teen-agers alone account for six hundred new cases of V.D. each day. That one thousand Americans die each month of V.D., and many more become blind, deaf, and insane. That of cases treated by private physicians, only about 11 percent are reported to public health authorities.

"The really frustrating thing is that today, for the first time in history, total eradication of venereal disease is a practical possibility, because a quick and certain cure *does* now exist," said Neuman. "The tragedy is that the people simply aren't getting the facts—and especially the young people." He was particularly struck with the inadequacy of V.D. education in the nation's public schools—in many areas nonexistent, in others spotty and often sadly ineffective. "Too often it's left up to an embarrassed gym teacher who shows a few slides," he said. "The only state with a competent system is Oregon, where they start in the sixth grade, and consequently the V.D. rate there is extremely low."

As the M-G-M production team investigated further, they were evidently seized with some of the crusading zeal of the health department workers who day in and day out wrestle with the problem of getting the facts about V.D. to an ignorant and apathetic public.

"We all felt obligated by the nature of the subject to do something about it," said Neuman. "It was a marvelous, rare opportunity to perform a public service." Leonard Freeman emphasized the need to remove the social onus that is attached to this particular disease, "so a young person would feel free to go to a doctor at the beginning. People should realize it's not the victim that's abhorrent, it's the disease. The terror of syphilis is that the symptoms are so brief—and painless. The victim can sit it out for two weeks, and then the symptoms disappear altogether—but he becomes a carrier, he isn't really cured. The disease goes underground but reappears in later life in the most deadly forms. The reasons for doing the show, to bring this to the light of day, seemed to us quite indisputable."

Furthermore they were convinced that the unusual and intriguing format of the proposed two-part drama, in which the stars of *Novak* and *Kildare* would appear together in both shows, would have increased the viewing audience enormously. "It would have been damn good showmanship and would have sprung the ratings way up, which means the life of the show," said Newman. "I have the same contempt for the ratings that everyone else has, but they're a fact of life, you have to live with them."

The next move for the producers of the two shows was to sell the idea of the two-part drama to the NBC officials in New York.

"Knowing the wariness of the networks in tackling this sort of subject, we realized it must be extraordinarily well and carefully done," said Freeman. "Neuman submitted an extended, unusually detailed outline of the drama so there'd be no surprises for the network—all the cards were on the table. The network considered the outline long and painfully, then gave the go-ahead, but with a proviso that there would be no carte-blanche approval until they saw the finished script."

This, it seems, was a departure from usual procedure. Generally proposals for episodes are accepted or rejected at the outline stage, after being considered by NBC's Programming Department for entertainment value and the Standards and Practices Department which rules on "matters of taste and propriety."

The draft screenplay, having won this tentative approval, was next subjected to the searching scrutiny of various experts. It was vetted for medical accuracy by public health educators in Atlanta, Washington, and Los Angeles; for English usage by a panel of the National Education Association (which acts in an advisory capacity to the *Novak* program); and for "taste and propriety" by NBC's own Broadcast Standards Department. The painstaking work of these groups is evidenced in a formidable stack of correspondence suggesting improvements in the draft.

The Los Angeles Health Department corrects Dr. Gillespie's discussion of symptoms: "It might be well to qualify Gillespie's statement, 'In the infectious stage syphilis is *often* simple to detect and diagnose.' "

The National Education Association punctiliously corrects Mr. Novak's English: "Improve Novak's English to 'here *are* a couple of unsatisfactory slips.' " "Novak's 'you sure need something' is too slangy and should be changed to 'you *certainly* need something.' " "Novak should say, '*whom* would they suspect,' not 'who.' " "Novak seems to be imitating Jimmy Cagney with his reply of 'yeh' to Dr. Kildare."

And Joyce's French: "Joyce should say to her French teacher, 'simplement, *mon ami*,' not 'amant,' which means 'lover.' "

And Mr. Peoples's arithmetic: "Forty-eight out of one hundred eighty school days is closer to *twenty-five percent* than thirty percent."

The Broadcast Standards Department anxiously urges prudence all down the line: "In the speech 'God knows how many unreported cases,' please delete 'God' and substitute '*who*.'" "As is your custom, please exercise caution when showing the interns staring appreciatively at the group of nurses passing by. In addition, please eliminate Dr. Tyler's speech, 'If she is not anybody's kin—and nobody's sister—I would like to scrub with her.'" "Please delete 'sexual intercourse' and substitute '*relations*.'" "Please delete 'a case of syphilis' and substitute '*this disease*.'" "Please delete 'your friendly backend' and substitute '*back*.'"

The finished script, pruned, pared, trimmed, tidied, polished, and sterilized, successfully cleared the NBC Standards and Practices Department, generally the last hurdle in the long obstacle race for writer and script. All was set in motion for production; Franciscus and the other leads had already learned their parts—when the word came. NBC had decided to kill the whole project.

"You're never told *who* decides these things. Nobody wants to stand up and be counted," said Leonard Freeman. "There was no memorandum with somebody's signature on it; we learned of the decision through a telephone call from the local NBC man who had got the word from New York." Neither, apparently, were any specific reasons given the producers for the sudden veto—merely the mysterious observation that the plays "were not in the best interests of the viewing public," and that the subject was not suitable for the early hour of the *Novak* show. "The ironic part of that reasoning is that the very audience that motivated the careful and arduous preparation of the two-part script was the audience chosen by the network to be sheltered—namely, teen-agers," remarked Freeman.

Understandably, the decision was received with anguish and frustration by the M-G-M producers, who saw the fruit of months of painstaking work arbitrarily discarded. "We pulled out every stop to persuade them to change their minds," said Neuman. "I was on the telephone upside down and backwards," said Norman

Felton. "I believed in this project. But there was no recourse." The Surgeon General's Office sent a full delegation to New York to plead with NBC executives, and the National Education Association threw the weight of its million members behind a request for reconsideration, but without success. "There was some talk that maybe, possibly, at some future time NBC might do a documentary on V.D.," said Freeman. "But obviously this would not have fulfilled the same purpose. As NBC well knows, teen-agers don't watch documentaries. They are watched by only a tiny fraction of the viewing audience, by the more sophisticated people who are least in need of this sort of information."

NBC now began to catch it from all sides. The *Saturday Review*, in an editorial entitled "NBC Turns Down a Golden Opportunity," pointed out: "If delicacy is the issue with NBC's Continuity Acceptance Department, it had better take a hard second look at much that goes out on its network. Sex at every extreme and brutality without precedent this side of the Grand Guignol are daily fare on television, including NBC." The Los Angeles *Times* called the decision ridiculous: "Why NBC should believe TV drama is not to deal with society and life escapes us." *Newsweek* said, "The network's open mind slammed shut."

Seeking further information on the sequence of events, I obtained audience with NBC in the person of Mr. Robert Kasmire, whose weighty title is Vice-President of Corporate Information. Mr. Kasmire was vague about who had actually delivered the *coup de grâce* to the two-part drama. He seemed to remember that there were about five people, including himself, involved in the decision, and that there was at first a difference of opinion among them. The disagreement was not resolved in any formalized fashion, he said, no votes are taken in these policy meetings. "It is rather a matter of discussion and concession. Our judgment was on the side of caution." I asked whether it would be possible to talk with somebody at NBC who felt deeply, as a matter of principle and rectitude, that the plays should *not* be shown, that to show them would be wrong and would do harm to the viewing audience. I should have liked to meet somebody who would de-fend this sort of position so that in all fairness his views could be set forth, but Mr. Kasmire was unable to produce such a person.

The finished script was rejected, he said, because "if the plays were to have substance and authenticity as a discussion of this serious problem, there would have to be reference to sexual in-timacy and a certain amount of clinical detail. The question arose as to whether this was fit and appropriate as entertainment. The determination was made that it was not."

This was getting curiouser and curiouser—for how could a play of substance and authenticity be written about syphilis *without* reference to sexual intimacy? "Some of us hadn't considered that at the beginning," said Mr. Kasmire uncomfortably. Was consider-ation given to asking the writer to rework certain passages? "Well, no; it would have looked silly to go back to the writer and say, 'We can't talk about sex.'"

Indeed it would, for the whole point of the script—and a major thrust of public health education about venereal disease—is to make it crystal clear that for all practical purposes sexual intimacy is the *only* way V.D. can be transmitted. The likelihood of becom-ing infected in any other way has been compared to the likelihood of being hit by a falling meteor. "Venereal disease is *not* spread from toilet seats or doorknobs or towels," say the high-school pamphlets on the subject. At Harvard, Dr. Alfred Worcester, in his famous freshman hygiene course, used to drive this fact home in a slightly different way. Invariably a student would ask, "Can you catch syphilis on a toilet seat?" And invariably the good doc-tor would pause reflectively before replying, "Well . . . I suppose you *could*, but it does seem to me it would be a rather uncom-fortable place. . . ."

I asked Mr. Kasmire who, exactly, among the viewing public might have been expected to object to the program; whether, for example, there were any particular religious groups that are known to take exception to this sort of subject being aired. No, said Mr. Kasmire; in fact, many of the protests against cancellation of the two-part play came from Protestant clergymen, and one of its strongest backers was Father Francis L. Filas, head of the theology department at Loyola, the well-known Catholic university. Would the sponsors have objected? Oh, no! They don't interfere with the content of shows. The advertisers are not a factor; most shows are sponsored by a large number of advertisers. Who, then? "It's hard to say. . . . I suppose, that section of the public that would feel the subject of V.D. is not a fit or suitable topic for an entertainment program."

Feeling slightly dizzy from going round in circles, I asked whether Mr. Kasmire and his colleagues at NBC had reconsidered their decision to ban "The Rich Who Are Poor" after the Surgeon General urged them to do so. "No, there was no formal rediscussion of the matter." A surprising answer. One might have thought that an official request from the government in a matter of vital concern to the nation's health should have merited at least a little get-together of NBC policymakers to talk it all over. But apparently it was not thought necessary.

Mr. Kasmire went on to explain that the question of taste and propriety is in a sort of "gray area" of television. That is to say, decisions in this area cannot be black or white, there are so many imponderables. . . .

In a last effort to get to grips with any real objections based on improprieties in the script, I asked Mr. Kasmire to mark the dirty passages in my copy. The script was returned to me with a note from Mr. Kasmire: "As I suspected, the passages I've put clips on will hardly qualify as 'dirty.' They do, however, represent the type of treatment—doubtless necessary to any valid dramatic treatment of venereal disease—that, it was felt, a great portion of the audience would find unsuitable within the context of family entertainment." The marked passages, I found, included all of those portions of the script which dealt with venereal disease. Once more we had come full circle.

Sleuthing for the villain in the gray area is an unrewarding task. There is, it seems, no bloated cigar-smoking moneybags behind the scenes who declares with cynical grin, "What's a few thousand syphilitic kids to me? I've got a million invested in this series." There are nothing but good guys at NBC, who operate in a veritable quagmire of nervous niceness, anxious to please everybody and anxious above all not to give offense to that mysterious nonentity, "the viewing public."

For further enlightenment I checked the *NBC Code of Radio and Television Broadcast Standards and Practices* (in which, needless to say, the word "censorship" nowhere occurs). Broadcasting, the booklet says, "brings a vivid world of fact and fancy into the privacy of scores of millions of individual homes. To this unique opportunity is linked unique responsibility." The codified standards "are intended to serve not as a strait-jacket but as a set of guidelines and principles which need never hinder genuine creativity." In the section on entertainment programs, it is affirmed that "the proper application of these standards should not preclude the presentation of programs of genuine artistic or literary merit dealing with valid moral and social issues even though they may be challenging or controversial, or present realities which some people might wish did not exist." So far so good. These ringing declarations about responsibility, valid moral and social issues, could indeed have been written to order as specifications for just such a drama as Mr. Neuman's two-part play.

The gray area in which the program foundered would appear to be defined in this thought-provoking clause: "The criterion used in reviewing programs is whether they would be regarded as acceptable in subject matter and treatment by a normal viewer under normal circumstances." The mind boggles at the thought of applying such a criterion. Is the normal viewer a Midwest businessman, a Southern farmer, a New York mechanic? Or is it a girl—a Mormon housewife, a black teacher, a Catholic beauty operator? Is he unemployed, is she on strike? Is he in debt, is she in analysis? Is he getting on well with the boss, is she getting on badly with the children? There are no given data; therefore the additional burden of deciding whether a program "would be regarded as acceptable in subject matter and treatment" by the normal viewer under normal circumstances would be enough to unstring the best of minds. Little wonder that, as Mr. Kasmire said, "Our judgment was on the side of caution."

Emerging from the gray area into the sunlit world of actual people, I went on a brief and unsuccessful search for a normal person under normal circumstances who would object to the subject of venereal disease being brought to the attention of teenagers. I started at a large and homogeneous California public school, Oakland Technical High. Mr. Jack Borum, the principal, told me that a Kansas State Health Department film called "The Innocent Party" is regularly shown to mixed classes of students and is followed by questions and discussion. The film is a fictionalized episode about a high-school boy who becomes infected with syphilis—very much like "The Rich Who Are Poor." Before the film is shown, notes are sent home to the parents explaining the subject matter and making it clear that attendance is optional. Never, ever, in all his years as principal, said Mr. Borum, has any parent objected or asked that his child be excused from seeing the film. Never, ever has any student objected. In fact the Parent-Teachers Association, both nationally and locally, is pressing for more extensive education in venereal disease.

In nearby Berkeley, California, state health educators who work year in and year out with the schools on V.D. education were also hard put to it to recall a case of protest against this type of instruction. Dr. Warren Ketterer, head of the venereal disease section, did remember that a couple of years ago in Marin County one P.-T.A. lady seemed to think it is a pity to reveal that venereal disease can easily be cured, as this may encourage promiscuity; but he did not consider her viewpoint either representative or particularly "normal." Mr. James Lovegren, health education consultant, described a number of educational talks given by his colleagues over local television stations. He said these stations have received many commendations and *no* protests. In his own travels he has run into school administrators who are reluctant to show the V.D. films for fear there may be some complaints; but, like Mr. Borum, he could cite no actual instance of parental objection. He even offered to telephone down to his colleagues in Los Angeles (a city regarded by all loyal Northern Californians as a reservoir of nuttiness) in the hopes of there uncovering a live and kicking objecting parent, but the Los Angeles health workers were also unable to furnish examples. Interestingly enough, Mr. Lovegren said that while there is a vocal minority of parents who strongly oppose sex education in schools, even this group has not expressed opposition to V.D. education. "Apparently they feel sex education as such belongs in the family, but that it's all right for the schools to teach the objective facts about a disease," he said.

Six months after Neuman's plays were banned, American Broadcasting Company (perhaps reacting to public indignation over NBC's action) presented a half-hour documentary called "VD Epidemic!" over ABC-SCOPE, a network program. The documentary contains far stronger stuff than Mr. Neuman's script, and it is prefaced with an appeal to parents to let their children watch because "the hugest rise of V.D. is among teen-agers." Actual V.D. patients tell their stories on the screen: an attractive woman graduate student who picked up V.D. in Italy ("I would have absolutely no idea how to say 'syphilis' in Italian") and who defends her own free-and-easy sexual mores, a married man who has infected his wife, a high-school student who started having sexual intercourse with girls at the age of eight. The even trickier point is then made that V.D. among homosexuals has risen to undreamt-of proportions, that their treatment is further hampered by ignorance, taboos, prejudice. I asked the producer of this documentary, Mr. Gordon Thomas, how it had been received and whether there had been much adverse reaction. He said that to his astonishment the program, which is not on prime time, attracted seven and a half million viewers, compared to an average two and a half million who generally watch ABC-SCOPE. Newspaper comment and letters to the network were uniformly laudatory, he said;

and not a single complaint was received: "Our publicity people have so far been unable to turn up any evidence of moral—or should I say immoral—indignation."

If the primary goal of broadcasting is to avoid giving offense, it seems reasonably certain that the NBC policymakers misread the signs and portents in the case of "The Rich Who Are Poor." The plays, far from offending anybody, would more likely have been warmly welcomed as an important contribution to the public welfare.

But according to the M-G-M producers in Hollywood, the sad fate of Neuman's plays is typical of the panicky response of the networks to current widespread criticism of television. The networks feel threatened on all sides: by legislative investigating committees and above all by the viewers whose likes and dislikes are supposedly reflected in the Nielsen ratings.

Neuman recalled that a few years ago the chairman of the Federal Communications Commission lambasted television as a wasteland of sex and violence. "This got all the broadcasters very nervous. In stupid panic a 'no violence' command went out from the Programming Departments to all writers and producers. It's ridiculous to ban violence per se—that's why we have this watered-down situation. Violence occurs in all drama and all literature from Shakespeare to Hemingway." Of the Nielsen ratings he said, "They are a lobotomy on the American public. The rating system is inaccurate, but it's a folly adhered to by all. Excellent shows like *The Defenders* are being replaced by ridiculous and imitative comedy and drama."

The easiest path for writer and producer, said Leonard Freeman, is simply to avoid any subject that might conceivably stir up fears in the network management. "The gray area leads to mental paralysis. For instance, according to the code, suicide is *verboten* if the intent is to show suicide as a solution to problems. It's easier for the man who above all wants to avoid trouble to turn down any reference to suicide in his productions on the ground it's against the code. A loose interpretation of the code can keep a subject matter locked up indefinitely. Gray area? It's more of a miasma." He said that the point of view of the creative workers who write and produce the programs and that of the network's Programming Department don't seem to match, they have different objectives: "Let's face it, commercial television is designed to sell products. It's a fact of life. No salesman wants to make the prospect angry. In the case of 'The Rich Who Are Poor' it was evidently felt that someone, somewhere, might not like it, might not be too receptive at the commercial break." However, he added, "We all go into this game with the rules afore spelled out, knowing that the final say-so of programming is in the hands of the network. Those are the Marquis of Queensberry rules of this particular game."

The type of programming that results from the gingerly approach of the networks to the television audience is best summed up in the gloomy words of Paul A. Porter, former chairman of the Federal Communications Commission. Speaking this year at the annual Peabody Television Awards luncheon, he said, "Some of the Peabody judges were tempted to take a sabbatical and not make any awards this year. A dreary sameness and deadly conformity seem to dominate the airwaves." A sentiment which, notwithstanding the corporate omniscience of NBC, will doubtless be echoed by many a normal viewer under normal circumstances.

COMMENT

The idea for this article was proposed by Vivian Cadden, an editor at *McCall's*, who wrote: "I don't know whether you happened to notice the stories about the 'Mr. Novak' and 'Dr. Kildare' programs on venereal disease that were planned, researched, written—and then suddenly canceled by the NBC network. The enclosed news clippings summarize the whole business. We'd like to have a story on how it all happened—from beginning to end, in the hope of illuminating some of the paradoxes, complexity and I think humor of the situation. . . ."

At first I was somewhat reluctant to take it on because the story had been covered in great detail, and the principals quoted at length, in newspapers and news weeklies, many of which had also run editorials blasting the network for its chicken-hearted about-face—so what was left for me to do? The editor had mentioned "paradoxes, complexity, humor." When I spotted in one of the news clippings that Robert D. Kasmire, spokesman for NBC, went by the Orwellesque title of "Vice-President of Corporate Information," I decided to have a try.

By the time I went to work on this article, I had already learned a fair amount about interviewing, and had developed certain techniques in the course of preparing *The American Way of Death,* published two years earlier. Accordingly, I plotted the sequence of my interviews with care: starting with the Friendly Witnesses, I set out to learn all I could about the program's origins and the circumstances of its cancellation before tackling my main target, the Veep of Corporate Info., who I hoped would furnish the icing on the cake.

From the news clippings I compiled a list of Friendlies—the Surgeon General, public health educators, school principals—to whom I wrote, and who eagerly plied me with more facts about symptoms and incidence of syphilis than I wanted to know. Needless to say, friendliest of all were the television writers who had spent close to a year researching their subject and developing their scripts, and who were ripe for sweet revenge against their network bosses.

Having acquired from the Friendlies an impressive stockpile of ammunition, I was ready to confront Mr. Kasmire. His Corporate Information was all I had hoped for, a steady stream of meaningless verbiage delivered in a studiedly obliging manner—he was at my service, he seemed to say, only too anxious to clarify the whole incident to my satisfaction. He was, I thought, about perfect for his job: master of the evasive answer, of the diplomatic lapse of memory as to who among his superiors had said what (if anything), of Corporate phrases such as "gray area" which I particularly liked. His reluctant yet long-winded comments were, as I had suspected they would be, the high point of the article.

The investigative reporter will often come up against some variant of Mr. Kasmire—the corporate spokesman, no matter what his title, who is there to act as a buffer between his bosses and the press. The role of such a person is to doggedly sidetrack the conversation, the role of the reporter to ever more doggedly stick to the points he wishes to develop. Thus the interview becomes an exercise in thrust and parry, requiring a degree of nerve and determination on both sides. In this case, who won? I think Mr. Kasmire scored at least one important point: my failure to press for the names of the other four network executives who participated in the decision to ban the program. Even if they had refused to talk to me and divulge their reasons, it would have been nice to list them in the piece and thus to publicize their pusillanimous role.

My one effort to go over Mr. Kasmire's head was firmly rebuffed. I wrote to Mr. Walter D. Scott, whose even weightier title was Executive Vice-President in Charge of the Television Network, asking for elaboration of the reasons given by Mr. Kasmire for cancellation of the program; predictably, his secretary answered that Mr. Scott was "out of the country on an extended trip." Very sensible of him, I thought; with Mr. Kasmire as a mouthpiece, who would want to compete?

Looking at the piece as a whole, I see it gets off to a rather slow start, probably because I was trying to lure *McCall's* readers gently into a subject that they (no less than the NBC network) might find unpalatable, through the device of quoting the views of Eminent Respectables like Dr. Parran and General Hugh S. Johnson.

I had some difficulty coping with the script of "The Rich Who

Are Poor," which I thought atrociously sophomoric. I could not bring myself to endorse it as an example of good playwriting. Not wishing to give offense to the authors—or to detract from their undeniably sincere, crusading efforts—I compromised by characterizing it as "innocuous in the extreme, relying as it does on the tried-and-true formulas of this sort of television play."

As in the case of " 'Something to Offend Everyone,' " some of the best copy in the piece was mined from the confidential interoffice memorandum from the Broadcast Standards Department slipped to me by the vengeful scriptwriters. I sometimes dream of compiling a whole book of such memoranda, if one could only get access to them. Who knows to what extent these deplorable Standards people have succeeded in watering down and emasculating the movies and TV programs that we, the audience, pay to see? What manner of people are they—dirty old men? Clean-cut young women? Or some combination? What do they do for recreation—jogging? Group sex? Transcendental meditation? I should love to know, and if somebody out there should decide to write a book about them I would be first in line to buy it.

MAINE CHANCE
DIARY

McCALL'S / *March, 1966*

From time to time over the years, word has leaked into the society columns and fashion magazines of a fabulous health and beauty resort where very rich women go to be slimmed and trimmed: Elizabeth Arden's Maine Chance in Arizona. There was a brief hullabaloo in the press during the Eisenhower Administration when Mamie Eisenhower commandeered the Presidential plane to make her annual safari there. It is rumored to be the most expensive retreat of its kind in the world.

One gathers from these tantalizing hints that Maine Chance stands at the apex of the whole vast pyramid of America's multibillion-dollar beauty industry—the *ne plus ultra* of beautification. Yet the particulars of this establishment are shrouded in mystery, for unlike Cartier jewels and Dior dresses it is never advertised.

I have long been curious about this place. It occurred to me that having investigated the American way of death, I should take a logical step backward and explore an aspect of the American way of aging; so I determined to go there and have a look.

Preliminary investigation led me to believe there are some points of similarity between the Maine Chance operation and the American funeral: an objective of both is what the undertakers' journals call "a body that can be shown with pride." There is the same business about prices: as in the mortuary world, the atmosphere is so heavy with discretion and graciousness, it seems crude to ask about the mundane matter of costs, and every time one does they go up, up, up.

I telephoned Arden's in New York to make my reservation. I had been told the cost was $400 a week. But no; the reservations lady (whose voice, like those of undertakers, exuded controlled inner peace and happiness) explained that this was some years ago. At the present time they have a few rooms with shower only at $600 a week; those with bathtub start at $750. A hundred and fifty dollars a week for renting a bathtub? But I decided to go whole hog, and booked one of those. She also told me that while the recommended length of stay is two or more weeks, much can be accomplished in one week.

My indoctrination into the Maine Chance way of life began with the literature sent to me from Arden's in New York. The descriptive brochure is full of this sort of thing:

The flowers in every room are breathlessly fresh. The carpet beneath your feet will be an Aubusson, the floor beneath the carpet, marble.

A big part of the therapy is a reversion to infantile ways:

There is the luxury of being told. Not asked, petitioned, begged to consider, requested to choose, just told. You do not have to make a single decision. You are lulled back into the life of childhood—the life of a good child. "Brush your hair, thus. Sleep now, and when you wake up your eyes will shine." What to wear? The Blue Number, sometimes called the Great Leveler, which serves as exercise and swim suit.

There is a certain amount of judicious name-dropping:

Such well-known dynamos as Cobina Wright, Beatrice Lillie and Theresa Helburn accomplish prodigies of work fifty weeks of the year on energy stored up at Maine Chance.

And flowery analogy:

There is time to think about yourself, perhaps in the beautifully tended bougainvillea gardens, where you may observe that it takes care and patience to make flowers blossom to perfection, but it can be done.

The brochure was supplemented by letters from the reservations desk: "We have reserved for you a charming room in the Upper Garden of Arden. A little bed-jacket is useful for breakfast in bed. For evening, tea gowns or simple evening dresses of short length. We do have a little boutique for shopping, should you forget anything!"

Friends greeted my plan with derision which ill concealed their secret envy. They threatened to take before-and-after pictures, and to stuff my suitcase with Arden lotion bottles filled with martinis (liquor is, of course, forbidden at Maine Chance). They made cruel remarks about what I would look like in the Great Leveler. They pointed out that I was least likely to succeed at Maine Chance, since my ideas of beauty care are pretty rudimentary: one lipstick until it is used up instead of the "color-correlated shades for each outfit" suggested in the ads; and although, like most people, I have resolved from time to time to do the Air Force Exercises or equivalent, the requisite nine minutes a day was always my undoing.

Oddly enough, while they deplored the whole preposterous idea of me at Maine Chance, their comments betrayed enormous curiosity as to what goes on there. "Write to me daily. Keep notes. We want every detail," they said. So one Sunday in mid-November I packed a large notebook in which to keep a daily journal along with my little bed-jacket, and, agog for the well-known dynamos, the breathlessly fresh flowers, the whole strange adventure, I boarded the plane for Phoenix.

JOURNAL: SUNDAY NIGHT

My plane was two hours late, a circumstance that rattled me terribly, but at the airport I was at once enfolded in the tranquilizing Maine Chance ambience. I was met by a gliding lady (they all glide at Maine Chance rather than walk), who turned me over to a driver—"our little driver," she called him, although he appeared to be of normal stature. The glider had to leave me to meet another arriving flower, so the little driver took me directly to the Upper Garden of Arden, which is at a short distance from the main buildings. It was too dark to see much but I discerned the outlines of a gatehouse at the entrance to the premises. The driver told me that a twenty-four-hour guard is posted there (evoking uneasy thoughts of Marie Antoinette's Versailles being stormed by the hungry populace). At the steps of the Upper Garden another gliding lady awaited me; in a sort of minuet progression, the little driver presented me to her and she in turn introduced me to "your maid," who escorted me to my room. Thus my first impression was of ineffable solicitude, service, courtesy.

My room is one of a row on a balcony overlooking the Upper Garden's own small private swimming pool. It is just like a very good motel room (white wool carpet and pink sateen curtains); the $150-a-week bath, alas! just like any bath; I had rather hoped for sunken lapis lazuli and gold taps. (I discovered later that there are other, far grander rooms up at the main house and at nearby Hilltop House, with canopied beds and flouncy satin all over, palace living with Hollywood overtones; these cost $800 a week and are generally reserved for the faithful old regulars.) On the dressing table are half a dozen jars of Arden preparations ("a gift for you," said my maid), face cream, hand lotion, deodorant, and so on, with prices on the bottoms, for a total retail value of about eleven dollars. Five breathlessly fresh roses on my bureau. I flopped into bed to the pleasant sound of my maid rustling about with my unpacking.

MONDAY

This morning my maid appeared early with breakfast (black coffee and grapefruit) and a card showing my schedule for the day. First, she explained, I must be examined by the doctor. He arrived, looked sadly at me, asked "How many years young are you," checked heart and blood pressure, and pronounced me fit for the rigors ahead.

The maid offered to have me driven to the main pool area, where all the action takes place, less than two city blocks away. I elected to hike, so she ushered me on foot across a shocking-pink wooden bridge, past some magnificent flower gardens where little gardeners were already at work, and over a sweeping lawn to the pool, where for the first time I set eyes on my fellow-inmates: one and a half tons of female forms in various stages of dilapidation, each in her little blue number and white terry-cloth robe. (I do not mean to exclude myself from this depressing description, for I fitted right into it. The fact is that middle-aged women in their natural state, sans girdle, bra, or make-up, do not present an attractive sight, particularly in the bright glare of the Arizona morning sun.)

There were about twenty of us round the pool, half of our total enrollment; the others had already disappeared into adjacent buildings, gymnasiums, massage rooms, steam cabinets, to start their chores of the day. The poolside sitters were having various things done to them by white-uniformed attendants: manicure, pedicure, scalp massage, hair brushing. Others were grimly submitting to various machines placed round the pool—electrically powered rollers against which they were pressing their behinds, or on which they were sitting for a walloping of the inner thighs.

I overheard one of our number gaily comparing our situation to that of a girls' boarding school. There may be something to it, the all-female company, the isolation from the outside world; but there the analogy ends. We are not (alas!) girls, neither are we scholars. The scene reminded me of another kind of institution, a well-appointed and expensive private lunatic asylum where I once visited a friend who had suffered a nervous breakdown. The inmates of that sad place, disheveled and drab in their housecoats and wrappers, were gathered in a pretty drawing room. As I looked more closely, I noticed that many were doing things to themselves, rhythmically brushing their hair, twisting or pleating their clothes, stroking their faces. One began to see that the poor spirits were utterly turned in on themselves; for the time being they had lost touch with the outside world.

The median age of my fellow-beauty-seekers is, I judge, around fifty-five. There are one or two of about thirty-five, regular tubs of butter and rather cross-looking tubs at that—or perhaps they are just stoically contemplating the tasks ahead. A few upward of sixty-five. One or two of those handsome, ageless women seen only in America—might be anywhere from early thirties to late forties. Quite a collection of bosoms, ranging from flat to pendulous, with abdomens to match. As Gypsy Rose Lee put it, "I have everything I had twenty years ago only it's all a little bit lower."

Seen in terms of art, there are many early Thurbers in our group (soft white turnips for faces and vaguely defined bodies), one or two possible Renoirs (pink and fleshy), some Helen Hokinsons (solid, imposing shapes evocative of a high degree of organizational leadership), one Mary Petty (a violet cloud of hair atop a finely wrinkled, birdlike face).

Surveying them, I wonder: Will they be transformed before my very eyes as the days go by? I much doubt it. The bovine, freckled woman with the insipid stare will (I predict) be ever bovine, freckled, and insipid; nor will the petulant, overblown brunette be noticeably different. As for me, time will tell.

As a newcomer I was first weighed in (at 140¾ pounds) and

measured in half a dozen strategic places. "A half-inch needs to come off here," murmured the measurer as she did my upper arm. Then the regime began in earnest.

We are doing or being done to (mostly the latter) from nine till five, a full working day, with everything planned to the exact minute, ten-minute intervals between treatments and one hour off for lunch. We glisten alternately with cream or sweat. It goes like this: Massage—a splendid Swedish masseuse of the old school rubs you all over with cream, rolls up her sleeves muttering "I'm going to get rrrrrrough," and proceeds to knead, pound, push, and pull you about for forty-five minutes. Exercise—two classes a day, about six of us in each, conducted by an elongated lady whose figure we should all like to emulate. We lie on mats or stretch to the ceiling to her cry of "Tuck it in, class! A nice, tight tuck. And now we stre-e-e-e-tch the rib cage, and walk our ears right up the wall for posture. Did you feel that? Goooooooood." The exercises are much like those a friend used to drag me to at the Y.W.C.A. Hair—daily brushing and scalp massage with cream, while a manicurist is going after feet or hands and digging about in the cuticles with more cream. No shampoo or setting until graduation day, I'm told. Mask—this is done in the nurse's office. She creams your face, covers it with a pinkish contraption so that you look like the victim of a mad doctor, and turns on some electricity. The mask, by remote control, gradually gets warm. Then she turns if off and it gradually gets cool. I asked her what it is for; she said good for circulation, also sinus trouble. Shortwave diathermy is the official name for this mysterious procedure. Facial—more cream, forty-five minutes of face massage, followed by iced lotion compresses. Ardena bath—pure torture chamber. The attendant pours some boiling hot wax into a bed sheet and makes you get in (responding with solicitous encouragement to cries of "ouch" and "too hot"), then pours more hot wax all over you (more than a gallon, I learned) until you are completely coated, then wraps you to the neck in sheets and warmed blankets; arms and legs are immobilized as with swaddling clothes. Thus pinned, one's nose at once starts tickling; you tell her, and she wipes off the face with icy lotion which feels pleasant but easily misses the tickle. You stay like that for twenty minutes, are peeled out of the wax which is now solidified, leaving a small pool of sweat in the waxy form. She says it draws all the poisons out of the body. "All *what* poisons?" I ask in alarm, but she is vague on that point. Steam cabinet—same idea, you are covered to the neck and slowly cooked, only in hot moist air instead of wax. Shakeaway—you are strapped into a sort of electric chair, the juice is turned on, and you sit there vibrating for twenty minutes.

The shakeaway chair is strategically located in the little boutique, to which the ladies flock during their ten-minute break between activities. As I sit there jiggling away, I see them clustered in twos and threes around the racks of negligées, bedjackets, tops, and slacks. "I'll take that, that, that, that, and two of those" is the standard cry, like a school cheer. There is an Arden Christmas stocking on display made of quilted white satin and filled with small gifts of Arden products. "I'll take twenty of those, they'll solve my Christmas gift problem," says one of the ladies. After she leaves, I ask the price (she didn't): the stockings are $27.50 each.

In the course of the day, the name of Miss Arden (as she is referred to hereabouts in reverent tones) is frequently invoked. "What sort of cream is that?" "A special formula that Miss Arden learned of years ago from a doctor in Rome." The mask is Miss Arden's own patented invention, as is the shakeaway contraption; Miss Arden has personally worked out the details of our 900-calorie diet.

Halfway through the proceedings, luncheon was served on an outdoor terrace by elegant parlormaids. It consisted of a single course, a very good rare hamburger and excellent salad, all prepared by a French chef who has been with Miss Arden for years. No water with meals; Miss Arden considers it bloating.

At dinnertime I got my first look at the main house. It is a riot of elegance, or a profusion of magnificence. This is where the

Aubusson carpets are, and the marble floors. It is like a small embassy: a large and splendid drawing room, another room called "the library" (in honor of a set of the Waverley Novels and the English Cyclopedia). There is a visitors' book in the library going back to 1958, which gives many a clue to the sources of income of the patrons of Maine Chance. The signatures read in part like a grocery shopping list (I found a popular ketchup, a famous cake flour, a brand of canned soup, a yeast, and a coffee), in part like a roster of the Republican National Committee. Mamie Eisenhower's large round hand appears over and over.

At seven o'clock we gathered in the drawing room, and for the first time I saw my fellow-guests in ordinary garb. Most reassuring —they looked *so* much better, so human for a change, in fact just like any other gathering of well-dressed ladies of uncertain age. Girdles, make-up, good clothes had done wonders. There was a fluttery chorus of "My, you look nice!" as flower after flower arrived in cocktail dress, tailored linen suit, flowing chiffon, or evening slacks. In fact, we found it hard to recognize each other as the forlorn, greasy creatures of the day.

An imposing six-foot butler and several parlormaids handed round the cocktails (small servings of carrot juice) and hors d'oeuvres (cut-up raw vegetables).

At dinner, all is elegance and formality, like a parody of a very grand English house party. Some sit round a huge, long table in the dining room, others at individual tables in an adjoining room. Lovely china, and delicious food—in *very* moderate amounts, for us dieters. The waitress discreetly indicates how much you are supposed to take (two slivers of saddle of lamb, a helping of squash and red cabbage, followed by fruit compote) as we wistfully notice wild rice, green peas, creamy desserts, and other delectables being placed before the three or four of our company who are trying to gain weight.

Circles are beginning to form, roughly along regional lines. A few came with a friend, a few others are acquainted from previous visits here. Most are strangers to each other. Tennessee, North Carolina, Texas have found each other, are making friends and discussing mutual loved ones in their soft Southern shriek and aberrant vowel sounds. "Wha, ah dew believe ah know yo' cuhsin, ma sister was brahdsmaid at her weddin'." The Middle Westerners are still uneasy, there are fewer of them. As there is only one of me, we make common cause, exchanging polite nothings about the activities of the day. ("Did *you* enjoy the Ardena bath? *I* didn't. But they say it's *very* beneficial." "Yes, I know, draws out the poisons. Rather sinister, I call it.") Then there's the International Set, with that snort-and-flounce voice with traces of English accent indigenous to Westchester County, Long Island, Newport. Pacesetters, I can tell at once. Predictably, *they* arrive in casual cottons (the rest of us having taken seriously the cocktail-dress injunction).

After dinner some play bridge, others knit or work at embroidery. Soon we are offered a nightcap of tea or Swiss Kriss laxative, and so to bed.

TUESDAY

I have lost two pounds already! Of course one is weighed at the most propitious moment, after being sweated in the steam cabinet and before luncheon. Nevertheless it seems miraculous.

The day's procedure is much like yesterday's: our bodies and faces are in turn kneaded, stretched, massaged, manipulated, creamed, steamed, cooled—from sunup to sundown.

There is perhaps little wonder that the prevailing mood is utterly, totally narcissistic—each is preoccupied only with herself, the pound lost (or in some sad cases the half-pound gained) at the daily weighing-in, the improving waistline, the tighter tuck at exercise class.

We get the newspaper with our breakfast trays. The headlines are full of bitter battles raging in Vietnam, the Rhodesia crisis, historic Supreme Court decisions. But we, who are being fiddled with while Rome burns, do not discuss these matters. At luncheon, conversation at my table goes like this: "*I* usually eat a very light lunch at home, just a sandwich." "*I* often skip lunch altogether, but may have a snack later on—perhaps just a piece of fruit." This proves to be contagious, for I hear myself saying in quite a loud and attention-getting voice, "*I* eat VERY LITTLE BREAKFAST. . . ." But not even a ho-hum greets this riveting announcement, for nobody is actually listening to anybody else.

The one in charge of all this lucrative avoirdupois (and the tender psyches that lurk beneath) is an elegant lady of French and English background. She comes as near perfection for the job as any human being could: a combination of ship's captain (her own simile, and she does run a *very* tight ship), English country house-party hostess, duenna. Her costumes subtly suggest her role of the moment. In the mornings, supervising staff and clients, she sports a chic modification of nautical attire, fitted blue trousers, gay silk shirt, and sailor hat. In late afternoon one may catch a glimpse of her in severe Italian knit. For dinner, she is transformed, the personification of charm and loveliness in silk, taffeta, or chiffon. How we long to be more like her! Slender, head erect, full of kindness. Although she did have some relatively brisk words for two ladies caught sneaking an apple (100 calories) into their room.

It is she, I think, who sets the tone for our psychological handling—the "good child" routine. We are treated ever, ever so gently and kindly by everyone—like half-witted children aged seven. You ask an attendant the way to the gym. Instead of pointing it out, she drops whatever she is doing, takes your arm, and leads you there. You are put into the Ardena bath for the first time (the thought "boiled in oil" dismally occurring to you), and the attendant soothes you, cajoles you, gets you in, wraps you up tenderly as you have never been wrapped since childhood bronchitis. We do not put on our shoes after a foot treatment, we do not pour our own potassium broth at 11 a.m., nor our grapefruit juice at 4 p.m. We do not fetch our own towels after swimming. Willing hands do it all.

The patrons seem to enjoy this kid-glove handling, they fall right in with the intense self-solicitude fostered by our custodians. I heard one woman arranging to be moved from her predominantly pink room, which she found somewhat too stimulating, to a blue room, a more tranquil color.

The second in command, and the only other staff member who takes her meals with us, is a very nice English governess type—she was in fact a schoolmistress in the north of England for many years. While she has gone far in acquiring the Maine Chance manner (the soothing, dulcet tones that could drive you faintly dotty in time), there is something a little incongruous in her presence here. I visualize her being more at home in a stout mackintosh, walking down a sopping-wet country lane with an assortment of cocker spaniels and retrievers.

She puts me in mind of my own far-off childhood in England—unsoothed and unlulled we were by our governess, who saw her primary task as knocking some sense into our heads. "Nobody's going to look at you," she would say if I was fussing about the way my sash was tied; or, approaching the drawing room at teatime, "Now, Jessica, remember you are the least important person in the room."

Maine Chance would not, I think, be a success in England. The aristocratic dowager, nearest English equivalent from a class standpoint to the ladies gathered here, is a hardier bloom whose upbringing has endowed her with an intractably matter-of-fact outlook on life. "Stuff and nonsense!" she would exclaim angrily, if asked to behave like a good child. While she might patronize a Continental health spa for a specific ailment—liver disease, gout, rheumatism are perennial English favorites—she would be unlikely to disburse a small fortune on going into retreat with a group of other women purely for the sake of sagging waistline and double chin.

In the late afternoon (the two hours of free time between the day's activities and dinner) I return to the Upper Garden of Arden. Maids are quietly padding to and fro with freshly pressed evening clothes. I say to myself, "*I* usually have a VERY DRY MARTINI about now," but settle for some tea brought by the maid to the pool.

Others from our snug dorm are gathered there, and we discuss rival beauty farms that have recently been in the news. There is the Greenhouse in Dallas, operated by Neiman-Marcus, and the Golden Door in California, where the exercise suits are pink instead of blue and where the tab is $1,100 for two weeks. "Very hilly-haley," says one of our little throng. "What does that mean?" I ask eagerly. "Oh, you know. . . . Inexpensive."

WEDNESDAY

Those in the know (the old-timers) tell me that by Wednesday one is for some reason at one's lowest ebb. I can see why: the miraculous shedding of weight has slowed down (I only lost half a pound today), the novelty of the day's routine has worn off, and there are still three days left until Sunday.

Perhaps reflecting the Wednesday slump, lunchtime talk today turned from food to liquor: how many calories in a whiskey sour? In an ounce of bourbon? The duenna smilingly instructed us in these matters, and added that if one must drink, plain Scotch and water is better than martinis.

A well-known dynamo (or at least the wife of one) arrived in our midst today—Mrs. Barry Goldwater. As we tucked it in together on adjacent mats and walked our ears up the wall for posture, I observed that she is a whiz at the exercises, and in my heart I knew she was far trimmer of figure than most of us. She is a day scholar, for her home is hard by and she returns there in the evenings. Here she is surrounded by her husband's admirers and former campaign contributors; I have yet to meet a Rockefeller supporter at Maine Chance. I asked my nice Swedish masseuse, "Do any Democrats come here?" "*Ach, ja,*" she answered. "Ve have very many of them, Mrs. Dwight Eisenhower, she come, and Mrs. John Foster Dulles, she always come for Christmas, and Mrs. Barry Goldwater . . ." "Any Johnsons, or Kennedys, or Humphreys?" She considered a moment. "No . . . I no know those names."

At dinner tonight there was a moment of perturbation to ruffle the calm. We had lamb chops, and the waitress, as is her custom, indicated that we might take two each. Halfway down the table, the platter was empty. Had she made a mistake? Would some diners have to go hungry? A Lord of the Flies look momentarily crossed some faces (while those who had already been served noticeably speeded up consumption, perhaps fearing the second chop would be called back); but another platter soon appeared, and the day was saved.

THURSDAY

As we become better acquainted, mealtime conversation takes on more range, and I am beginning to acquire some insight into the affluent mind. F. Scott Fitzgerald is supposed to have said, "The rich are different from us," and Ernest Hemingway to have answered, "Yes, they have more money." One wonders.

There is the lady from Florida who has six darling poodles at home. She couldn't bear to leave *all* of them for two whole weeks, so she brought her favorite one and a maid to look after it, rented an apartment for them in Phoenix, and visits twice daily. Today, at lunch, she swiped a piece of steak to take to Doggie. This set us talking about bowser bags. Another lady at our table complained about a queer thing that happens at her parties: guests bring along bowser bags, and behind her back get the servants to fill them up with food—but she knows the food isn't really for their dogs, they take it home and eat it. I was startled into saying that I must say nothing like that has ever happened to me when I give a party; she said, "My dear, check with your butler, I'm sure he'll admit to you that it goes on all the time." There is the lady whose husband sends her fresh flowers every day, flown here from Honolulu. Another has just returned from Portugal where she took her eight grand-children for a little treat—and allowed each to bring a friend along for company, so they wouldn't fight. Yet another sometimes flies from New York to London *for the day*, to see the races—her race horse lives in England with its trainer.

They are all nonstop shoppers. In the few free daytime mo-ments they are at the boutique; after the daily routine they dash to Phoenix for more shopping before dinner. The International Set-ters regularly show up in the evening in darling look-alike outfits bought that day at Saks or Magnin.

FRIDAY

Tonight, after dinner, we played Bingo for house prizes, wrapped packages of bubble bath and other gifts in the range of $1.25 to $5. The Bingo almost led to a nasty row; it is amazing how close to the surface lurk some of the cruder passions in the bosoms of our flowers. The duenna, looking smashing in flowered organza, gaily presided and announced the games. "A straight line in any direction, horizontal, vertical, or diagonal," she sang out. It took a little time to explain these concepts to some of the less alert ladies, but they finally got it. We played, there was a winner, her prize was ceremoniously handed.

As the games progressed, the duenna varied the rules to add to the suspense—at one point she gave *three* prizes to a single winner for a full board. The rivalry soon became intense, each furiously concentrating on her board. Now Mrs. C., a large motherly lady sitting next to me, won twice in a row. Somebody said, in a stage whisper heard all over the room, "I think Mrs. C. should disqualify herself now she's won two prizes." There was an awkward silence. Mrs. C. looked about her uncertainly, then rose and said in frigid tones, "Very well, I'll disqualify myself. But I think I should say Mrs. X. got *three* prizes for one game and *she* wasn't disqualified." Everybody rallied: "Oh, don't go, Mrs. C.," they cooed. She was persuaded, and sat down. The duenna, perhaps fearing we were getting overexcited, soon declared the fun over and we retired to bed.

SATURDAY

For those of us who are leaving tomorrow, this is the day for the final garnish. We are like well-done cakes, out of the oven, cooled and ready for icing. Hair is now cut, washed, tinted, and set: nails (both toe and finger) coated with pink polish. Faces are painstakingly dealt with: eyebrows are plucked, lashes touched up with black dye and mascara on top of that; foundation lotion, rouge, and powder carefully applied. Legs are coated from ankle to upper thigh with a hot thick brown wax which is ripped off after cooling, leaving the legs hairless and gleaming. Rather to my terror, the same procedure is followed for the armpits; surprisingly, it hardly hurts at all, so quickly and skillfully is it done. But (I think gloomily) it is all very much like taking old Tray to the vet for a clip and bath; he looks marvelous for a few days, but quickly reverts to his usual state.

Now we get our report cards. I am alleged to have lost two inches round the waist and the promised half-inch off upper arm, with corresponding reduction of hips, thighs, legs. I have also lost five pounds.

This evening, at dinner, those of us who had done well were each allowed a tiny sliver of a magnificent cheesecake, a speciality of our chef. One of the International Setters was so moved by the appearance of this dessert that she did some rapid calorie calculation and dined off cheesecake alone—forgoing her first course entirely in order to be entitled to an extra piece.

SUNDAY

My last day. A super-lull has fallen over these hushed precincts. The place is almost deserted: some patrons have already departed, and those who are staying on have rented cars or chartered planes for a little Sunday outing. I took advantage of the inactivity to seek out a higher-echelon staff member who told me something of the history and operation of Maine Chance.

The original Maine Chance, a farmhouse in Mount Vernon, Maine, was acquired by Elizabeth Arden before World War II, and is open each year from June to September. The Arizona establishment, which operates in winter only, opened in 1948 with 9 clients; it has expanded over the years, several new buildings have been added, and today the average enrollment is 40 to 45. In a six-month period, some 750 flowers are processed.

The staff numbers about 60. There are 27 beautifiers (masseuses, hairdressers, and so on), 25 household help (kitchen personnel, maids, drivers), 2 hostesses, 2 office workers, several gardeners. Most of the staff migrate to Mount Vernon in summer. They work a six-day week and for three months of the year, when both establishments are closed, they are on leave.

My informant explained that the reason Maine Chance is never advertised is that it is "definitely noncommercial." "You mean, it doesn't make money?" I asked, incredulous. She said that it might break even or might lose money, but it is not a profit-making proposition. "A charitable enterprise?" "No, not exactly, more an accommodation for clients." "Any camperships under the Poverty Program?" "You must be joking." (I was, for once.)

Maine Chance is, she went on, the fulfillment of a dream—an expression of Miss Arden's personality, her beliefs, her life's dedication to principles of health and beauty, cleanliness inside and out, serenity, simplicity of regimen carried out in beautiful, peaceful surroundings.

Yet from the prosaic viewpoint of an innkeeper, Maine Chance has much going for it. There are no men, children, drunks, dogs, or other misusers of furnishings among the clientele. While the food is delicious (and French chefs come high), there are no substitutions on the $750 dinners, and no second servings. For the sake of restfulness and serenity, lights go out at 10 p.m. and the telephone switchboard closes for the night—a practice also highly compatible with economy.

Later, sitting in the Phoenix airport coffee shop, I felt as though I had awakened from a curious dream. Although I had been gone from the real world for only a week, somehow it seemed much longer. It was a wonderful feeling to be once more surrounded by ordinary people with ordinary preoccupations, hurrying about carrying things, looking at watches, coping with little children. The coffee-shop hostess, with her iron-gray bouffant hairdo and lamé dress, could have stepped right out of the Maine Chance dining room—right age, right clothes, same incipient figure problems—only she probably makes eighty dollars a week, paid forty dollars for the dress, sets her own hair, and really does do the Air Force exercises.

Waiting for my plane, I did some simple sums. My week at Maine Chance, including tips (15 percent of my bill) and transportation, cost roughly $1,000. I had lost five pounds, at $200 per pound. The forty of us at Maine Chance represented a total investment of some $40,000 in a one-week effort to jack up sagging muscles and restore the fading roses to aging cheeks. A poignant thought.

Friends met me at the airport. "Do I look different?" I asked hopefully. "Well . . . not really. But you've lost some weight, haven't you?" And at least I could say that, like Poor Jud in *Oklahoma!,* my fingernails have never been so clean.

COMMENT

A major part of the magazine editor's job is to think up ideas for articles with which to fill those flapping pages of text that serve as the fragile connective tissue for the many more pages of advertisements. Some editors will bombard the "established writer" with article proposals without much regard for that particular writer's sphere of interest or expertise. I have a large file of such proposals, ranging from a story on Queen Elizabeth's coronation to ecological advances in the Midwest. Because I make my living by writing, I do not lightly turn down article assignments; I consider them very carefully. But I also know that if I cannot, after earnest contemplation, warm up to a subject, the finished piece will please nobody: I shall be dissatisfied, so will the editor, so will the reader.

There are exceptional editors who have an instinct for matching the story with the writer. Such a one is Vivian Cadden of *McCall's*. "Honestly! Maine Chance—for *me?*" I roared in astonishment when she called up to suggest this subject. Of course, she said; it will be a giggle all the way, do go; besides, you might lose some weight. That last observation, while not exactly kind, was persuasive.

"How do I go about getting accepted?" I asked.

"Oh, come *on*," said Vivian. "You know better than that. Just do it."

Of course she was right. Yet a slight feeling of paranoia took hold at the moment of actually picking up the phone to call Elizabeth Arden's for a reservation. Maine Chance would surely be, for me, enemy territory; what if my identity were discovered by the reservations people? Would they refuse my application? I could use my married name, but this would be scanty cover at the local Arden salon in San Francisco, where they might easily make the connection with Jessica Mitford. So I telephoned to the New York office and announced myself as Mrs. Robert Treuhaft, which was how I was introduced to the other slimmers at Maine Chance. One day at lunch I overheard a woman asking another, "Who is that?" "Oh, that's Mrs. Fruehauf" came the reply. "Her husband is very big in trucking." This, for me one of the major giggles, I omitted from the article as too much of an in-joke for *McCall's* readers.

The other giggle was the bathtub. I really loathe not having a proper bath, and had even asked Reservations if there was a bath somewhere in the building to which I could nip in my dressing gown, as is often the case in the cheap European hotels where I sometimes stay. Reservations, sounding very reserved, answered in the negative. Although *McCall's* are generous about expenses —and were well aware that the outlay for this piece was going to be large—I did think it advisable to check with them about the $150 bathtub, and wrote to Vivian anxiously inquiring if they would underwrite this extra expense. The reply came by telegram:

"MCCALL'S WOULD NOT WANT YOU TO BE WITHOUT A BATHTUB."

LET US NOW
APPRAISE
FAMOUS WRITERS

ATLANTIC / *July, 1970*

> Beware of the scribes who like
> to go about in long robes, and
> love salutations in the market
> places . . . and the places of
> honor at feasts; who devour
> widows' houses . . .
>
> Luke 20:46, 47

In recent years I have become aware of fifteen Famous Faces looking me straight in the eye from the pages of innumerable magazines, newspapers, fold-out advertisements, sometimes in black-and-white, sometimes in living color, sometimes posed in a group around a table, sometimes shown singly, pipe in hand in book-lined study or strolling through a woodsy countryside: the Guiding Faculty of the Famous Writers School.*

Here is Bennett Cerf, most famous of them all, his kindly,

---

* They are: Faith Baldwin, John Caples, Bruce Catton, Bennett Cerf, Mignon G. Eberhart, Paul Engle, Bergen Evans, Clifton Fadiman, Rudolf Flesch, Phyllis McGinley, J. D. Ratcliff, Rod Serling, Max Shulman, Red Smith, Mark Wiseman.

humorous face aglow with sincerity, speaking to us in the first person from a mini-billboard tucked into our Sunday newspaper: "If you want to write, my colleagues and I would like to test your writing aptitude. We'll help you find out whether you can be trained to become a successful writer." And Faith Baldwin, looking up from her typewriter with an expression of ardent concern for that vast, unfulfilled sisterhood of nonwriters: "It's a shame more women don't take up writing. Writing can be an ideal profession for women. . . . Beyond the thrill of that first sale, writing brings intangible rewards." J. D. Ratcliff, billed in the ads as "one of America's highest-paid free-lance authors," thinks it's a shame, too: "I can't understand why more beginners don't take the short road to publication by writing articles for magazines and newspapers. It's a wonderful life."

The short road is attained, the ads imply, via the aptitude test which Bennett Cerf and his colleagues would like you to take so they may "grade it free of charge." If you are one of the fortunate ones who do well on the test, you may "enroll for professional training." After that, your future is virtually assured, for the ads promise that "Fifteen Famous Writers will teach you to write successfully at home."

These offers are motivated, the ads make clear, by a degree of altruism not often found in those at the top of the ladder. The Fifteen have never forgotten the tough times—the "sheer blood, sweat and rejection slips," as J. D. Ratcliff puts it—through which they suffered as beginning writers; and now they want to extend a helping hand to those still at the bottom rung. "When I look back, I can't help thinking of all the time and agony I would have saved if I could have found a real 'pro' to work with me," says Ratcliff.

How can Bennett Cerf—Chairman of the Board of Random House, columnist, television personality—and his renowned colleagues find time to grade all the thousands of aptitude tests that must come pouring in, and on top of that fulfill their pledge to "teach you to write successfully at home"? What are the standards for admission to the school? How many graduates actually find their way into the "huge market that will pay well for pieces of almost any length" which, says J. D. Ratcliff, exists for the beginning writer? What are the "secrets of success" that the Famous Fifteen say they have "poured into a set of specially created textbooks"? And how much does it cost to be initiated into these secrets?

My mild curiosity about these matters might never have been satisfied had I not learned, coincidentally, about two candidates for the professional training offered by the Famous Writers who passed the aptitude test with flying colors: a seventy-two-year-old foreign-born widow living on Social Security, and a fictitious character named Louella Mae Burns.

The adventures of these two impelled me to talk with Bennett Cerf and other members of the Guiding Faculty, to interview former students, to examine the "set of specially created textbooks" (and the annual stockholders' reports, which proved in some ways more instructive), and eventually to visit the school's headquarters in Westport, Connecticut.

An Oakland lawyer told me about the seventy-two-year-old widow. She had come to him in some distress: a salesman had charmed his way into her home and at the end of his sales pitch had relieved her of $200 (her entire bank account) as down payment on a $900 contract, the balance of which would be paid off in monthly installments. A familiar story, for like all urban communities ours is fertile ground for roving commission salesmen skilled in unloading on the unwary housewife anything from vacuum cleaners to deep freezers to encyclopedias to grave plots, at vastly inflated prices. The unusual aspect of this old lady's tale was the merchandise she had been sold. No sooner had the salesman left than she thought better of it, and when the lessons arrived she returned them unopened.

To her pleas to be released from the contract, the Famous Writers replied: "Please understand that you are involved in a legal and binding contract," and added that the school's policy requires a doctor's certificate attesting to the ill health of a student before she is permitted to withdraw.

There was a short, sharp struggle. The lawyer wrote an angry letter to the school demanding prompt return of the $200 "fraudulently taken" from the widow, and got an equally stiff refusal in reply. He then asked the old lady to write out in her own words a description of the salesman's visit. She produced a garbled, semi-literate account, which he forwarded to the school with the comment "This is the lady whom your salesman found to be 'very qualified' to take your writing course. I wonder if Mr. Cerf is aware of the cruel deceptions to which he lends his name?" At the bottom of his letter, the lawyer wrote the magic words "Carbon copies to Bennett Cerf and to Consumer Frauds Division, U.S. Attorney's Office." Presto! The school suddenly caved in and returned the money in full.

Louella Mae Burns, the other successful candidate, is the brainchild of Robert Byrne and his wife. I met her in the pages of Byrne's informative and often hilarious book *Writing Rackets* (Lyle Stuart, 1969, $3.95), which treats of the lures held out to would-be writers by high-priced correspondence schools, phony agents who demand a fee for reading manuscripts, the "vanity" presses that will publish your book for a price.

Mrs. Byrne set out to discover at how low a level of talent one might be accepted as a candidate for "professional training" by the Famous Writers. Assuming the personality of a sixty-three-year-old widow of little education, she tackled the aptitude test.

The crux of the test is the essay, in which the applicant is invited to "tell of an experience you have had at some time in your life." Here Louella Mae outdid herself: "I think I can truthfully say to the best of my knowledge that the following is truly the most arresting experience I have ever undergone. My husband, Fred, and I, had only been married but a short time . . ." Continuing in this vein, she describes "one beautiful cloudless day in springtime" and "a flock of people who started merging along the sidewalk . . . When out of the blue came a honking and cars and motorcycles and policemen. It was really something! Everybody started shouting and waving and we finally essayed to see the reason of all this. In a sleek black limousine we saw real close Mr. Calvin Coolidge, the President Himself! It was truly an unforgettable experience and one which I shall surely long remember."

This effort drew a two-and-a-half-page typewritten letter from Donald T. Clark, registrar of Famous Writers School, which read in part: "Dear Mrs. Burns, Congratulations! The enclosed Test unquestionably qualifies you for enrollment . . . only a fraction of our students receive higher grades. . . . In our opinion, you have a basic writing aptitude which justifies professional training." And the clincher: "You couldn't consider breaking into writing at a better time than today. Everything indicates that the demand for good prose is growing much faster than the supply of trained talent. Just consider how a single article can cause a magazine's newsstand sales to soar; how a novel can bring hundreds of thousands in movie rights. . . ."

There is something spooky about this exchange, for I later found out that letters to successful applicants are written not by a "registrar" but by copywriters in the Madison Avenue office of the school's advertising department. Here we have Donald T. Clark's ghost writer in earnest correspondence with ghost Louella Mae Burns.

Perhaps these two applicants are not typical of the student body. What of students who show genuine promise, those capable of "mastering the basic skills" and achieving a level of professional competence? Will they, as the school suggests, find their way into "glamorous careers" and be "launched on a secure future" as writers?

Robert Byrne gives a gloomy account of the true state of the market for "good prose" and "trained talent." He says that of all lines of work free-lance writing is one of the most precarious and worst paid (as who should know better than Bennett Cerf & Co.?). He cites a survey of the country's top twenty-six magazines. Of 79,812 unsolicited article manuscripts, fewer than a thousand were accepted. Unsolicited fiction manuscripts fared far worse. Of 182,505 submitted, only 560 were accepted. Furthermore, a study based on the earnings of established writers, members of the Authors League with published books to their credit, shows that the average free-lance earns just over $3,000 a year—an income which, Byrne points out, "very nearly qualifies him for emergency welfare assistance."

What have the Famous Fifteen to say for themselves about all this? Precious little, it turns out. Most of those with whom I spoke were quick to disavow any responsibility for the school's day-to-day operating methods and were unable to answer the most rudimentary questions: qualifications for admission, teacher-student ratio, cost of the course. They seemed astonished, even pained, to think people might be naïve enough to take the advertising at face value.

"If anyone thinks we've got time to look at the aptitude tests that come in, they're out of their mind!" said Bennett Cerf. And Phyllis McGinley: "I'm only a figurehead. I thought a person had to be qualified to take the course, but since I never see any of the applications or the lessons, I don't know. Of course, somebody with a real gift for writing wouldn't have to be taught to write."

One of the FWS brochures says, "On a short story or novel you have at hand the professional counsel of Faith Baldwin . . . all these eminent authors in effect are looking over your shoulder as you learn." Doesn't that mean in plain English, I asked Miss Baldwin, that she will personally counsel students? "Oh, that's just one of those things about advertising; most advertisements are somewhat misleading," she replied. "Anyone with common sense would know that the fifteen of us are much too busy to read the manuscripts the students send in."

Famous Writer Mark Wiseman, himself an ad man, explained the alluring promises of "financial success and independence," the "secure future as a writer" held out in the school's advertising. "That's just a fault of our civilization," he said. "You have to overpersuade people, make it all look optimistic, not mention obstacles and hurdles. That's true of all advertising." Why does the school send out fleets of salesmen instead of handling all applications by mail? "If we didn't have salesmen, not nearly as many sales would be made. It's impossible, you see, to explain it all by mail, or answer questions people may have about the course." (It seems strange that while the school is able to impart the techniques requisite to become a best-selling author by mail, it cannot explain the details of its course to prospects and answer their questions in the same fashion; but perhaps that is just another fault of our civilization.)

Professor Paul Engle, a poet who directed the Writers' Workshop at the University of Iowa, is the only professional educator among the fifteen. But like his colleagues he pleads ignorance of the basics. The school's admissions policy, its teaching methods and selling techniques are a closed book to him. "I'm the least informed of all people," he said. "I only go there once in a great while. There's a distinction between the *Guiding* Faculty, which doesn't do very much, and the *Teaching* Faculty, which actually works with the students—who've spent really quite a lot of money on the course!" Professor Engle has only met once with the Guiding Faculty, to pose for a publicity photograph: "It was no meeting in the sense of gathering for the exchange of useful ideas. But I think the school is not so much interested in the work done by the Guiding Faculty as in the prestige of the names. When Bennett Cerf was on *What's My Line?* his name was a household word!"

How did Professor Engle become a member of the Guiding Faculty in the first place? "That fascinated *me!*" he said. "I got a letter from a man named Gordon Carroll, asking me to come to Westport the next time I was in New York. So I did go and see him. He asked me if I would join the Guiding Faculty. I said, 'What do I guide?' We talked awhile, and I said well it seems all right, so I signed on." How could it come about that the Oakland widow and Louella Mae Burns were judged "highly qualified" to enroll? "I'm not trying to weasel out, or evade your questions, but I'm so very far away from all that."

Bennett Cerf received me most cordially in his wonderfully posh office at Random House. Each of us was (I think, in retrospect) bent on putting the other thoroughly at ease. "May I call you Jessica?" he said at one point. "I don't see why not, *Mortuary Management* always does." We had a good laugh over that. He told me that the school was first organized in the late fifties (it opened for business in February, 1961) as an offshoot of the immensely profitable Famous Artists correspondence school, after which it was closely modeled. Prime movers in recruiting Famous Writers for the Guiding Faculty were the late Albert Dorne, an illustrator and president of Famous Artists; Gordon Carroll, sometime editor of *Coronet* and *Reader's Digest;* and Mr. Cerf. "We approached representative writers, the best we could get in each field: fiction, advertising, sportswriting, television. The idea was to give the school some prestige."

Like his colleagues on the Guiding Faculty, Mr. Cerf does no teaching, takes no hand in recruiting instructors or establishing standards for the teaching program, does not pass on advertising copy except that which purports to quote him, does not supervise the school's business practices: "I know *nothing* about the business and selling end and I care *less.* I've nothing to do with how the school is run, I can't put that too strongly to you. But it's been run extremely cleanly. I mean that from my heart, Jessica." What, then, is his guiding role? "I go up there once or twice a year to talk to the staff." The Guiding Faculty, he said, helped to write the original textbooks. His own contribution to these was a section on how to prepare a manuscript for publication: "I spent about a week talking into a tape machine about how a manuscript is turned into a book—practical advice about double-spacing the typescript, how it is turned into galleys, through every stage until publication." How many books by FWS students has Random House published? "Oh, come on, you must be pulling my leg—no person of any sophistication whose book we'd publish would have to take a mail order course to learn how to write."

However, the school does serve an extremely valuable purpose, he said, in teaching history professors, chemistry professors, lawyers, and businessmen to write intelligibly. I was curious to know why a professor would take a correspondence course in preference to writing classes available in the English department of his own university—who are all these professors? Mr. Cerf did not know their names, nor at which colleges they are presently teaching.

While Mr. Cerf is by no means uncritical of some aspects of mail order selling, he philosophically accepts them as inevitable in the cold-blooded world of big business—so different, one gathers, from his own cultured world of letters. "I think mail order selling has several built-in deficiencies," he said. "The crux of it is a very hard sales pitch, an appeal to the gullible. Of course, once somebody has signed a contract with Famous Writers he can't get out of it, but that's true with every business in the country." Noticing that I was writing this down, he said in alarm, "For God's sake, don't quote me on that 'gullible' business—you'll have all the mail order houses in the country down on my neck!" "Then would you like to paraphrase it?" I asked, suddenly getting very firm. "Well —you could say in general I don't like the hard sell, yet it's the basis of all American business." "Sorry, I don't call that a paraphrase, I shall have to use both of them," I said in a positively governessy tone of voice. "Anyway, why do you lend your name to this hard-sell proposition?" Bennett Cerf (with his melting grin): "Frankly, if you must know, I'm an awful ham—I love to see my name in the papers!"

On the delicate question of their compensation, the Famous ones are understandably reticent. "That's a private matter," Bennett Cerf said, "but it's quite generous and we were given stock in the company, which has enhanced a great deal." I asked Phyllis McGinley about a report in *Business Week* some years ago that in addition to their substantial stock holdings each member of the Guiding Faculty receives 1.6 percent of the school's annual gross revenue, which then amounted to $4,400 apiece. "Oh? Well, I may have a price on my soul, but it's not *that* low, we get a lot more than that!" she answered gaily.

With one accord the Famous Writers urged me to seek answers to questions about advertising policy, enrollment figures, costs, and the like from the director of the school, Mr. John Lawrence, former president of William Morrow publishing company. Mr. Lawrence invited me to Westport so that I could see the school in operation, and meet Mr. Gordon Carroll, who is now serving as director of International Famous Writers schools.

The Famous Schools are housed in a row of boxlike buildings at the edge of Westport ("It's Westport's leading industry," a former resident told me), which look from the outside like a small modern factory. Inside, everything reflects expansion and progress. The spacious reception rooms are decorated with the works of Famous Artists, the parent school, and Famous Photographers, organized in 1964.

The success story, and something of the *modus operandi,* can be read at a glance in the annual shareholders' reports and the daily stock market quotations. (The schools have gone public and are now listed on the New York Stock Exchange as FAS International.)

Tuition revenue for the schools zoomed from $7,000,000 in 1960 to $48,000,000 in 1969. During this period, the price per share of common stock rose from $5 to $40. (It has fallen sharply, however, in recent months.)

The schools' interest in selling as compared with teaching is reflected more accurately in the corporate balance sheets than in the brochures sent to prospective students. In 1966 (the last time this revealing breakdown was given), when total tuition revenue was $28,000,000, $10,800,000 was spent on "advertising and selling" compared with $4,800,000 on "cost of grading and materials."

The Famous Schools have picked up many another property along the way: they now own the Evelyn Wood Speed Reading

Course, Welcome Wagon, International Accountants Society (also a correspondence school), Linguaphone Institute, Computer College Selection Service. Their empire extends to Japan, Australia, Sweden, France, Germany, Switzerland, Austria. An invasion of Great Britain is planned (the report warns) as soon as the English prove themselves worthy of it by stabilizing their currency situation. In the "market testing stage" are plans for a Famous Musicians School, Business Courses for Women, a Writing for Young Readers Course.

Summarizing these accomplishments, the shareholders' report states: "We are in the vanguard of education throughout the world, the acknowledged leader in independent study and an innovator in all types of learning. We will continue to think boldly, to act with wisdom and daring, to be simultaneously visionary and effective." The schools, mindful of "the deepening of the worldwide crisis in education," are casting predatory looks in the direction of "the total educational establishment, both academic and industrial." The shareholders' report observes sententiously, "As grave times produce great men to cope with them, so do they produce great ideas."

From Messrs. Lawrence and Carroll I learned these salient facts about Famous Writers School:

The cost of the course (never mentioned in the advertising, nor in the letters to successful applicants, revealed only by the salesman at the point where the prospect is ready to sign the contract): $785, if the student makes a one-time payment. But only about 10 percent pay in a lump sum. The cost to the 90 percent who make time payments, including interest, is about $900, or roughly twenty times the cost of extension and correspondence courses offered by universities.

Current enrollment is 65,000, of which three-quarters are enrolled in the fiction course, the balance in nonfiction, advertising, business writing. Almost 2,000 veterans are taking the course at the taxpayers' expense through the GI Bill. Teaching faculty: 55, for a ratio of 1,181 ⅘ students per instructor.

There are 800 salesmen deployed throughout the country (for a ratio of 14⅗ salesmen for every instructor) working on a straight commission basis. I asked about the salesmen's kits: might I have one? "You'd need a dray horse to carry it!" Mr. Carroll assured me. He added that they are currently experimenting with a movie of the school, prepared by Famous Writer Rod Serling, to show in prospects' homes.

I was surprised to learn that despite the fact the schools are accredited by such public agencies as the Veterans Administration and the National Home Study Council, they preserve considerable secrecy about some sectors of their operation. Included in the "confidential" category, which school personnel told me could not be divulged, are:

The amount of commission paid to salesmen.

Breakdown of the $22,000,000 "sales and advertising" item in the shareholders' report as between sales commissions and advertising budget.

Breakdown of the $48,000,000 income from tuition fees as between Writers, Artists, Photographers.

Terms of the schools' contract with Guiding Faculty members.

If Bennett Cerf and his colleagues haven't time to grade the aptitude tests, who has? Their stand-ins are two full-timers and some forty pieceworkers, mostly housewives, who "help you find out whether you can be trained to become a successful writer" in the privacy of their homes. There are no standards for admission to FWS, one of the full-timers explained. "It's not the same thing as a grade on a college theme. The test is designed to indicate your *potential* as a writer, not your present ability." Only about 10 percent of the applicants are advised they lack this "potential," and are rejected.

The instructors guide the students from cheerful little cubicles equipped with machines into which they dictate the "two-page letter of criticism and advice" promised in the advertising. They

are, Gordon Carroll told me, former free-lance writers and people
with editorial background: "We never hire professional teachers,
they're too *dull!* Deadly dull. Ph.D.s are the worst of all!" (Con-
versely, a trained teacher accustomed to all that the classroom
offers might find an unrelieved diet of FWS students' manuscripts
somewhat monotonous.) The annual starting salary for instructors
is $8,500 for a seven-hour day, something of a comedown from the
affluent and glamorous life dangled before their students in the
school's advertising.

As I watched the instructors at work, I detected a generous
inclination to accentuate the positive in the material submitted.
Given an assignment to describe a period in time, a student had
chosen 1933. Her first paragraph, about the election of F.D.R.
and the economic situation in the country, could have been copied
out of any almanac. She had followed this with "There were
breadlines everywhere." I watched the instructor underline the
breadlines in red, and write in the margin: "Good work, Mrs.
Smith! It's a pleasure working with you. You have recaptured the
atmosphere of those days."

Although the key to the school's financial success is its huge
dropout rate ("We couldn't make any money if all the students
finished," Famous Writer Phyllis McGinley had told me in her
candid fashion), the precise percentage of dropouts is hard to
come by. "I don't know exactly what it is, or where to get the
figures," said Mr. Lawrence. "The last time we analyzed it, it
related to the national figure for high-school and college dropouts,
let's say about two-thirds of the enrollments."

However, according to my arithmetic based on figures furnished by the school, the dropout rate must be closer to 90 percent. Each student is supposed to send in 24 assignments over a
three-year period, an average of 8 a year. With 65,000 enrolled,
this would amount to more than half a million lessons a year, and
the 55 instructors would have to race along correcting these at a
clip of one every few minutes. But in fact (the instructors assured
me) they spend an hour or more on each lesson, and grade a total

of only about 50,000 a year. What happens to the other 470,000 lessons? "That's baffling," said Mr. Carroll. "I guess you can take a horse to the water, but you can't make him drink."

These balky nags are, however, legally bound by the contract whether or not they ever crack a textbook or send in an assignment. What happens to the defaulter who refuses to pay? Are many taken to court? "None," said Mr. Lawrence. "It's against our policy to sue in court." Why, if the school considers the contract legally binding? "Well—there's a question of morality involved. You'd hardly take a person to court for failing to complete a correspondence course."

Mrs. Virginia Knauer, the President's Assistant for Consumer Affairs, with whom I discussed this later, suspects there is another question involved. "The Famous Writers would never win in court," she said indignantly. "A lawsuit would expose them—somebody should take *them* to court. Their advertising is reprehensible, it's very close to being misleading." Needless to say, the debtors are not informed of the school's moral scruples against lawsuits. On the contrary, a Finnish immigrant, whose husband complained to Mrs. Knauer that although she speaks little English she had been coerced into signing for the course by an importunate salesman, was bombarded with dunning letters and telegrams full of implied threats to sue.

A fanciful idea occurred to me: since the school avers that it does not sue delinquents, I could make a fortune by advertising in the literary monthlies: "For $10 I will tell you how to take the Famous Writers' course for nothing." To those who sent in their ten dollars, I would return a postcard saying merely, "Enroll in the course and make no payments." I tried this out on Mr. Carroll, and subsequently on Bennett Cerf. Their reactions were identical. "You'd find yourself behind bars if you did that!" "Why? Whom would I have defrauded?" A question they were unable to answer, although Bennett Cerf, in mock horror, declared that the inventive mail order industry would certainly find *some* legal means to frustrate my iniquitous plan.

Both Mr. Lawrence and Mr. Carroll were unhappy about the case of the seventy-two-year-old widow when I told them about it—it had not previously come to their attention. It was an unfortunate and unusual occurrence, they assured me, one of those slip-ups that may happen from time to time in any large corporation.

On the whole, they said, FWS salesmen are very carefully screened; only one applicant in ten is accepted. They receive a rigorous training in ethical salesmanship; every effort is made to see that they do not "oversell" the course or stray from the truth in their home presentation.

Eventually I had the opportunity to observe the presentation in the home of a neighbor who conjured up a salesman for me by sending in the aptitude test. A few days after she had mailed it in, my neighbor got a printed form letter (undated) saying that a field representative of the school would be in the area next week for a very short while and asking her to specify a convenient time when he might telephone for an appointment. There was something a little fuzzy around the edges here—for she had not yet heard from the school about her test—but she let that pass.

The "field representative" (like the cemetery industry, the Famous Writers avoid the term "salesman") when he arrived had a ready explanation: the school had telephoned to notify him that my neighbor had passed the test, and to tell him that luckily for her there were "a few openings still left in this enrollment period" —it might be months before this opportunity came again!

The fantasy he spun for us, which far outstripped anything in the advertising, would have done credit to the school's fiction course.

Pressed for facts and figures, he told us that two or three of the Famous Fifteen are in Westport at all times working with "a staff of forty or fifty experts in their specialty" evaluating and correcting student manuscripts. . . . Your Guiding Faculty member, could be Bennett Cerf, could be Rod Serling depending on your subject, will review at least one of your manuscripts, and may suggest a publisher for it. . . . There are 300 instructors for 3,000 students ("You mean, one teacher for every ten students?" I asked. "That's correct, it's a ratio unexcelled by any college in the country," said the field representative without batting an eye). . . . Hundreds of university professors are currently enrolled . . . 75 percent of the students publish in their first year, and the majority more than pay for the course through their sales. . . . There are very few dropouts because only serious, qualified applicants (like my neighbor) are permitted to enroll. . . .

During his two-hour discourse, he casually mentioned three books recently published by students he personally enrolled—one is already being made into a movie! "Do tell us the names, so we can order them?" But he couldn't remember, offhand: "I get so darn many announcements of books published by our students."

Oh, clean-cut young man, does your mother know how you earn your living? (And, Famous Fifteen, do yours?)

The course itself is packaged for maximum eye-appeal in four hefty "two-toned, buckram-bound" volumes with matching loose-leaf binders for the lessons. The textbooks contain all sorts of curious and disconnected matter: examples of advertisements that "pull"; right and wrong ways of ending business letters; paragraphs from the *Saturday Evening Post, This Week, Reader's Digest;* quotations from successful writers like William Shakespeare, Faith Baldwin, Mark Twain, Mark Wiseman, Winston Churchill, Red Smith; an elementary grammar lesson ("*Verbs* are action words. A *noun* is the name of a person, place or thing"); a glossary of commonly misspelled words; a standard list of printer's proof-marking symbols.

There is many a homespun suggestion for the would-be Famous Writer on what to write about, how to start writing: "Writing ideas—ready-made aids for the writer—are available everywhere. In every waking hour you hear and see and feel. . . ." "How do you get started on a piece of writing? One successful author writes down the word 'The' the moment he gets to the typewriter in the morning. He follows 'The' with another word, then another. . . ." (But the text writer, ignoring his own good advice, starts a sentence with "As," and trips himself in an imparsable sentence: "As with so many professional writers, Marjorie Holmes keeps a notebook handy. . . .")

Throughout the course the illusion is fostered that the student is, or soon will be, writing for publication: "Suppose you're sitting in the office of a magazine editor discussing an assignment for next month's issue . . ." The set of books includes a volume entitled "How to Turn Your Writing Into Dollars," which winds up on a triumphal note with a sample publisher's contract and a sample agreement with a Hollywood agent.

In short, there is really nothing useful in these books that could not be found in any number of writing and style manuals, grammar texts, marketing guides, free for the asking in the public library.

Thrown in as part of the $785–$900 course is a "free" subscription to *Famous Writers* magazine, a quarterly in which stories written by students appear under this hyperbolic caption: "Writers Worth Watching: In this section, magazine editors and book publishers can appraise the quality of work being done by FWS students." According to the school's literature, "Each issue of the magazine is received and read by some 2,000 editors, publishers and other key figures in the writing world." However, Messrs. Carroll and Lawrence were unable to enlighten me about these key figures—who they are, how it is known that they read each issue, whether they have ever bought manuscripts from students after appraising the quality of their work.

The student sales department of the magazine is also worth watching. Presumably the school puts its best foot forward here, yet the total of all success stories recorded therein each year is only about thirty-five, heavily weighted in the direction of small denominational magazines, local newspapers, pet-lovers' journals, and the like. Once in a while a student strikes it rich with a sale to *Reader's Digest*, *Redbook*, *McCall's*, generally in "discovery" departments of these magazines that specifically solicit first-person anecdotes by their readers as distinct from professional writers:

Most Unforgettable Character, Turning-Point, Suddenly It Happens to You.

The school gets enormous mileage out of these few student sales. The same old successful students turn up time and again in the promotional literature. Thus an ad in the January 4, 1970, issue of *The New York Times* Magazine features seven testimonials: "I've just received a big, beautiful check from the *Reader's Digest.* . . ." "I've just received good news and a check from *Ellery Queen's Mystery Magazine.* . . ." "Recently, I've sold three more articles. . . ." How recently? Checking back through old copies of *Famous Writers* magazine, I found the latest of these success stories had appeared in the student sales department of a 1968 issue; the rest had been lifted from issues of 1964 and 1965.

As for the quality of individual instruction, the reactions of several former FWS students with whom I spoke were varied. Only one—a "success story" lady featured in FWS advertising who has published four juvenile books—expressed unqualified enthusiasm. Two other successes of yesteryear, featured in the school's 1970 ad, said they had never finished the course and had published nothing since 1965.

A FWS graduate who had completed the entire course (and has not, to date, sold any of her stories) echoed the views of many: "It's tremendously overblown, there's a lot of busywork, unnecessary padding to make you think you're getting your money's worth. One peculiar thing is you get a different instructor for each assignment, so there's not much of the 'personal attention' promised in the brochures." However, she added, "I have to be fair. It did get me started, and it did make me keep writing."

I showed some corrected lessons that fell into my hands to an English professor. One assignment: "To inject new life and color and dimension into a simple declarative sentence." From the sentence "The cat washed its paws," the student had fashioned this: "With fastidious fussiness, the cat flicked his pink tongue over his paws, laying the fur down neatly and symmetrically." The instructor had crossed out "cat" and substituted "the burly gray tomcat."

With fastidious fussiness, the lanky, tweed-suited English professor clutched at his balding, pink pate and emitted a low, agonized
groan of bleak, undisguised despair: "Exactly the sort of wordy
stuff we try to get students to *avoid*."

The staggering dropout rate cannot, I was soon convinced, be
laid entirely at the door of rapacious salesmen who sign up semi-
literates and other incompetents. Many of those who told me of
their experience with the school are articulate, intelligent people,
manifestly capable of disciplined self-study that could help them to
improve their prose style. Why should adults of sound mind and
resolute purpose first enroll in FWS and then throw away their
substantial investment? One letter goes far to explain:

My husband and I bought the course for two main reasons. The
first was that we were in the boondocks of Arkansas and we truly felt
that the Famous Writers School under the sponsorship of Bennett Cerf
etc. was new in concept and would have more to offer than other
courses we had seen advertised. The second was the fact that we had
a definite project in mind: a fictionalized account of our experiences in
the American labor movement.

I guess the worst part of our experience was the realization that the
school could not live up to its advertised promise. It is in the area of
the assignments and criticism that the course falls down. Because you
get a different instructor each time, there is no continuity. This results
in the student failing to get any understanding of story and structure
from the very beginning.

My husband completed about eight assignments, but felt so intensely
frustrated with the course that he could not go on. He couldn't get
any satisfaction from the criticism.

While the school is careful to advise that no one can teach writing
talent they constantly encourage their students towards a belief in a
market that doesn't exist for beginning writers. For us, it was an expensive and disappointing experience.

The phenomenal success of FWS in attracting students (if not
in holding them) does point to an undeniable yearning on the part

of large numbers of people not only to see their work published, but also for the sort of self-improvement the school purports to offer. As Robert Byrne points out, what can be learned about writing from a writing course can be of great value in many areas of life, "from love letters to suicide notes." For shut-ins, people living in remote rural areas, and others unable to get classroom instruction, correspondence courses may provide the only opportunity for supervised study.

Recognizing the need, some fifteen state universities offer correspondence courses that seem to me superior to the Famous Writers course for a fraction of the cost. True, the universities neither package nor push their courses, they provide no handsome buckram-bound two-tone loose-leaf binders, no matching textbooks, no sample Hollywood contract.

Unobtrusively tucked away in the *Lifelong Learning* bulletin of the University of California Extension at Berkeley are two such offerings: Magazine Article Writing, 18 assignments, fee $55; and Short Story Theory and Practice, 15 assignments, fee $35 ($5 more for out-of-state enrollees). There are no academic requirements for these courses, anybody can enroll. Those who, in the instructor's opinion, prove to be unqualified are advised to switch to an elementary course in grammar and composition.

Cecilia Bartholomew, who has taught the short-story course by correspondence for the past twelve years, is herself the author of two novels and numerous short stories. She cringes at the thought of drumming up business for the course: "I'd be a terrible double-dealer to try to *sell* people on it," she said. Like the Famous Writers instructors, Mrs. Bartholomew sends her students a lengthy criticism of each assignment, but unlike them she does not cast herself in the role of editor revising stories for publication: "It's the improvement in their writing technique that's important. The aim of my course is to develop in each student a professional standard of writing. I'll tell him when a piece is good enough to submit to an editor, but I'll never tell him it will sell." Have any of her students sold their pieces? "Yes, quite a few. Some have published in volumes of juvenile stories, some in *Hitchcock Mysteries.* But we don't stress this at all."

In contrast, Louise Boggess, who teaches Magazine Article Writing by correspondence in addition to her classes in "professional writing" at the College of San Mateo, exudes go-ahead salesmanship: she believes that most of her students will eventually find a market for their work. The author of several how-to-do-it books (among them *Writing Articles That Sell,* which she uses as the text for her course), she points her students straight toward the mass writing market. In her streamlined, practical lessons the emphasis is unabashedly on formula writing that will sell. Her very first assignment is how to write a "hook," meaning an arresting opening sentence. What does she think of the word "The" for openers? It doesn't exactly grab her, she admitted.

During the eighteen months she has been teaching the correspondence course, several of her 102 students have already sold pieces to such magazines as *Pageant, Parents, Ladies Circle, Family Weekly.* She has had but six dropouts, an enviable record by FWS standards.

My brief excursion into correspondence-school-land taught me little, after all, that the canny consumer does not already know about the difference between buying and being sold. As Faith Baldwin said, most advertising is somewhat misleading; as Bennett Cerf said, the crux of mail order selling is a hard pitch to the gullible. We know that the commission salesman will, if we let him into our homes, dazzle and bemuse us with the beauty, durability, unexcelled value of his product, whatever it is. As for the tens of thousands who sign up with FWS when they could get a better and cheaper correspondence course through the universities (or, if they live in a city, Adult Education Extension courses), we know from reading Vance Packard that people tend to prefer things that come in fancy packages and cost more.

There is probably nothing actually illegal in the FWS operation, although the consumer watchdogs have their eye on it.

Robert Hughes, counsel for the Federal Trade Commission's

Bureau of Deceptive Practices, told me he has received a number of complaints about the school, mostly relating to the high-pressure and misleading sales pitch. "The real evil is in the solicitation and enrollment procedures," he said. "There's a basic contradiction involved when you have profit-making organizations in the field of education. There's pressure to maximize the number of enrollments to make more profit. Surgery is needed in the enrollment procedure."

There is also something askew with the cast of characters in the foregoing drama which would no doubt be quickly spotted by FWS instructors in television scriptwriting ("where the greatest market lies for the beginning writer," as the school tells us).

I can visualize the helpful comment on my paper: "Good work, Miss Mitford. The Oakland widow's problem was well thought through. But characterization is weak. You could have made your script more believable had you chosen a group of shifty-eyed hucksters out to make a buck, one step ahead of the sheriff, instead of these fifteen eminently successful and solidly respectable writers, who are well liked and admired by the American viewing public. For pointers on how to make your characters come to life in a way we can all identify with, I suggest you study Rod Serling's script *The Twilight Zone*, in the kit you received from us. Your grade is D–. It has been a pleasure working with you. Good luck!"

OBJECT LESSON

"Every writer worth his salt develops, after a time, his own style." Faith Baldwin, *Principles of Good Writing*, FWS textbook.

(But Famous Writers Write Alike)

By Faith Baldwin	By Bennett Cerf
If you want to write, my colleagues and I would like to test your writing aptitude. We'll help you find out if you can be	If you want to write and see your work published, my colleagues and I would like to test your writing aptitude.

trained to become a successful writer. We know that many men and women who could become writers—and *should* become writers—never do. Some are uncertain of their talent and have no reliable way of finding out if it's worth developing. Others simply can't get topnotch professional training without leaving their homes or giving up their jobs.	We'll help you find out whether you can be trained to become a successful writer. We know that many men and women who could become writers—and *should* become writers—never do. Some are uncertain of their talent and have no reliable way of finding out if it's worth developing. Others simply can't get topnotch professional training without leaving their homes or giving up their jobs.

(Reprinted from postcard inserts currently being circulated in millions of paperback books.)

COMMENT

This article gave me more pleasure, from start to finish, than any other I have written. Its preparation afforded the opportunity to apply everything I had thus far learned about investigative techniques. My efforts to get it published, a series of dizzying ups and downs, gave me an insight into the policymaking process of magazines that I should never otherwise have acquired. The aftermath of publication filled my normally uneventful life with drama of many months' duration. It was also one of the few clear-cut successes, however temporary, of my muckraking career, so I pray forgiveness if an unseemly note of self-congratulation becomes apparent in what follows.

At first it was a mere twinkle in the eye. By some fortunate confluence of the stars, the "Oakland lawyer" (who was in fact my husband, Bob Treuhaft) happened to tell me about his case of the aged widow vs. Famous Writers School on the very same day that Robert Byrne's excellent and amusing book *Writing Rackets* appeared in my mailbox. Lunching soon after with William Abrahams, then West Coast editor of the *Atlantic*, I regaled him with stories of the misdeeds of these Famous Frauds. Why not do a short piece for the *Atlantic*, suggested Abrahams, about seven hundred words, combining an account of the Oakland widow's unhappy experience with a review of Byrne's book? And so it was settled.

Here my publishing troubles began. The next day Abrahams called up to say that Robert Manning, editor of the *Atlantic*, had second thoughts about the piece: while Manning agreed that the Famous Writers School advertising was "probably unethical," the *Atlantic* had profited by it to the tune of many thousands of dollars, hence it would be equally "unethical" for the magazine to run a piece blasting the school. I was aghast at this reasoning; would it not, then, be "unethical" for a magazine to publish an article linking smoking to lung cancer while accepting ads from the tobacco companies? I asked Abrahams. Well, yes, he saw the point. If Manning changed his mind, he would get back to me.

A week went by; no word from the *Atlantic*. By now adrenalin was flowing (easily the most effective stimulant for the muckraker); those Famous Writers, I was beginning to see, were a power to be reckoned with if they could so easily influence the policy of a major magazine. Without much hope, I queried the articles editor at *McCall's*. She replied that *McCall's* would welcome a full-scale rundown on the school's operation, six to seven thousand words, no holds barred. This put the matter in an entirely new light; with *McCall's* lavish backing for a piece of that length, I could afford to go all out in pursuit of the story.

For weeks thereafter I lived in what turned out to be a fool's paradise, traveling back East at *McCall's* expense to see the school in Westport and to visit its Madison Avenue advertising headquarters in New York, interviewing the Famous ones, poring over the textbooks and the stockholders' reports. The finished article drew extravagant praise from the articles editor and her associates at *McCall's*, but when the editor-in-chief returned a week later from a trip out of town she rejected it. *Why?* I sternly asked her. "Well—I don't think it's very good," she answered, a comment to which there is, of course, no possible rejoinder. However, she promptly paid not only my large expense account but the full agreed-on fee, rather than the "kill fee" that is usual in such circumstances. Did she have a guilty conscience? Had the Famous Writers got to her? Yes, it turned out, but I only learned this much later.

Furious at this turn of events and in a black mood of revenge, I submitted the piece to *Life*, whose editor immediately responded: he would be delighted to have it, photographers would be deployed to take pictures of the school and its Famous Faculty, it would be a major *Life* story. But the next day the editor happened to drop by the office of *Life*'s advertising manager, who mentioned that the school had contracted for half a million dollars' worth of advertising over the next six months. End of that pipe dream.

By now the article, Xeroxed copies of which were floating around in New York publishing circles, had achieved a sort of underground notoriety; my editor at Knopf got a wire from Willie Morris, then editor of *Harper's*, saying he would love to publish it. I was on the point of turning it over to Morris when William Abrahams at last did "get back" to me: the *Atlantic* wanted it after all. Furthermore, Manning had canceled the magazine's advertising contract with FWS.

How does one go about researching such an article? My first step, before laying siege to the Famous Faculty, was to accumulate and absorb every available scrap of information about the school, my objective being to know more about its operating methods than did the Famous Writers themselves—which, as I soon discovered, was not hard. Via the *Readers' Guide to Periodical Literature*, I found articles in back issues of *Business Week*, *Advertising Age,* the *Wall Street Journal* from which I was able to trace the school's phenomenal growth over the years. Robert

Byrne lent me his vast file containing among other treasures the school's glossy promotional brochures, its annual financial reports, and the original correspondence between "Louella Mae Burns" and the "registrar."

Wishing to make contact with some live ones who had actually enrolled in FWS, I hit on the idea of taking an ad in the *Saturday Review*'s classified columns, giving my name and a box number: "Wanted: Experiences, good, bad or indifferent, with Famous Writers School." I chose *SR* for the purpose because it seemed just the kind of middlebrow magazine whose readership might include likely victims. Nor was I disappointed; my ad drew several letters from dissatisfied students. Faced with the agony of selection from these, I decided eventually to use the one that seemed most representative—from the couple in "the boondocks of Arkansas," as they put it, conveying in authentic tones of frustration their earnest expectations of the school and their dashed hopes. (My Yale students, to whom I imparted this story, loved the idea of using the classified columns as a research tool. I was told that during my stint there as instructor, the advertising revenues of the *Yale Daily* soared as a result of ads placed by members of my journalism seminar.)

Thus prepared, I set about interviewing those of the Guiding Faculty whose home addresses were listed in *Who's Who* and whose phone numbers I got from Information. Early one Sunday morning my husband found me at the telephone. "What are you doing?" "Dialing Famous Writers." He insisted I was wasting my time: "They won't talk to you, why should they?" "No harm in trying," I said. "Wait and see." He stood by fascinated as one after another they talked on interminably—it was hard to shut them up. Needless to say, their off-the-cuff comments—and their unanimously admitted ignorance of the school's operating methods—made for some of the most successful passages in the piece.

I was now ready to advance on the ultimate stronghold, the school itself. Armed with my list of questions, carefully graduated from Kind to Cruel, I called the director, Mr. John Lawrence, and explained that Miss Faith Baldwin, Mr. Paul Engle, and other faculty members had suggested he could help me with an article I was writing about the value of correspondence schools. He immediately offered to pay my fare, first class, to New York where I would be put up at the hotel of my choice, and to set aside a day to show me around the school. (When I reported this to the articles editor at *McCall's*, she insisted that as a matter of principle *McCall's* should pay. I suppressed the fleeting and unworthy thought that I might collect the price of the fare from both.)

My day at the school was long, grueling, and on the whole satisfactory. Late in the afternoon, having elicited through persistent questioning Mr. Lawrence's firm and unqualified assurance that *never* had the school demanded a medical certificate of ill health as the condition of a student's withdrawal, I sprung the final Cruel: Bob's file on the Oakland widow, which contained a letter stating, "It is the policy of the School that when difficulties such as yours arise that we require a statement from the physician in attendance attesting to the inability of the student to continue on with the studies. . . ." After listening to Mr. Lawrence's murky attempt at an explanation—"unfortunate occurrence . . . a slip-up"—I took my leave. There seemed to be nothing more to say.

I saved Bennett Cerf for the last. My interview with him in New York went as described in the piece; the high point his illuminating remark about mail order selling: "a very hard sales pitch, an appeal to the gullible," which he immediately regretted and asked me not to quote.

How, then, could I justify quoting it? I have been asked this many times by my students, and even by other working journalists. Was it not "unethical" of me? The technical answer is that at no time had Mr. Cerf indicated that his conversation was to be off the record, hence I had violated no agreement. Yet there is more to it than that. I can easily visualize interviewing an average citizen who is unused to dealing with the press, and acceding to his plea not to quote some spontaneous and injudicious comment. But—Bennett Cerf, at the top of the heap in publishing, television

star performer, founder of FWS, who was cynically extracting
tuition payments from the "gullible" for the augmentation of his
already vast fortune? This hard heart felt then, and feels now, not
the slightest compunction for having recorded his words as
spoken.

We had one more brief encounter. I had just submitted the
finished article to *McCall's* and was showing a Xerox of it to a
friend at Knopf, up on the twenty-first floor of the Random House
building. We were giggling away about the Famous Writers when
who should pop in but Bennett Cerf. The Random House offices
are on the twelfth floor. What was he doing up here, I wondered
—had somebody tipped him off to my presence? Genial as ever,
Mr. Cerf took a chair and remarked jovially, "So HERE'S the
archvillain. I hope you're not going to murder us in that piece of
yours."

"Murder you? Of course not," I answered. "It's just a factual
account of the school, how it operates, and your role in it."

"I don't like the look in your eye as you say that," said Cerf.
"Where are you going to publish it?"

Three possible answers flashed through my mind: (1) I haven't
decided, (2) I'd rather not say, (3) the truth. I reluctantly settled
on the last. "If I tell you, do you promise not to try to stop publication?" I asked. Cerf made pooh-poohing sounds at the very
suggestion. "It was commissioned by *McCall's*," I said. He sprang
out of his chair: "*McCall's!* They're out of their mind if they think
they can get away with this."

By the time the article had finally found safe haven at the *Atlantic*, I was aglow with unbecoming pride which, as we know,
precedes a fall. It seemed to me I had diligently and fully explored
every facet of the school's operation. The luck factor had been
with me all the way; short of reading matter in a motel where I
was staying, I had picked up the Gideon Bible, which miracu-
lously fell open at the very passage in St. Luke's gospel quoted in
the epigraph, "Beware of the scribes . . ." And somebody in Robert Manning's office had spotted and forwarded to me the postcard

inserts in paperback books, an incomparable example of FWS's sloppy yet devious methods, which I used for the box, "Object Lesson."

The fall came after the piece was published, and it still gives me nightmares. The *Atlantic* ran a letter from Cecelia Holland, a young novelist, who once when in financial straits had taken a job as instructor for FWS. She wrote: "Students are led to believe that each letter of criticism is personally written by the instructor. It is not. The instructor has a notebook full of prewritten paragraphs, identified by number. He consults this book and types out, not personal comments, but a series of numbers. Later, the paragraphs are written out in full by a computer-typewriter."

How could I have missed this stunning bit of chicanery which so neatly epitomized the ultimate swindle perpetrated by the school? I shall ever regret not having set eyes on those automated typewriters, sincerely clacking out "This opening is effective. It captures the reader's interest. . . ." "I can see you made a try at writing a satisfactory ending, but you only partially succeeded. . . ." I had spent much of my day at the school watching the instructors at work—why had I not asked to see some of the "two-page personal letters of criticism and advice" promised in the advertising? Why had I not quizzed Mr. Lawrence as to whether I had been shown the entire premises—was there anything interesting in the basement that I might have overlooked? To this day it pains me to think of this lapse in my investigation, and I only relate it here as a solemn warning to the would-be muckraker to take nothing for granted, and never to be lulled into the assumption that one's research is beyond reproach.

Robert Manning scheduled the article for publication in July. Once having taken up arms against the school, he proved himself a most effective ally. It was he who thought of the clever and apposite title, "Let Us Now Appraise Famous Writers," and who commissioned the brilliant cover cartoon by Edward Sorel, depicting Famous Writers William Shakespeare, Oscar Wilde, Samuel

Johnson, Gertrude Stein, Voltaire, Ernest Hemingway, Mark Twain, Leo Tolstoy, Edgar Allan Poe, and Dylan Thomas gathered to pose for their publicity photograph.

Before the July issue appeared on the newsstands, Manning telephoned to say the *Atlantic* had already received fifty letters about the school from subscribers, who get their copies early. He was amazed—generally, he said, even a controversial article draws no more than a dozen letters during the whole life of the issue. (I can attest to this, having often published in the *Atlantic* on far more important subjects, such as the Spock trial and prisons, which generated maybe six to ten letters apiece. What stirs up readers to the point of writing letters to the editor will ever remain a mystery to me.) Before the month was over, more than three hundred letters arrived, all of which were forwarded to me and all of which I answered. Most of them were from FWS students who felt they had been swindled and who wanted to get out of the contract. To these I replied, "Don't make any more payments and tell the school I advised this."

Developments now came thick and fast. Manning reported that the July issue of the *Atlantic* had the largest newsstand sale of any in the magazine's history—which recalled to me a line in the "registrar's" letter to "Louella Mae Burns": "Just consider how a single article can cause a magazine's newsstand sales to soar. . . ." Both the Washington *Post* and the Des Moines *Register* ran the piece in their Sunday editions, the first and only time one of my magazine articles has been picked up and republished in a daily paper. It was subsequently reprinted in England and West Germany, both countries in which the school was trying to establish a foothold. The state universities of Washington and Indiana ordered reprints for distribution to all secondary-school principals and counselors, and all university directors of independent study. Television producers invited me to discuss the school on programs ranging from the *Dick Cavett Show* to ABC's *Chicago*.

As a result of all this, the controversy heated up in the most exhilarating fashion, reaching an audience far beyond the readership of the *Atlantic*. I put up a map of the United States and began shading in the battle areas as they developed: D.C., Virginia, Maryland, covered by the Washington *Post;* Middle Western states, the Des Moines *Register;* and so on.

Soon the consumer watchdogs got into the act, and my map filled up accordingly. Congressman Laurence J. Burton of Utah read the whole thing into the *Congressional Record* as a warning to the public. The Attorney General of Iowa filed suit to enjoin the school from sending its literature into that state, charging use of the mails to defraud. Louis J. Lefkowitz, New York State Attorney General, announced a crackdown on the school's "deceptive practices" and, adding injury to insult, ordered the school to pay $10,000 in costs. The New York City Department of Consumer Affairs demanded "substantial revisions" in FWS advertising and required the school to pay $3,000 to cover the cost of the investigation. The Federal Trade Commission launched a full-scale inquiry, sending investigators around the country to take depositions of the school personnel, the Famous Faculty, and disgruntled students.

Cartoonists merrily joined the fray. A drawing in *The New York Times Book Review* portrayed an amply proportioned middle-aged lady writing a letter at her desk: "Dear Bennett Cerf and Faith Baldwin, Yes! I have a strong desire, nay, a *lust* to write. . . ." The *National Lampoon* ran a caricature of a disheveled Cerf, red pencil in hand, captioned: "Unlikely Events of 1971: Bennett Cerf Stays Up All Night Correcting Student Papers from the Famous Writers School." A *New Yorker* cartoon showed a scowling husband at the typewriter, saying to his smirking wife: "Go ahead, scoff. Bennett Cerf and Faith Baldwin say I have writing aptitude, and they know more about it than you do." *Screw* magazine ran a full-page ad for the Famous Fuckers School: "We're Looking for People Who Like to Fuck. Earn money at home. We know that many people who could become professionals—and *should* become professionals—never do."

The letters, the media interest, the cartoons filled me with nostalgia—they were so reminiscent of the response to *The American Way of Death,* published seven years earlier. So, too, was the school's counteroffensive, which was not long in coming, its opening shot a letter to the *Atlantic* saying that my article contained "at least twenty-three errors according to our latest count." Famous Writer Bergen Evans repeated this libel on the *Dick Cavett Show*, where he was given equal time to rebut my remarks. Pressed for what the errors were, Evans was unable to answer, nor were they ever revealed by the school; although *Time,* in its roundup of the story, said the list was "long but quibbling." The Evans effort drew a sharp comment from Harriet Van Horne, television critic for the New York *Post:* "One might have expected a professor of English to refute Miss Mitford objectively and efficiently. One expected wrong. Dr. Evans leveled a purely personal attack."

There was more of the same to come. In October, an outraged employee of Congressman (later Senator) Lowell P. Weicker, Jr., of Connecticut sent me a Xerox copy of a letter to Weicker from John J. Frey, president of FWS. Drawing attention to the fact that I had just been listed by Congressman Ichord, chairman of the House Internal Security Committee, as one of sixty-five radical campus speakers, Mr. Frey suggested that Congressman Weicker should read this information into the *Congressional Record* to counteract the damage done by Congressman Burton: "Most interesting is her association with the Communist Party, USA. We would like to visit you to discuss the nature and depth of damage to our reputation and with a suggestion that may set the *Congressional Record* straight. . . . We feel that this matter has assumed urgent proportions and would like to take counteraction quickly." (Weicker, the employee assured me, had no intention of participating in the "counteraction.")

Had Mr. Frey borrowed this idea from the undertaking fraternity, whose response to *The American Way of Death* had been to get an ally in Congress, James B. Utt of Santa Ana, California, to read into the *Record* a lengthy report by the House Committee on

Un-American Activities about my subversive background? In any event, it set me thinking about what undertakers and Famous Writers have in common: both promise their customers a measure of immortality, overcharge for it, and then fail to produce.

While all the attention lavished on the fracas in the popular press and on television was most gratifying, even more so were accounts of the school's growing financial difficulties as reported in the daily stock market quotations, *The New York Times* financial pages, the *Wall Street Journal*, and *Advertising Age*. Having in the past been a resolute nonreader of stock market reports, I now swooped down on that page in the San Francisco *Chronicle* first thing each morning to see how the school was doing. For some months after my article appeared, FAS International stock declined consistently and precipitately, plunging from 35 to 5. But then it started creeping up again: $5\frac{1}{4}$, $5\frac{3}{8}$, $5\frac{1}{2}$ . . . I was in despair. "What can I *do?*" I wailed to my husband. When the stock reached 6, fearing perhaps for my mental well-being, he presented me with a certificate for ten shares of stock bought in my name as a special surprise: "That way, you won't mind so much if it does go up a bit," he said sympathetically.

In May, 1971, I was staying in Washington, doing research for my book on prisons. One morning I got a telegram from my husband: "SORRY, YOUR FAMOUS WRITERS STOCK WIPED OUT. SUSPENDED FROM TRADING ON THE STOCK EXCHANGE." Later, he told me that when he had phoned in the telegram to Western Union, the operator had suggested, "Don't you think you should phrase that more gently? Your wife might do something drastic—jump out of the window—if you tell her she's been wiped out."

Early the following year the school filed for bankruptcy. The final windup was reported in *More* magazine's Hellbox column for January, 1972: "Rosebuds (late blooming) to Jessica Mitford, whose devastating dissection of the Famous Writers School in the *Atlantic* has produced what all exposés aim at but so few achieve: tangible results. . . . The Mitford article and all the nosing around it prompted has staggered the school financially. Earnings dropped from $3,466,000 in 1969 to $1,611,000 in 1970. . . .

"A wilted rosebud should also go to the editor-in-chief of *Mc-Call's*, who originally assigned the piece and then rejected it because, she explains, 'I did not want to offend Bennett Cerf at a time when *McCall's* was trying to improve the caliber of its fiction.' "

There is, however, a sad addendum: the Famous Writers School is creeping back.

I first became aware of this in 1974 when Justin Kaplan, the distinguished biographer and a long-time friend of mine, sent me a letter he had received from Famous Writer Robin Moore inviting him to join the Advisory Board of the "new" FWS: "The emoluments are not inconsiderable," Mr. Moore had written. Justin replied, "I am interested in hearing more about the Advisory Board. I do need to find out how the new operation differs from the old, which as a friend of Jessica Mitford's I followed with more than routine interest." But answer came there none; on this matter, Mr. Moore "stood mute," as lawyers say.

More recently friends have clipped and sent me ads for the school—not the huge full-page clarion calls of yore, rather discreet columns headed "Are You One of the 'Quiet Ones' Who Should Be a Writer?"

Seeking to make a cursory check of the school's comeback, I asked a friend in San Francisco to write for the Aptitude Test. It arrived: the same old Aptitude Test. She sent it in, and within days a "Field Representative" appeared at her house: same old pitch, almost indistinguishable from the one I described in my article.

Some of the "Advisory Board" members listed in the current 1978 brochure are holdovers from the same old Guiding Faculty, although as a regular reader of the obit page I have noted that quite a few of these have gone to join the Famous Faculty in the Sky. I mentioned this circumstance to Cecelia Holland, who replied, "Oh—well, but surely you've heard of ghost writers."

A TALK WITH
GEORGE JACKSON

THE NEW YORK TIMES BOOK REVIEW / *June, 1971*

The idea of interviewing George Jackson about his writing occurred to me last autumn when I read *Soledad Brother*, his
remarkable and moving collection of prison letters. Although I
had never done an author interview, I have read many and know
roughly how they go: "When do you do your best work?" "At
dusk, in a Paris bistro, over a glass of Pernod." "What childhood
influences shaped your literary tastes?" "My parents' home was a
gathering place for the foremost writers of the day. . . ."

But authors are sometimes elusive and this one, through no
wish of his own, proved exceptionally so. Prison walls, I soon
discovered, are not only to keep convicts in but to keep reporters
out. After months of frustrating and fruitless negotiations with
prison officials, who refused to permit the interview, Jackson's
lawyer, at his request, secured a court order for my visit.

George Jackson, now aged twenty-nine, has been in prison
almost continuously since he was fifteen. Seven of those years
were spent in solitary confinement. In his introduction to *Soledad
Brother*, Jean Genêt calls it "a striking poem of love and combat,"
and says the letters "perfectly articulate the road traveled by their

author—first the rather clumsy letters to his mother and his brother, then letters to his lawyer which become something extraordinary, half-poem, half-essay, and then the last letters, of an extreme delicacy. . . ." What was that road, and what kind of person is the author?

As to the latter question, the San Quentin guard in charge of visitors undertook to enlighten me. "We have to set up this interview for you," he said. "You'll be seeing Jackson in the attorney's room. Now we suggest posting a guard in the room for your protection. He's an extremely dangerous, desperate man, liable to try *anything*." I replied, a trifle stiffly, that I preferred a private interview as specified in the court order. "Then we can post a guard by the window—he won't hear the conversation, but he'll be able to look through and see everything that goes on." No thanks. "We can erect a heavy wire screen between you and the prisoner?" No wire screen, thank you. Thus my interlocutor unwittingly acted out for my benefit the most pervasive cliché in all prisondom: "They treat the convicts like caged animals."

Jackson's appearance surprised me in two respects: unlike other prisoners I have met, whose stooped, impoverished physique attests to their long years of confinement, he has the bearing of an athlete. Nor does he affect the stony, ungiving glare of so many of his black revolutionary contemporaries on the outside; on the contrary, he came forward with both hands outstretched, face wreathed in smiles, and exclaimed, "How wonderful to see you!"

I had been warned by no less an authority than Alex Haley, author of *The Autobiography of Malcolm X*, that it is extremely difficult to get political, revolutionary people to talk about themselves. This proved true in Jackson's case. From a long discussion, ranging across the globe and over the centuries, I distilled the following "author interview":

Q. What time of day do you do your writing?
A. I don't stick to any regimen. I generally get two or three hours of sleep a day, six hours of exercise, and the rest reading

and writing. [In the letters, Jackson describes the exercises possible in his tiny solitary cell: "One thousand fingertip push-ups a day. I probably have the world's record on push-ups completed. . . ."]

Q. Do you get a certain number of hours of writing in each day?

A. Of course. After my six and three, I write. At present I'm engaged in a study of the working-class movement here in the United States and an in-depth investigation of history of the last fifty years, when Fascism swept the Western world. I split my writing time between that and correspondence with people I love.

Q. Do you revise much?

A. I write strictly off the top of my head. I don't go over it because I haven't time.

Q. What about writing equipment? I noticed that the letter you sent me was written with a very stubby pencil.

A. That's all they allow you. I have thirty pencils in my cell right now. But keeping them sharp—the complication is I have to ask the pigs to sharpen them.

Q. Yes, I see. But do they sharpen them?

A. Sometimes yes, sometimes no, depending on whim.

Q. Typewriters are not allowed?

A. No, of course not. There's metal in typewriters.

Q. Your book has been hailed here and in Europe as a superb piece of writing. How did you become such a good writer?

A. You've got to understand that I'm from the lumpen, that every part came real hard. I spend a lot of time with the dictionary. I spend forty-five minutes a day learning new words. I'll read, and I'll come across words that I'm not familiar with. I record them on a piece of paper, in a notebook I have laying beside me. I look them up in a dictionary and familiarize myself with the entire meaning.

Q. Were there any problems about sending out the original letters to your family that make up the bulk of *Soledad Brother?*

A. The letters that went to the family had to go through the censor, of course, and they were all watered down. Three-fourths of the letters were returned. There's a rule here stipulating one cannot make criticisms of the institution or society in general.*

Q. What's the mechanism for censorship of letters? It starts with the guard, right?

A. They go through about three censorships. The first one is the unit officer who picks the mail up. He reads them. Then they go to the mail room and a couple of people over there read them. And in special cases—when it was a question of whether I was attacking the institution or the social system—they go from the mail room to the Warden or the Assistant Warden, and he reads them. Every one of my letters has been photostated or Xeroxed, and placed in my central file folder.

Q. If the warden decides he doesn't want a letter to go out, does it come back to you with notations, or what?

A. Either that or they'll just put it in my file and I'll never hear anything else about it.

Q. In other words, you eventually find out from the person you wrote it to that it was never received?

A. That's all.

Q. In *Soledad Brother* you describe your grandfather, the stories and allegories he made up to tell you. Did anyone else stimulate your imagination as a child?

A. Well, my mother. She had bourgeois ideas, but she did help me. I can't give all the credit to my grandfather, Papa Davis. My mother had a slightly different motivation than my grandfather. Her idea, you know, was to assimilate me through the general

---

* In January, 1970, Jackson's lawyers secured an injunction prohibiting the authorities from tampering with prisoners' letters to them, which explains those letters in *Soledad Brother* described by Genêt as "a call to rebellion."

training of a black bourgeois. Consequently, her whole presentation to me was read, read, read. "Don't be like those niggers." We
had a terrible conflict, she and I. Of course I wanted a life on the
street with guys on the block and she wanted me to sit on the
couch and read. We lived in a three-story duplex and the only way
out was through the kitchen. It was well guarded by Big Mama.
I'd throw my coat out the window and volunteer to carry out the
garbage and she wouldn't see me any more for a couple of days.
But while I was home, Mom made me read.

Q.   What books did she give you?

A.   *Black Boy*, by Richard Wright, was one. All of her life she
had the contradictions of black people living in this country. She
favored W. E. B. Dubois. She tried to get me interested in black
intellectualism with overtones of integration. When I was twelve
or thirteen, I'd read maybe two books a week, also newspapers
and periodicals.

Q.   Can you think back and remember a favorite book you read
as a child?

A.   Strangely enough, *The Red and the Black*. I read that when I
was about thirteen. I got a deep, let's say, understanding of some
of the degenerate, contradictory elements of Western culture from
reading *The Red and the Black*.

Q.   What about reading in prison? In your book you mention
reading Sabatini and Jack London.

A.   I was about fifteen in Paso Robles [Youth Authority facil-
ity] when I read those light things. I like Sabatini. Sabatini is
fabulous. I read Shakespeare, Sabatini, Jack London with my
bathrobe on. I played dummy. Went along with what they told me
to do; pretended I was hard of hearing, an absent-minded book-
worm, an idiot. And I got by with it. I've read *thousands* of books.
Of course years ago I read Dostoevski's *Crime and Punishment*,
but mainly my interests are economics and political economy.

Q.   What are the books that you'd say impressed you most of all?

A.   A brother gave me a copy of Engels' *Anti-Duhring*.

Q.   About what year—how old would you have been then?

A.   It was in '61. I struggled with that, it took me three months. The same brother gave me a copy of the *Communist Manifesto*. Then I went deep into such things as William J. Pomeroy—*The Forest, On Resistance*. And then Nkrumah. And do you know who I was really impressed with, although he isn't a Socialist or a Communist? I was impressed with Henry George's stuff. I've read all his stuff.

Q.   Oh, really? His theories of economics?

A.   Yes. His single-tax idea is not correct. But I like his presentation—I like the explanation he advanced explaining how the ruling class over the years managed through machinations to rob and despoil the people.

Q.   What particular books are you reading for your historical study?

A.   *The Nature of Fascism*, edited by Woolf; and then Wilhelm Reich's *Mass Psychology of Fascism*. That's a beautiful book. I think it should be required reading for all of us, and there's one statement in there that appeals to me in a very, very, very significant way. It goes like this: "Man is biologically sick."

Q.   What about black poetry, fiction, biography?

A.   Poetry is not my bag. Not my medium. I have no sense of poetry at all. You know, the formalistic meter-type poetry. But I like some of the Langston Hughes stuff. Nice old guy. I like some of his stuff. Of course, I read the outstanding poems—and I've quoted them, such as the one that arose out of the riot written by Claude McKay. I like such things as "Invictus." But as a student of poetry—no.

Q.   What black biographies have you read?

A.   Malcolm's, of course. And let me think. Several. I've had Wright's stuff. And—what's his name?— Little skinny guy. James Baldwin.

Q.   Now, since the book has been published, who do you feel you have reached with this book; what do you think the effect has been on readers?

A.   Well, I have mixed opinions, mixed emotions about the whole thing. But one strange thing has evolved out of the whole incident: it seems that parts of the book appeal to the right-wing blacks and parts appeal to the left. I've had letters of commendation from a hundred different sects that represent the whole black political spectrum from right to left. So there's parts in there that the progressive left, black left, can relate to. I've gotten letters from black people eight feet tall, celebrities, entertainers, et cetera.

Q.   What were the prisoners' reactions?

A.   Well, the prisoners accepted it, of course. They loved it, especially the sections near the end. Well, you know we're all considered trapped in here, without voice, and they seem to be gratified that one of us had the opportunity to express himself. For one, you understand we're an oppressed people. And that events lik that, you know, a prisoner getting a book published, getting ideas across, speaking for them, speaking for us—all that's appreciated.

Q.   Did the guards ever say anything to you about the book?

A.   Well, you have a difference of character, a character difference. Some laughed and said, "I'm reading, I'm learning about myself," and then there are others that look at me with daggers in their eyes. And it's pretty clear that what they're saying is that "First chance I get, nigger, I'm going to kill you." They're saying, "Look, we have a mutual understanding." When I use the word "pig," one officer will take it as a terrible, terrible attack on him, whereas another will laugh.

Q. When Greg Armstrong [senior editor at Bantam Books] presented you with the first copy of your book on the day it was published, it was immediately confiscated by a guard, is that true?

A. True. Later on my lawyers raised a fuss and they finally let me have a hardback and softback copy. But without the fuss, I'd never have gotten them.

Q. Is your book available in the prison library at the present time?

A. No. The publisher sent a hundred copies to the prison library. The librarian distributed the books, but one month later, after the officials had read the book, they started confiscating it, so now it's underground. It's being picked up by the search-and-destroy squad. They invade the cells and look for contraband. It's considered contraband, but there's copies circulating around, underground. Now I'm locked up, but that's the way I heard it.

[I checked with Officer McHenry, librarian at San Quentin. He told me the prison had received thirty-five copies of *Soledad Brother*, they were checked out immediately to inmates who wanted to read them, there was never any censorship of the book so far as he knew. The mystery was further compounded by Jackson's lawyer, John Thorne, who told me his copy of *Soledad Brother* was taken from his briefcase by a guard and held as contraband when he went to visit his client—what is the truth of the matter? With Jackson locked up, and me locked out, we can each but report what we are told.]

Q. Now, at the time of publication Greg Armstrong flew out here for the customary publisher's champagne party—which, in this case, was held at the gates of San Quentin. What did the prisoners think about that?

A. They love that sort of thing. You know, after years of isolation, all of a sudden to find out that people really are interested in you and that people can relate to you in spite of the fact that sociology books call us antisocial and brand us as criminals, when actually the criminals are in the *Social Register*—well, we did relate to that, to the whole incident.

COMMENT

At the time of this interview I was deep in my book on prisons, *Kind and Usual Punishment*. The year before, I had published an article in the *Atlantic* about the California prison system, which had achieved a considerable underground circulation among the inmates. George Jackson, who for good reason had in general a deep mistrust of journalists and who thus far had rebuffed their efforts to interview him, had read the piece and sent word through his lawyer that he would welcome an interview by me.

I knew something of the prison administrators' opinion of Jackson from a confidential memorandum by L. H. Fudge, Associate Superintendent of a California prison camp, that was mailed to me in a plain envelope by—a convict trustee? A disaffected prison staff member? I shall never know. The memorandum might, I suppose, pass for what publishers' advertising departments call "a selling review" of *Soledad Brother:* "This book provides remarkable insight into the personality makeup of a highly dangerous sociopath. . . . This type individual is not uncommon in several of our institutions. Because of his potential and the growing numbers, it is imperative that we in Corrections know as much as we can about his personality makeup and are able to correctly identify his kind. . . . This is one of the most self-revealing and insightful books I have ever read concerning a criminal personality."

Among the prison officials quoted at length in my *Atlantic* article was James Park, Associate Warden at San Quentin—he had not, I gathered, been pleased with the piece nor with my rendition of his conversation. It was to him that I was obliged to apply for permission to interview Jackson, refused until Jackson's lawyer obtained a court order compelling Park to allow my visit.

When the court order came through, I telephoned Park to make arrangements for the interview. I could hear him over the phone fussing away at his secretary: "Where's that fucking court order for Jessica?" (Like *Mortuary Management* and Bennett Cerf, the Corrections crowd all called me "Jessica.") "Mr. Park," said I sternly, "don't you know it's a misdemeanor in California to use obscene language in the presence of women and children?" Which it is; a silly and sexist law that my husband is challenging in the courts, but that came in handy at that moment.

This is one of the very few interviews in which I used a tape recorder. I am mistrustful of these gadgets, which might break down at any moment and which necessitate tedious hours of transcription. But somehow—while I am on the whole confident of my ability to scribble down accurate notes of conversations—in the case of a person behind bars, helpless to challenge any possible misquotation, it seemed important to get the interview on tape. Fortunately George Jackson knew how to work the recorder. He took charge and it went off without a hitch.

When three months later Jackson was gunned down in the San Quentin shoot-out, his words, to which I had listened over and over again in the course of my laborious transcription of the interview, came back to me in his distinctive tone of voice: "And it's pretty clear that what they're saying is that 'First chance I get, nigger, I'm going to kill you.'"

MY SHORT
AND HAPPY LIFE
AS A DISTINGUISHED
PROFESSOR

ATLANTIC / *October, 1974*

The memory of my brief excursion into academia is fast fading into a wild, improbable, yet wonderful fantasy, a confused medley of classrooms, courtrooms, student demonstrations, television cameras, the gloomy faces of college administrators. . . . Were it not for the journal I kept sporadically, and assorted memorabilia such as clippings from the student newspaper, some toeprint labels, some exam papers, I might begin to think I dreamed the whole thing.

It all started in May, 1973, when I received a letter from San Jose State University which began: "Dear Ms. Mitford: I am writing to inquire whether you would be interested in being considered for an appointment as a Distinguished Professor for fall semester 1973." Signed "Snell Putney, Ph.D., Acting Chairman, Department of Sociology," it was sprinkled with many an oddly turned phrase: "We are wanting someone such as yourself. . . ." "The period of responsibility would be from late September, 1973, through late January, 1974. . . ." "More importantly, we seem to be in a period of rather active intellectual ferment. . . ." "The honorarium for the semester would be slightly over $11,000. . . ."

What on earth, I thought. Was somebody pulling my leg—which of my fun-loving friends would have access to San Jose State University writing paper? And if Snell Putney, Ph.D., indeed exists, what is his native tongue? "That's easy, Sociologese," said my husband. "You'd probably love being a Distinguished Professor, you'd better go after it." So I did.

The pursuit gave rise to many an anxious moment. A professor of my acquaintance, privy to the subtleties of university parlance, was quick to point out that Mr. Putney had not actually offered me the job but merely asked if I would be *interested in being considered*, the clear implication being that the same letter had been dispatched far and wide to other possible candidates. Furthermore, he cautioned, there would be political hurdles. Any appointment would doubtless have to be confirmed by Dr. John Bunzel, president of the university, who in his prior capacity as head of the political science department at San Francisco State University had proved to be "one of those 'responsible liberals' who always end up opting for law and order" and who, because of his equivocating role in the student strike of 1968, had incurred the enmity of militant students and faculty alike.

Then came the day when Snell Putney, Ph.D., with whom I was soon in constant communication, asked the dread but inevitable question, "What is your academic background?" I sadly told him it could best be summed up in one word: nil. My mother, who did not approve of girls going to school, had brought us up at home; to my deep regret, I had never attended a university, a high school, or even an elementary school. "Oh-ho, that's delightful," said Mr. Putney with his scholarly chuckle, and assured me that this odd upbringing would make no difference to my chances.

Much later, I learned that I was indeed one of some twenty-five to whom identical letters had been sent. Of these, three came down to the wire as possible choices for the job: Paul Jacobs, who had been involved with the strike at San Francisco State when Mr. Bunzel was there; David Horowitz, editor of *Ramparts;* and myself. When the short list was presented to President Bunzel with the department's recommendation that I be appointed, he said, my informant reported, "Well, I'm glad it's not Jacobs or Horowitz, they could be troublemakers."

The contract safely inked, I was interviewed at some length by a reporter from the San Francisco *Chronicle*, who made great sport of my singular lack of academic preparation for the appointment, and of the fact that only three years before I had been listed along with some sixty-five others by the House Internal Security Committee as an "undesirable radical campus speaker." The following day a cloud no bigger than a man's hand appeared on my otherwise serene horizon; the *Chronicle* reported that Frank P. Adams, former president of the ultraconservative California Republican Assembly and currently a trustee of the state university system, had "hotly contested" my status as Distinguished Professor in the sociology department, remarking indignantly that "to me, if she's an authority on death she should be in the morticians' department." Which, I thought, was rather a good point.

One of my new-found colleagues in the sociology department told me the news stories had triggered a flurry of student applications for my classes and a few crank telephone calls. "What kind of crank calls?" I asked. "Oh, just irate citizens demanding to know what an uneducated radical like you is doing on our campus." I observed I did not consider that crank, as the same question had occurred to me.

I was to have two classes, I was told: a large lecture course of some two hundred students, and an honors seminar limited to twenty. But what, exactly, was I to teach? What *is* sociology, anyway? I put these questions to a professor in the department, but it seemed he hadn't a clue either. "Sociology is a very broad term," he said. "You can structure your classes any way you choose, hopefully based on your own social action research." Ahem, thought I, and it is to be hoped that I may be able to squeeze in a few pointers on talking plain English.

Actually, I found that I was both excited and apprehensive at the thought of assuming my new duties. I had given many a one-time lecture to college audiences, on a hit-and-run basis in which one disappears forever immediately after the event—but a sustained course to students whose future careers might depend on the quality of their college preparation? This was an alarming, yet challenging prospect.

I spent the summer hopefully structuring away in collaboration with my student assistant, Novelle Johnson, a reformed airline stewardess from South Carolina, who proved to be an accomplished and experienced guide to the academic scene. She patiently led me through the ABCs of classroom procedure; it would be desirable, she explained, to prepare class outlines, reading lists, examination questions, so together we got these ready. The lecture course would be called "The American Way," a title vague and flexible enough to enable us to explore the American way of all sorts of things, based on my "own social action research" which I hoped meant I would not have to read any sociology texts but would merely draw on subjects I already knew about: caskets, courts, convicts, con men, the rise and fall of Bennett Cerf's Famous Writers School. . . . The final section would be "Water-buggers of Yesteryear," the point here being that the Watergate gang and their counterparts of twenty to thirty years ago cut their teeth in the witch hunt against the Left following World War II. Under this heading we would present the reminiscences of some Old Left victims of the McCarthy era, New Left comments on same, and try generally to link the radical politics of the two eras. To top it off, we would invite the head of the San Francisco FBI to tell all about electronic surveillance of suspected subversives. In the section on criminal justice we would bring in as guest lecturers lawyers, judges, and ex-convicts. In short, we hoped the lecture course would turn into something resembling a variety show.

The exams, I decided, should be designed to bring out the multiplicity of talents I expected to find among my students. Those more at home in some medium other than prose could turn in a poem, song, one-act play, a cartoon strip. All would be invited to translate into English a paragraph taken from a sociology textbook—with the caveat, however, that if they were hoping for a graduate degree in that discipline they might find themselves at a disadvantage if they learned this lesson too well.

The small seminar (honor students, no less! Horrors!) would be a workshop in "Techniques of Muckraking" in which students, working alone or in teams according to preference, would investigate some local institution of their choice such as a nursing home, jail, police department, radio station, and so on.

San Jose is a big sprawling industrial area about an hour's drive from San Francisco. The university, a unit of the state system presided over from far-off Southern California by Chancellor Glenn S. Dumke and a board of trustees, is vast: enrollment is close to 27,000, comparable in size to the Berkeley campus of the University of California, where entrance requirements are stiffer and where the student body, with its long history as bellwether of radical youth movements, is more sophisticated, more cosmopolitan, and perhaps more world-weary.

Looking back over my journal, I see that events of my first week in San Jose pretty much foreshadowed the shape of things to come.

NOTES FROM JOURNAL, SEPTEMBER 24TH

Arrived in a state of high nerves to take up lodgings in the Faculty Club—classes begin tomorrow. Checking in at Prof. Mitford's mailbox, I found assorted sociological memoranda and announcements, copies of the student newspaper *Spartan Daily* full of wise sayings of deans and information about parking regulations, a penciled note from the secretary of the department saying "Miss Mitford, please go to personnel to take the loyalty oath and be fingerprinted" which I threw straight into the wastepaper basket, and—joy of unanticipated joys!— a letter from a local funeral director saying he had read in the papers that I was coming to teach in San Jose and would "be pleased to put my staff at your disposal to tell your students how we care for the dead." My class outlines are ready, all neatly dittoed. To my annoyance, Somebody Up There has ordered the title "Techniques of Muckraking" deleted from the seminar outline and replaced with "Sociology 196H," which sounds boring as hell, so they all had to be redone with the title put back in. Novelle, who is good at ferreting out campus politics, discovered that the order to strike the muckraking had come from Chancellor Dumke's office.

Some women faculty members took me and Novelle out to lunch in San Jose's finest eatery—nerves much assuaged by their kindness and several preprandial drinks. In mid-lunch two men came over to our table: a dean, and a spruce young fellow, something like a composite of the junior Watergate set we'd seen on television, who introduced himself as lawyer for the university trustees. I said oh good, I need a lawyer, I just got this absurd note about a loyalty oath and fingerprinting, there's not a word about either in my contract, so please tell your bosses, whoever they are, to cut out the one-line jokes as I don't intend to do any of that. He replied sternly that it's a rule, I would have to comply with these requirements. The dean, looking grave, concurred. "Then . . . see you in court!" said I gaily, and on this note we parted.

SEPTEMBER 25TH

My first lecture—at last I've found my true vocation! There were over two hundred students, ranging from fresh-faced late teens to grizzled heads; I loved them on sight. All nerves vanished, I gave them a brief rundown on How I Came to Be a Distinguished Professor (throwing myself on their mercy), and a short intro. to funerals, throwing in all the jokes I could think of about different layaway plans and how one wouldn't be caught dead in one of the cheaper lines of caskets, showed samples of the Fit-a-Fut Oxford that I'd ordered from the Practical Burial Footwear Company of Columbus, Ohio, passed round copies of my favorite trade mags. *Mortuary Management* and *Casket & Sunnyside,* explained the uses of various embalmers' aids like the Natural Expression Former (a plastic device which, inserted into the mouth after rig-mo, as we call it in the trade, sets in, can produce a seraphic smile on the deceased face). . . . It all went off like gangbusters, they were in fits of laughter.

The university public relations office telephoned in the afternoon to say they would be having a press conference to announce my appointment as Dist. Prof., which I thought incredibly cordial of them; and one of the deans called to warn me that the loyalty oath and fingerprinting are ironclad conditions of employment, so I'd better get along to personnel to comply with these. I stiffly replied that I should be consulting the American Civil Liberties Union about that.

SEPTEMBER 26TH

My muckraking seminar, limited to twenty, is a very different cup of tea from the lecture course. Three of the students, it turns out, are not enrolled in the university, hence are attending illegally, which I find flattering. We've decided to meet in the Faculty Club (also, no doubt, illegal, who knows?) where we can have lunch and bring wine to enliven the three and a half hours of class time. My plan: to spend the first several sessions exploring methods of gathering information, which will give everyone time to figure out what particular muckraking project each wishes to pursue. Today, discussed techniques I've found useful in interviewing funeral directors, prison administrators, Famous Writers, and so on—how to get them to talk, how to assume various fictional identities to help loosen tongues: pre-need cemetery-plot buyer? Nervous citizen anxious about crime control and prison security? Aspirant Famous Writers School student? And how to double-check information thus adduced by seeking out those on the receiving end, so to speak: survivors who have had to foot the funeral bill, convicts, students actually enrolled in the Famous Writers School. . . .

Another deanish telephone call: Had I gone down to personnel yet? I explained I hadn't time to think about all that or to consult the ACLU, I'd been too busy preparing my classes and meeting with students, so the oath and fingerprint matters had rather slipped my mind. Professor Alvin Rudoff, head of the sociology department, called to say there is a big flurry going on in the administration about all this, and they've been after him to persuade me to comply. He agrees both requirements are absurd and demeaning. I said I'd be back in touch after talking with some lawyers.

OCTOBER 2ND

The two funeral directors came to address my lecture class—they were more than up to expectations. "We are in the business of serving people," one announced mournfully, and averred that all this talk of the high cost of dying is nonsense—they would furnish a funeral for as little as $119.50. This sounded like an odd price, and the students demanded a breakdown; the information that the actual price is $117 and the $2.50 for sales tax was greeted with gales of hilarity. A long wrangle ensued between students and guest lecturers about the wholesale cost of caskets—why is it a closely held trade secret? Our undertakers fumbled and fudged over this one, with students in hot pursuit. Novelle's Roarometer, a device she proposes to invent to measure decibels of laughter in my classroom, would have been wagging its head off during this interchange.

Teaching, then, was heady stuff; so was the fracas over the loyalty oath and fingerprinting that began to build up between me and the college administration. To be perfectly truthful about this, I believe that had these requirements been explicitly set forth in my original dealings with the university, I might after some grumbling have complied; for are we not all inured to such bureaucratic absurdities in myriad aspects of life, from obtaining a driving license to applying for a government job? And what of my colleagues, professional teachers whom I had learned to respect as men and women of principle, and their thousands of counterparts in the state university system—who was I to set myself up as some sort of political purist and initiate a challenge when they had not seen fit to do so? Nor was I seeking, as was later charged, a "confrontation"—I had been through enough of those in my time, and yearned only to be left in peace, taken up as I was with the rigorous requirements of my new job. Yet, having stumbled into this arena, I was reluctant to withdraw. Thus the warp and woof of my days in San Jose consisted of trying to learn more about the mysterious, fascinating process of teaching, and locking horns with the authorities in a series of ever-increasing skirmishes.

The first of these had to do with the loyalty oath. There is something weird about the wording of the California Oath of Allegiance; although extremely brief, it manages to encompass a number of bewildering and contradictory propositions. If it reads like a truncated version of something, this may be because in the middle sixties the ACLU, after arduous battle, succeeded in excising the most objectionable portion, that which required all state employees to swear that they are not now nor ever have been. As it now stands, one must swear to "uphold and defend" the Constitutions of the United States and California "against all enemies foreign and domestic," and further to swear that the oath was taken "freely and without any mental reservation." Well (said I to the deans), I think I have done my best to uphold and defend the Constitution of the United States against enemies, especially domestic ones like you; but the annotated Constitution of the State of California runs to three hefty volumes and covers all manner of subjects. Do I uphold and defend, for example, Article 4, Section 25¾, limiting boxing and wrestling matches to fifteen rounds? I don't know. Perhaps it should be fourteen, or sixteen? I do know that I cannot uphold and defend the recent amendment which reinstates the death penalty, since in my view it runs counter to the U.S. Constitution's prohibition against cruel and unusual punishment. Nor can I uphold and defend the section requiring the loyalty oath, which I regard as an abridgment of First Amendment rights. But (said they) you must sign if you want to work here, it's the law. What if I strike out the words "freely and without any mental reservation" and substitute "under duress"? No, that won't do, you can't tamper with the oath. Then . . . you are requiring me to swear falsely as a condition of employment?

The section of the Penal Code giving the penalty for perjury, one to fourteen years in state prison, is printed right above the oath. But the same Penal Code would seem to contain an equally stiff caveat for university administrators who require employees to perjure themselves as a condition of employment: subornation of perjury also carries a penalty of one to fourteen years in stir. . . . What, then, if we all end up behind bars as a consequence of my signing? Will it be a race between me and the administrators to see who is rehabilitated first?

We went round and round on this for several days. Eventually I consulted Paul Halvonik, counsel for the ACLU. He advised that since the Oath of Allegiance is a requirement built into the California Constitution, it would take a deal of toppling in court; it might be years before such litigation would be resolved. Meanwhile, refusal to sign would be cause for my immediate dismissal, an event that would doubtless be hailed with unalloyed glee by the trustees. It boiled down to a choice, then, between continuing to teach or being fired and embarking on an interminable court fight over the oath. Why not sign, making it clear I was doing so under protest? Fingerprinting is another matter, said Halvonik; it is not a constitutional requirement, we could probably win that one.

I had not yet broached the oath matter to my classes—we were far too busy with funerals, Famous Writers, and related subjects —but I discussed it at length with Novelle and Professor Rudoff, who agreed with Halvonik's approach; so on Monday, October 1st (a date that later was to become significant), I went to the personnel office and signed. The previously scheduled press conference to announce my appointment was held a couple of days later; it was surprisingly well attended by TV, all the local press, even stringers from New York and London papers. I took the occasion (to the consternation of the university P.R. people who had called the conference) to explain my position on the loyalty oath and to denounce the perjury-suborning administration.

There followed a few days of press hoopla. The *Spartan Daily*, to my gratification, published two pages of letters from faculty members supporting my attack on the oath requirement; then it all subsided, and with some relief I settled back into my new occupation. But somehow, in the process of clarifying my position on the loyalty oath, I had forgotten all about the fingerprinting. It was soon brought sharply back to my attention.

NOTES FROM JOURNAL, OCTOBER 10TH

My horoscope in today's paper says "Higher-ups may cause problems . . . do not overspend . . . rely more on colleagues . . . p.m., enjoy social activity, relax with mate." It turned out to be pretty accurate. The deans were after me all last week to come in for a discussion of the fingerprinting issue, but since the whole thing seems to have turned dead serious and they are holding up my paycheck, I said I would have to wait until I could get a lawyer to accompany me to the meeting. Today was kaleidoscopic: a book report which I'd been asked to give at a noon faculty luncheon, the meeting with the deans, an afternoon reception given for me by women faculty members.

Following the book report, I braced the assembled professors with a brief polemic on fingerprinting: an arbitrary, demeaning rule promulgated by the chancellor, part of a general policy of Big Brotherism, the dossier-building process through which our life histories can all be stored eventually in giant computers; was much fortified by their expressions of agreement and support.

Bob [Treuhaft, my husband, who is a lawyer] came down from Oakland and together with Novelle and Professor Rudoff we breached the deanly stronghold in the administration building, there to confront the massed deans: Dr. Hobart Burns, Academic Vice-President; Dr. James Sawrey, Dean of School of Social Sciences; Dr. Robert Sasseen, Dean of Faculty. With one accord, these worthies pronounced themselves opposed in principle to the fingerprinting requirement—they even commended me for bringing the issue to their attention. *But*, I must comply at once or leave the campus. "Then . . . you mean to tell me that you support my stand,. but you are firing me for refusing to be fingerprinted?" I asked in some astonishment. With one accord, they glumly nodded assent.

Novelle and Professor Rudoff pleaded the cause of my students, who would be subjected to real hardship: we were now three weeks into the semester, books had been bought, projects and assignments undertaken —some two hundred and twenty students would be faced with the prospect of losing credits for my courses, some might fail to graduate as a consequence, others would lose grants.

We proffered some face-saving compromises. Professor Rudoff proposed to invite me out for a drink and turn over my glass to a friend of his in the sheriff's office who would lift the prints. Bob suggested that I might continue to teach, so that my students would not be penalized by loss of credits, and agree to forgo my salary until the issue had been decided in court. The deans were immovable; these higher-ups conceded they were acting on instructions from President Bunzel, who in turn was almost certainly actuated by higher-higher-ups, the trustees and possibly the chancellor. As we left, they had already begun to discuss my replacement—I learned later that the leading candidate for my job was Clinton Duffy, retired warden of San Quentin prison.

Off to the Faculty Club where two or three hundred women were gathered for the reception. I took the sponsors aside and told them what had just happened—I had been fired, I intended however to meet my class as usual the next morning, but I had no idea what to expect; would the administration try to remove me forcibly? I asked if I might make a brief statement to the gathering explaining my position on the fingerprinting issue and asking their support. The sponsors were dubious; many of the women there, they said, were not "politically aware" enough to understand these matters, there were teachers from the athletic department, from nursing and homemaking. . . . So, in the receiving line, as guests came up with words of welcome I confided to each one, "I've just been fired." This was greeted with uneasy titters; was it some sort of unfunny joke? Finally, I prevailed upon the sponsors to let me speak to the assemblage. The response was overwhelming. Women shouted their encouragement and support—some left to prepare leaflets calling for a campuswide mobilization at my lecture, others said they would alert the press to these developments, the women's coach came up to say she would bring along the whole football team to be bodyguards and prevent my eviction!

P.m., relaxed with mate, who agreed to stay overnight and come to class with me tomorrow to explain the legal aspects of the matter to my students.

The unexpected intransigence of the administration, their rejection of every offer of compromise, made me pause to consider my legal position. Having swallowed the oath, I had gagged on the fingerprinting. What now?

My lawyers told me I had a very strong case. My contract said nothing about fingerprinting; the law which establishes the fingerprinting requirement for teachers in the California system from grade-school level through junior college had, possibly through oversight, not been extended to include the state universities. The administration had been unable to cite any statutory basis for the requirement; the best their lawyers could come up with was a 1962 memo from the chancellor's office to all state college presidents instructing them to continue "the existing policy" of requiring all employees to be fingerprinted. The origins of that policy had, it seems, been lost in antiquity.

I could refuse to be fingerprinted, let the university fire me, then sue for breach of contract. "You can just take a long vacation and get paid for not teaching," I was assured. My lawyers were surprised, as I was, when I blurted out, "But I *want* to teach, I can't bear the thought of giving it up."

My insistence on continuing to teach ("your inexplicable attachment to your new calling" was the way one lawyer put it) made the lawyers' task much more difficult, however, and the outcome more uncertain. It meant racing to court to find a judge willing, on the basis of affidavits alone, to sign a temporary restraining order commanding the university, pending a full-scale hearing to be held later, to reinstate me with full pay and to restore course credits for my students. They would try, they said, but were not at all confident that a judge would be willing to stick his neck out that far. If the judge refused to do anything without a full-scale hearing—and that would require at least two weeks' notice—there would be a further period of uncertainty as to my status and that of my students.

For my own part, I was fully prepared to weather it. The four-month teaching job in San Jose was, after all, merely an unforeseen and enjoyable episode in a long and crowded life. Win or lose the court case, I should have plenty of other things to do. But what about my students, whose academic careers could be seriously disrupted while litigation meandered on? How would they react to this predicament? And my colleagues in the sociology department, many of whom I had never met? These nagging questions dominated my waking hours.

NOTES FROM JOURNAL, OCTOBER 11TH

Today was what Novelle calls, in her soft Southern drawl, "the Da-a-a-y of Infamy." She came over early with her trusty tape recorder (she is preserving all this for History), and accompanied by a dozen students we walked over to the lecture hall. Rumors abounded—some said there was a sign on the door posted by the administration saying "Mitford Lecture Canceled," others warned that security police were on hand to prevent the class from assembling and to drag me off the platform. To forestall a lockout, we decided to arrive fifteen minutes early and seat ourselves with the previous class held in that hall. As we approached the building, we saw hundreds of students assembled on the lawn, some with placards reading "We Want Jessica, Not Her Fingerprints," a forest of television equipment, swarms of reporters. We made our way through and into the classroom, which was packed to the rafters—my usual attendance of two hundred students augmented to seven or eight hundred. A cheer went up as we came in, and a young man introduced himself as Student Body president—could he make a brief statement from the platform? Yes, indeed, said I. Dean Sawrey was on hand looking most uncomfortable—might he read a brief statement from the platform? Yes, Dean Sawrey, in this classroom we defend and uphold First Amendment rights of free speech for all; anybody can have his or her say without fear of censorship.

I called the class to order at the appointed hour, and announced

that we were fortunate to have several distinguished guest speakers
with us today; first Rudi Leonardi, president of the Student Body.
Leonardi (whom I had rather expected to take a middle-of-the-road
position—possibly try to mediate my differences with the administration) came on like an avenging angel: "On behalf of students searching for new ideas on this campus, we offer support to Jessica Mitford.
. . . This university, whose primary role is one of disseminating information to students, has resorted to academic back-stabbing. . . ."

When the roar of applause died down, I reminded the class that we
are studying The American Way, and said that our next distinguished
speaker would doubtless shed some light on the American Way of
College Administration—Dean Sawrey. Shaking like H*Y*M*A*N
K*A*P*L*A*N's aspirin leaf, Dean Sawrey (Novelle pronounces it
"Sor-ry"!) read a six-line statement, the burden of which was that I
have been removed from the faculty and am unauthorized to teach, no
credits will be given for my classes, the sociology department is seeking
a qualified replacement. To a crescendo of boos, and shouts of "She *is*
qualified!" he hurried off the platform. "Dean Sawrey!" I called after
him. "There are several hands up—it's customary in this class to respond to students' questions." But he made rapidly for the exit, for
which I apologized to the students, observing that there were apparently lots of questions but no answers.

Bob gave a rundown on the legal situation and the complexities of
the forthcoming court battle. There followed impassioned discussion
from the floor. A thirtyish student, veteran of SNCC and draft resistance: "These cases can't be won in court alone; success depends on
mass support of the students, beginning with everybody in this room!"
Roars of approval. A young political activist: "What about the Angela
Davis case, right here in San Jose? Doesn't that prove something about
the importance of mass movements against injustice?" A serious and
usually reserved young woman who seldom speaks up in class: "The
fight is up to us! We can show the administration we're not going to be
pushed around by maintaining the integrity of this class." And so it
went, until even hardboiled old me felt slightly overcome by emotion,
so for the first time in my teaching career I adjourned the class early.

Following the Day of Infamy, there were these developments.
After much classroom discussion I polled my students to learn

their wishes—how many would transfer into alternative classes, as proposed by the administration? The overwhelming majority indicated they would refuse to transfer and would stick with me even though it meant risking their academic credits. The sociology department met and voted unanimously to defy the administration's order to seek a replacement and to support my stand and that of my students. "We consider Jessica Mitford to be a member of the sociology department," said their official statement. The student government announced they would invite my class to meet in the Student Union should we be locked out of our regular lecture hall. The academic council, advisory body to the university president, passed a unanimous resolution declaring that fingerprinting is "an infringement of human sensibilities" and "irrelevant to academic endeavor." The *Spartan Daily*'s thunderous editorial denunciation of the administration for kowtowing to right-wing pressures of chancellor and trustees was echoed by the San Francisco *Chronicle,* which said the fingerprinting requirement is a "breach of ordinary freedoms" exemplifying "a preposterous timidity in the scholastic authority," and the far-off Atlanta *Journal:* "This presumes, we suppose, the students are well-protected from unsafe ideas with fingerprints stashed away in some administrator's file. We don't know whether to laugh or cry." For many days students all over the campus sported labels of my toeprints with the legend "MITFORD THUMBS HER TOES AT THE TRUSTEES."

The administration in turn tried to cool things by announcing I had not been "fired" but merely "de-hired" (a word not in any dictionary), and President Bunzel told the press "We cannot always accommodate conscience when it conflicts with policy," statements that became the object of editorials and general unmerciful spoofing in the *Spartan Daily.* As one *Spartan* columnist had it, positively bristling with indignation over Dr. Bunzel's remark: "Dr. Bunzel has said that he opposes the fingerprint policy—if not in public then at least in private. As a matter of fact almost everyone does—faculty and students. I say to Dr.

Bunzel you are making a fool of yourself. You are crumbling into a quagmire of lofty, conservative, status quo thought. You are afraid to take a stand . . . and worst of all, you are betraying a fellow scholar who has brought to the surface a grossly superfluous policy which you know is all wrong."

I was, I must confess, enjoying every minute of this enormously.

On the whole, I was surprised by the impassioned response of the campus to the "Finger-Flap," as my students called it. When school had resumed that autumn, there had been the usual newspaper soundings of the campus mood across the country. According to these reports, universities had by and large subsided into the political apathy of the fifties; "student unrest" was a thing of the past. If this was true of such former strongholds of student militancy as the University of California and Columbia, surely sleepy San Jose would be the last place one would expect a rebellion of such dimensions to erupt, and the fingerprint issue an unlikely rallying point.

Thus in the early days of the controversy, when I first realized I was set on a collision course with the administration, I hardly expected the campuswide demonstrations and near-unanimous support of students and faculty. I had thought they would divide into roughly three categories: a minority of militant supporters, a certain amount of hard-hat reaction of the why-don't-you-go-back-where-you-came-from variety, and a large middle group who would feel that while compulsory fingerprinting as a condition of employment was silly and distasteful, the issue was trivial, possibly even contrived. As the sponsors of the women's reception had miscalculated the response of that gathering, so I had misread the temper of the campus as a whole.

It seemed to me, a newcomer to the academic scene, that the Finger-Flap, and the administration's handling of it, struck a sensitive nerve and ignited long-smoldering, deeply felt resentments that far transcended this one issue. For many students and faculty members, it apparently symbolized the petty, arbitrary, bureaucratic treatment they receive in daily doses from those in authority.

In court my lawyer, David Nawi, argued for a temporary restraining order to compel the university to give the students their credits and pay my salary. The judge offered a Solomon-like compromise: I should place a set of my fingerprints in a sealed envelope, and submit them not to the university but to the court, there to repose until the litigation was finally resolved. The lucky winner, the trustees or I, would eventually be awarded custody of the prints in perpetuity. Meanwhile my full status as professor would be restored, the university would pay my back wages, I would continue teaching, and my students would get their credits.

David Nawi explained this proposition to the students and I put it up to a vote. The prevailing view was that the so-called compromise was in fact a clear victory for us, since it exposed the absurdity of the university's rationale for the fingerprinting requirement. According to the chancellor's office, the prints are needed to establish identity of the employee and to divulge any criminal record. It might be months before the court ruled on the matter, by which time my stint as Distinguished Professor would be long since over. Meanwhile, I would be teaching on, and the university authorities would not get so much as a sniff of those fingerprints which, they claimed, were prerequisite for this work. The students having voted in favor of accepting the judge's proposal, we once more got down to our regular class work.

NOTES FROM JOURNAL, NOVEMBER 12TH

Novelle and I spent the weekend correcting and grading some two hundred exam papers—actually, the total haul was more like a huge Christmas stocking than the sere fruits of academic endeavor. Taking me at my word, students had turned in posters, collages, tape recordings, comic strips, scrapbooks—one had composed a crossword puzzle consisting entirely of words that had come up in class ("Lawn in Smog City" = "Forest," "Goodnight, sweet—" = "prints"), another had constructed a miniature velvet-lined casket with dinky bronze handles. We held an exhibition of the artifacts in class, and I read out a selection of the more brilliant papers on subjects ranging from funerals to fingerprints—but oh, their spelling! Since we are now in the habit of taking a vote on everything, I wrote on the blackboard "CEMETARY or CEMETERY?" and asked for a show of hands; fortunately for the future of the language, the latter won by a hair's-breadth. Most have trouble with "it's" and "its," so I proposed a mnemonic device: "When is it its? When it's not it is. When is it it's? When it is it is." I begged them not to say "hopefully" when they mean "I hope," and pleaded the cause of "structure" as a noun, not a verb—losing battles, I fear, since their instructors perpetrate these abuses. But a good time was had by all.

NOVEMBER 25TH

My muckrakers are taking to their work like ducks to water, and are fast turning into devious super-sleuths. The illegally enrolled are doing best. One of these, a baby-faced, bearded lad in his early twenties, is trying to ferret out the industrial secrets of Mace manufacturers and handcuff suppliers, and has assumed the role of director of a Citizens' Committee for More Secure Jails. In this improbable guise he visits factories and interviews executives, obtaining price lists, specification manuals, promotion material which he gleefully spills out of his brief-case in class like a conjurer producing rabbits from a hat. Predictably, one team has chosen to investigate the origin and application of the fingerprinting requirement and is attacking the subject from a number of angles: How much does the procedure cost? (Four dollars and twenty cents a person, levied against the university by the California Criminal Investigation Department.) Is the policy adhered to by all state colleges? (No. San Francisco State University, for example, has never bothered to apply it, so presumably on that campus unidentified persons with criminal records may teach and roam at will.)

I'm afraid, though, muckraking is beginning to get out of hand on this campus. A reporter from the *Spartan Daily* telephoned to say she was conducting a survey of faculty members who had assigned their own books as reading—how much had I netted in royalties from sales to my students of *The American Way of Death* and *Kind and Usual*

Punishment, both on my reading list? So my teaching is beginning to have some impact, though I must say in an unforeseen direction. The muckraker raked, this time.

In my lecture course on The American Way, the variety-show idea, its theme a study in contrasts, was working rather successfully. Students seemed to enjoy the diverse—often diametrically opposed—views presented, and began to relish the opportunity to match wits with the guest speakers. We arranged a special showing of *The Loved One* after the funeral directors' lecture. During sessions on the criminal justice system, some ex-convicts from the San Francisco Prisoners Union discussed their firsthand experiences with cops, courts, and "corrections." Our next guest lecturer, a superior court judge, tried valiantly to give a convincing picture of the courts as even-handed dispensers of justice for all, and was vociferously challenged by several students who, at the urging of the ex-cons, had done their homework by going to see for themselves what goes on in the local courthouse.

The Waterbuggers of Yesteryear section was introduced by a tape of *Are You Now or Have You Ever Been?,* Eric Bentley's dramatization of actual transcripts of House Un-American Activities Committee hearings in the fifties, and this was followed in subsequent sessions by Al Richmond, author of *A Long View from the Left* and for three decades editor of the *Peoples World;* Bettina Aptheker, a leader of the 1964 Free Speech Movement at the University of California; Frank Bardacke, draft resister and defendant in the "Oakland 7" conspiracy trial of 1968. Our final guest speaker in this section was Charles W. Bates, San Francisco bureau chief of the FBI. In introducing him I explained we were studying Waterbuggers and invited him to tell the students all about FBI surveillance of suspected subversives. Instead, perhaps from force of habit, Mr. Bates launched into a history of the FBI, beginning in 1908. Restless students soon began raising their hands demanding to know how many agents in his jurisdiction are assigned to shadowing radicals. Why was Bettina Aptheker followed by an FBI agent for many months during Free Speech Movement activities in Berkeley? How many telephones are now being tapped in the San Francisco area? How many operatives are assigned to college campuses? "I'm not trying to weasel out, but I can't answer that" was Mr. Bates's response to most questions, which caused a student to ponder out loud, "What do funeral directors and the FBI have in common?"

While on the classroom front all seemed to be progressing satis-factorily—in fact, far better than I had hoped—there was more infamy to come: "The Case of the Disappearing Paycheck," as the *Spartan Daily* called it. It was in the course of this new develop-ment that I began dimly to apprehend the elusive mentality of the academic bureaucrat—akin, no doubt, to that of his counterpart in government or industry, yet having distinct and subtle pecu-liarities of its own.

Judge John McInerny's order had specified that once I had delivered my prints to the court I was to be paid "all monies due and past due," which seemed pretty clear. So I was surprised (and annoyed) to discover that my September paycheck had been withheld. Why, and on whose command? There was a great deal of buck-passing on this, seized upon by *Spartan Daily* newshounds who sensed a mini-Watergate, complete with credibility gaps, in the making. Dean Sawrey disavowed responsibility; he said the university lawyers had decided to withhold the check "on their own initiative." President Bunzel by implication washed his hands of it, for he wrote in his San Jose *Mercury* column that pursuant to the court ruling I would get my pay and the students their credits, "which," said he, "is what the university wanted all along." Larry Frierson, lawyer for the trustees and a party to the court agreement to pay "all monies due and past due," told the *Spartan Daily* he couldn't recall who first questioned the propriety of paying me for September, but said, "we feel we cannot legally pay her."

A few days later (lo and behold!) President Bunzel admitted to the *Spartan Daily* that it was he who had called Frierson and suggested that my September pay could be stopped on the ground that I had not signed the loyalty oath until October 1st. "If she had signed the oath one day earlier, on September 30th, she would have been paid for September with no problem, but she went one day too long," he said, adding that state employees who don't sign because of negligence are not paid for the period before the oath is signed. But *Spartan Daily* reporters, hot on the trail, learned "from sources," as they put it, that Dr. Bunzel had told the academic council in a closed meeting that "approximately 40 faculty members did not sign the loyalty oath in September and the only distinction between Mitford and the other faculty members was her unwillingness to sign"—a prize entry for the "How's That Again?" column of *The New Yorker*.

So, back to court, accompanied by the usual phalanx of students and reporters. Proceedings were brief, for the judge asked the university lawyers only one question: "Has she performed the duties for which she was hired?" Yes, said they. *"Then pay the lady her money!"* roared the judge, words immortalized in headlines in the next day's *Spartan Daily*.

The decision on the fingerprinting case, when it was finally handed down in late January, came as an anticlimax and attracted little notice. My classes were over—culminating in a farewell wine-and-cheese bash attended by five hundred students and faculty members—and since school was in recess, the *Spartan Daily* was not publishing.

Judge William A. Ingram ruled that the university's fingerprint requirement was unsupported by any "validly adopted statute, rule or regulation." Thus, he said, although he personally viewed fingerprinting as "desirable and constitutional," he was constrained to rule that the requirement was legally unenforceable. The effect of the decision is to invalidate the fingerprinting requirement throughout California's state university system—and, of course, to restore to me the sealed envelope with its hard-won contents. This arrived too late, alas, for the public ceremony I had envisaged in which my students would cremate the prints, place the ashes in a suitable urn, and donate them to the university.

COMMENT

This is organized as a straightforward narrative of the events as they unfolded—to me, always the easiest format. On the whole I avoid flashbacks and other fancy stylistic tricks in which one can get hopelessly tangled. However, I wrote some of it in the guise of "Notes from Journal"—much as I had used "Trip Notes" in "You-All and Non-You-All"—although actually in this case I had kept no journal; the spurious "Notes" are merely a device to achieve change of pace and speed things up where necessary.

As usual, I had considerable difficulty with the first paragraph, which I worked over, wrote and rewrote, for several days. In the end the editor, with my reluctant concurrence, cut out that paragraph, so that the published version began "It all started in May, 1973 . . ." Perhaps it is better that way? A borderline case of a murdered darling, sacrificed for a quicker lead-in to the story? But having gone to all that trouble I have put it back in for this collection. The editor also deleted the description of Dr. Bunzel at the end of the fourth paragraph, and the reference to the order from Chancellor Dumke's office to strike the muckraking on page 197. He told me he felt I had been hard enough on the university administration without these extra pinpricks. Again I reluctantly agreed to the cuts, although I detected a certain squeamishness on the part of the editor, who evidently did not want to go too far in offending those eminences.

After the piece was published, the *Atlantic* ran a long letter from Dean Robert Sasseen, together with my reply. Mr. Sasseen's letter was full of deanish attempts at biting sarcasm: "Surely all but the most insensitive must suffer with a Lady-in-Exile, thrill to her heroic struggle, wonder at her enchanting ways and rejoice in her eventual triumph over the evils of fingerprinting. Surely one must envy the fortunate students who were enrolled in her 'variety show'. . . ." But of the fingerprinting requirement he said, "The requirement was found to be valid. . . ."

I replied that the Dean was wrong about this, that the decision was general in its application and by no means confined to my case; and that the ACLU lawyers who filed amicus briefs could find no ambiguity in Judge Ingram's ruling that the university's fingerprinting requirement is unsupported "by any validly adopted statute, rule or regulation."

The university trustees made no move to appeal from Judge Ingram's decision, presumably fearing that it would be upheld in the appellate court. Consequently the Ingram ruling invalidating the print requirement stands to this day as the law governing this issue. But it seems that college administrators, like prison officials, consider themselves exempt from the laws which ordinary mortals are expected to obey. Curious to know whether the Finger-Flap, the clear-cut judicial decision, and my article relating all this had resulted in any policy changes, I checked recently (in October, 1978) with the personnel officers at San Jose and San Francisco State to find out what is happening on the finger front.

Sam Milioto, San Jose personnel officer, said, "We still have the same policy, the only difference is that since your case we don't let anyone *start* working until they've been fingerprinted." And Joseph Glynn of San Francisco State told me, "Before your case came along, although fingerprinting was required we didn't enforce it, because we hadn't enough staff to monitor and follow up, so we were unable to insure compliance. We now send the newly hired employees to the Public Safety Office, and Public Safety sends us back a notice confirming that fingerprinting is completed."

Thus, unhappily, it seems that the net result of my effort was a tightening up of the illegal fingerprint procedure at San Jose State, enforcement of the illegal policy at San Francisco State where it was formerly ignored, and the creation at San Francisco State of that prize grotesquerie the "Public Safety Office." This, an example of muckraking that not only fizzled but backfired, illustrates the limitations of the genre: absent an ongoing protest movement, which in this case failed to materialize, the mere exposure of bureaucratic absurdities is insufficient in and of itself to force change.

For me there was, however, a considerable consolation prize. A month after "My Short and Happy Life" was published, I had a letter from the dean of Calhoun College at Yale, saying that he had read the piece and proposing that I teach a seminar on "Muckraking and Investigative Journalism." "Let me assure you at the outset that neither a loyalty oath nor fingerprints are considered to be prerequisites or requirements for the position," he wrote. Thus was initiated a most fascinating and illuminating experience: a semester at Yale in the spring of 1976, during which I not only had the pleasure of teaching some exceptionally bright and inventive students, but also of learning from them something of the politics of power, money, and corruption that lurks in the corridors of Ivy League Academe. That, of course, would be another story, more appropriately told by the students themselves.

THE BEST OF
FRENEMIES

DAILY MAIL / *August, 1977*

English newspaper readers were accorded a rare treat this summer when the press discovered that Mr. Ted Heath, former British Prime Minister, maintained a "Friends List" of 110 names, with revealing notations to enable his secretary to identify callers. Among his graphic comments: "Smooth stockbroker," "Old lady, not too nice," "Sends goodies," "Very rich—fork lift trucks," "We owe dinner."

Reading in far-off California about Mr. Heath's Friends List, I visualize that it must have created a new parlour game being played nightly in sitting-rooms all over England: the capsule characterisation of Friends. I know it sent me scurrying for my address book, to scrutinize the names therein for appropriate one-line comment on each: "Lunch, not dinner, too drunk by then." "Good for $100 contribution Prisoners Support Committee if approached right." "Gone guru, alas." "Into ceramics, health foods. Bother." [*Into?* Yes, unfortunately—a new and deplorable shorthand for interested in or working at.] "An adorable creature, pity lives New York." "Moderately good Scrabble, not much cop anything else."

Actually, I soon discovered that a substantial number of the names listed in my address book belong in the category of Frenemy, an incredibly useful word that should be in every dictionary, coined by one of my sisters when she was a small child to describe a rather dull little girl who lived near us. My sister and the Frenemy played together constantly, invited each other to tea at least once a week, were inseparable companions, all the time disliking each other heartily.

I wonder whether most of us do not, in fact, spend more time with frenemies than with actual friends or outright enemies? Those fringy folks whose proximity, either territorial or work-related, demands the frequent dinner invitation and acceptance of their return hospitality? Pondering the potential guest list, dear reader, how often have you and your spouse bickered on in this fashion: "Well, if we ask Geraldine, we'll have to ask Mary and her awful boy-friend." "We can't just ask Peter from my office and not the others—makes for bad blood. If we ask Peter, we've got to have the lot."

The return invitation of the frenemy is always cause for alarm, although generally not immediate alarm: "It's three weeks off, darling, and anyway it's a free dinner so let's go," one says hopefully. In our neighbourhood, the evening too often involves the showing of slides of the frenemies' trip to Europe. In California, where the threat of earthquakes is ever present, one can take out "slide insurance" on one's house; but this does not, as I have ascertained from my insurance agent, apply to such gatherings. "There is no such thing as a free dinner," my husband once gloomily remarked as we staggered, exhausted, from the interminable click-click of the slides being put into their slot: "Oh, sorry, upside down, but this is Maudie at the Kremlin—you can just see her skirt on the left. . . ."

But real friends—ah! Who are they? Mostly people, boys and girls, whom we knew and laughed with and loved passionately *circa* age twenty. Only rarely does one make new friends in later life; I have some, and I cherish them dearly. The point about the friends of our youth, though, is that no matter how divergent our interests, viewpoints, ways of life have become over the years we can pick straight up with them and carry on as before: "Your pugs, darling, they are *too* smashing," I will exclaim to such a friend who knows I actually loathe pugs, and she will counter with "Well darling I haven't actually read your book [she actually loathes books] but I do think it's marvellous anyway . . ." and from then on it is very plain sailing: a sort of basking in mutual fondness that has nothing to do with her pugs or my books, just the heaven of each other's company for the sake of it.

Enemies are, to me, as important as friends in my life, and when they die I mourn their passing. For example, when I was writing *The American Way of Death,* some of my very best quotations of the funeral industry spokesmen were those of Mr. Wilber Krieger, Managing Director of the National Selected Morticians. His pronouncements were always absolutely sure-fire, marvellous copy. I could never have done without him; his "selection room for Merchandising Research to demonstrate lighting to show arrangements and decoration through the 25-unit balanced line of caskets," and so on; he made my book. After the book came out, his denunciations of it in *Casket & Sunnyside* made my day. How very sad, then, to read in *Mortuary Management* that Mr. Krieger has gone on to a balanced-line casket. The news filled me with gloom; lifelong enemies are, I think, as hard to make and as important to one's well-being as lifelong friends.

Our former President, Mr. Richard Nixon, evidently recognizing this universal human need, maintained an official Enemies List. Surely Mr. Heath could produce one of those? But perhaps it would turn out to be not all that different from his old Friends List, with the same occasional notation "We Owe Dinner."

COMMENT

There is no muck in this one. I include it because of the difficulties it presented as a commissioned piece on a subject far afield from my normal proclivities.

The telephone rang at 6:30 a.m., London calling. Because of the eight-hour time difference, the Londoner who telephones to California generally contrives to rouse one from that deep and satisfying sleep that comes just before dawn. It was the editor of the *Daily Mail*, who in a charming Scottish accent explained what was wanted: Ted Heath's "Friends List" had made headlines all over England. Would I do a short essay for the *Mail* on the subject of Friendship? Well, no, I said, I'd be hopeless on the subject of Friendship, that sort of thing isn't my speed at all. But the editor would not take no for an answer; with many an "Och!" and "Ay!" he pressed on, and let drop the fact that the fee would be substantial. He did sound sweet, and so did the substantial fee; so I weakly said all right, I'll have a try. When will the piece be due?

"Och, today, my dear lady." *Today?* In that case, said I, I cannot possibly do it, I am a very slow writer, it would take me at least a week.

"Ay, but the *Mail* is a daily paper, we should have it in hand no later than tomorrow morning at this time, ye can telephone it in."

"Och, then, O.K., I'll do my best."

Friendship. Friendship. Friendship. I had some coffee (always a good mind-jolter), and hung around miserably until about 10:30; nothing came to mind. I had a hot bath (another effective stimulant) and thought again. Still nothing. I am not an essayist by nature; the word evokes high-level scholarship and rich, thoughtful prose on some abstract subject—like Friendship. But for the *Daily Mail*, Yellow Press personified with one of the largest circulations in England, I reflected that I would virtually have to turn into Dear Abby or Erma Bombeck to produce the kind of comment on Friendship they would want. Either way, it was beyond my capabilities.

At noon, I wrote out a telegram to the editor: "TERRIBLY SORRY TO HAVE INCONVENIENCED YOU BUT CANNOT WRITE FRIENDSHIP PIECE." I dialed Western Union and got a recorded announcement that all lines were busy. Reading over my telegram while waiting for Western Union to become un-busy, I thought that this was really an extremely unprofessional thing to do, and hung up.

Friendship. What about *enemies*, in some ways far more interesting and memorable than friends? Or Frenemies? I remembered my sister's Frenemy and got to work. By nightfall I had finished.

Promptly at 6:30 a.m. I telephoned to the *Daily Mail* and dictated the article to a typist. There is something rather pleasurable in calling London collect and lolling all relaxed in one's dressing gown with a cup of coffee and a cigarette while the huge bill inexorably ticks up minute by minute.

After the piece appeared in the *Daily Mail*, my canny braw agent, Scott Meredith, flogged it to *The New York Times* Op-Ed page, thus garnering yet another fee—whereupon numerous New York friends wrote to say they recognized themselves as the "adorable creature, pity lives New York."

All in all, a lucrative and satisfying day's work.

CHECKS
AND BALANCES
AT THE SIGN
OF THE DOVE

NEW YORK / *May 30, 1977*

This is a cautionary tale in five acts for out-of-towners, as New Yorkers call provincials, like me, who venture into Manhattan only once in a great while. (I should hasten to hedge: some of my happiest moments have been spent in New York restaurants, from plain to fancy.)

Act I. I invite a friend who works in the fashion industry to have dinner with me. As she is (I presume) a sophisticate who knows the city, I ask her to choose the restaurant. "Let's go somewhere *really* nice," I say expansively. She proposes the Sign of the Dove, once recommended to her by somebody; so thither we repair at 8 p.m.

Act II. We are seated in an absurdly done-up place, its décor like a pink wedding scene, but, determined to enjoy ourselves, we remark how very elegant it is. Menus arrive; rather to my sorrow, I note the entrées are in the range of $16 to $18.50. We order frugally: one drink each; my friend gets the $18.50 lamb chops, I get the plat du jour (not on the menu), which is shad roe; half a bottle of Chablis to share; no starters or desserts. She has two small coffees, I none. The shad roe is overcooked, with a charred piece of bacon on top; my friend's potatoes are cold. We ask for some proper bacon and some string beans to replace the cold potatoes. After a longish interval, these are brought. The restaurant, fairly empty when we first arrived, is filling up rapidly with persons of the gold-brocade-pantsuit type and their male counterparts, who blend nicely with the décor.

Act III. The bill comes; it is for $76.10. I am inwardly fuming, especially since the two entrées are lumped as $50, with no further explanation. (Was the unlisted shad roe $31.50? Had the restaurant charged extra for the new piece of bacon? For the string beans in lieu of the unacceptable potatoes?) The two drinks are $5.50; the half-bottle of Chablis, $10.50; my friend's coffee, $3.50. Cover charge and sales tax account for the balance. Not wishing to embarrass my friend—TSOTD having been her suggestion—I choke down my fury, say nothing, and write a check (with a measly $9 tip) for $85. My only desire now is to get out of this beastly place and write the whole thing off as one of life's more dismal experiences.

Act IV. Waiter says he cannot accept a personal check. I counter crossly that I haven't got that much cash. Manager looms; have I no credit card? No, but I have tons of identification. He says *on no account* will he take personal checks—a check is just a piece of paper. So is a dollar bill, I point out. He beckons us into the lobby, where we are surrounded by menacing waiters, acting with the precision of trained guards. The manager, directing this B-movie scene, says he is going to call the police. I furiously demand that he should do so immediately; we'll wait until they come and *then* he'll find out what trouble is. He changes his mind about the police but swoops up our coat checks and says we won't get our coats until we pay cash. I snatch back my $85 check, which he is holding, and we storm out, coatless, into the cold night.

Act V. Back at the apartment, we start telephoning, first to a lawyer renowned for his consistent, militant defense of the underdog, then to a famous food columnist. The lawyer grumpily says I should have realized there's no law requiring a businessman to accept a personal check, and there's nothing he can do. The food columnist says I should have known better than to go there, that the place is notorious for its absurd prices and awful food. I am beginning to feel like the rape victim who is told she asked for it.

Epilogue.   My friend, who went back the next day bearing cash to ransom our coats, demanded an itemized breakdown of the $76.10 bill. After a long, whispered huddle between manager and waiters, this was produced. Except for its total, it bore no relation to our original bill. The "two entrées, $50" had disappeared, replaced by chops and roe at $18.50 apiece. Coffee, previously charged at $3.50, was now $4.50, and two desserts had been added for $10. My persevering friend managed to make them knock off the unordered, unserved desserts plus a dollar for the coffee. The new total, including tax and cover charge, was $63.72, already a saving of $12.38 over the original bill. But this time my friend proffered not even the mingiest tip; thus, if one deducts $63.72 from the $85 I tried to pay, I saved a grand total of $21.28—thanks entirely to the inhospitable behavior of the management. What a windfall! Nevertheless, I think I shall not soon return to the Sign of the Dove.

THE DOVE STRIKES BACK—
A MORALITY PLAY
IN FIVE ACTS

NEW YORK / *September 19, 1977*

> Now I will show myself to have more of the serpent than the dove;
> that is, more knave than fool.
>
> *Christopher Marlowe*

Prologue: Some weeks ago (*New York* magazine, May 30th) I described an unhappy evening at the Sign of the Dove, located at 1110 Third Avenue. To recapitulate for Faithless Readers who do not read, or remember, every golden word we writers inflict upon them: I had invited a woman friend to dine there with me. Seeing the prices on the menu, we ordered frugally, one pre-dinner drink apiece, a half-bottle of Chablis to share, two entrées, one coffee. The food was pretty awful, but the bill was worse: $76.10, including "cover charge" and tax, the two entrées lumped as $50. Not having that much cash on me, I tried to pay by check, refused by waiter. The manager threatened to call police unless I produced cash or credit card; he changed his mind about the police but, holding our coats as hostage, sent us shivering into the cold night air. The next day my friend, who went back bearing cash to ransom our coats, demanded a breakdown of the $76.10 bill. This was eventually produced; except for its total, it bore no relation to our original bill. Entrées were now listed at $18.50 apiece, desserts and extra coffee had been added. My friend made them knock off the unordered, unserved items, reducing the total to $63.72. In short, an unpleasant and debilitating experience.

Now, it seems to me that an honest and appropriate response to my article (and one that could have saved much trouble in that dovecote) might have been a letter from the restaurant to *New York* magazine admitting error and promising to shape up in the future. But that, it seems, is not the way of businesses that are run by their public relations departments. What follows is an account of the Dove's highly un-colombine counterattack.

Act I. *New York* magazine reports a fair deluge of letters to the editor about my article. Most of them say "Good for you!" or words to that effect; a few come to the wounded bird's defense: ". . . she has maligned one of the finest restaurants in New York . . ." "I was shocked at your recent article about the Sign of the Dove and its lack of credibility. . . ." (Do we already detect the fine hand of P.R. at work here?) Two communications addressed to editor James Brady appear to be of more than passing interest: a postcard signed Patti Fink, Westport, Connecticut, which starts, "I happened to be at The Dove the evening Miss Mitford recalls in her article. Unfortunately she did not mention what a scene she made and was *drunk*"; and a letter signed by Anne Williams of Kew Gardens, New York: ". . . I would like to tell it as I saw it from the table next door. I feel obliged to say that Miss Mitford was inebriated upon being seated. . . ."

Here the mystery begins, for a sharp-eyed secretary has noticed that these are both postmarked in New York City and bear the same postal meter number: 1147184! Ms. Fink of Westport and Ms. Williams of Kew Gardens sharing a postal meter in Manhattan? How cozy! Do these ladies actually exist? If so, could they be Dove-connected?

Act II. I send an inquiry to the Postmaster of New York, who replies: "Kindly be advised that the holder of Postage Meter #1147184 is Med-Den, Inc., 1110—3rd Avenue, New York,

N.Y." This is indeed kindly advice, for that is the address of the Dove. Who, then, is Med-Den? The trail now leads to Dr. Santo, a dentist who owns the Sign of the Dove, doing business under the corporate name of Med-Den Enterprises.

Act III. I discover via telephone Information that Mss. Fink and Williams are indeed corporeal entities. I get Patti Fink on the phone and ask her about the postcard. She sounds totally mystified —she never sent any such card, she has never been to the Sign of the Dove, she hardly knows anyone in New York. "I'm getting a little paranoid," she says. "I don't know who could have used my name." I observe that I am getting a little paranoid myself, and give her my address in case some clue should occur to her later. In a few days, her letter comes giving the name of a childhood friend, Jane Porter, who works at Med-Den—and who has confessed to forging the postcard! "To say that I am annoyed about this whole situation is putting it mildly," writes Patti.

Act IV. Forward to Jane Porter. For the first half of our twenty-minute telephone conversation, she is extremely cool. I learn that she works for a public relations agency but is "not at liberty" to tell me which one; that she signed Patti's name to the postcard because she did not want to get her agency in trouble; that she was at the Dove on the evening in question with a girl friend, sitting about three tables away from me; that she noticed I was "being kind of loud" and that "everyone was looking your way"; that she recognized me from a photo on one of my books; that she had read all my books but couldn't remember any of their titles. Furthermore she reiterates that the Patti Fink postcard is the only communication she has sent to *New York* magazine. "You're quite sure that you haven't written another letter?" I ask sternly. "That's the only one, Miss Mitford." "You're absolutely certain?" "Yes."

I feel I am not getting very far, so I make vague noises about the law of libel; I mention the Postal Inspectors and the dim view they might take of this use of the U.S. mails. I suggest to Jane that somebody has been using her. Does she not in fact work for Med-

Den? "Yes, ma'am," she answers despondently and floods of tears follow. From now on it is plain sailing.

The second half of our discussion unwinds like a movie going in reverse. Jane now tells me (between sobs) that she was *not* at the Dove that evening; that she does public relations work for Dr. Santo at Med-Den; that there were terrible goings-on after my article came out: "Everybody was running around screaming, and everybody was trying to get people to write letters as I guess a form of retaliation, and *New York* magazine wouldn't print any of them." Business fell off, she says; the restaurant is no longer open for lunch. "Oh, like your article caused a lot of hoo-ha," she wails. I realize that I am behaving like a prosecuting attorney, not my favorite role—I long to comfort her, but there is one other thing I must find out. "*Please* stop crying, Jane," I implore. "Just answer this, and you've absolutely got to answer truthfully. Did you write another letter and sign it with the name of Anne Williams?" "Yes." Oh, dear. I beg Jane to pull herself together, we murmur soft goodbyes, we hang up.

Act V.   James Brady, editor of *New York*, tells me he has been approached by Brenda Johnson of the Johnson & Morton Associates agency, who does public relations for the Sign of the Dove. Ms. Johnson had quite a long chat with Mr. Brady, in the course of which she divulged that my friend and I had been very drunk that evening; that I have a reputation in New York restaurants for getting drunk; that I was once kicked out of the Four Seasons for that reason; that my friend had now repudiated my version of what happened that evening. Curiouser and curiouser!

So, back to the telephone for the Tale of Brenda Johnson, who answers with a sprightly "Oh, hi, Miss Mitford!" But as with Jane, the sprightliness first dims then vanishes and despondency takes over.

Brenda Johnson tells me she has represented the Sign of the Dove for about two months—she works with Dr. Santos a couple of days a week. "He's a wonderful man with broad interests, travels extensively . . ." and she tells me all about his recent trip to

Japan, but I want to get back to the article. What about the arithmetic on the bill? Well, "Dr. Santo does one hundred percent realize there was an error on the bill, he's the first to admit that." So far so good.

Brenda, who is amazingly long-winded, now rattles off a great deal of other information: there were five bomb scares in the restaurant after my article, hundreds of letters and angry phone calls, "Kooks saying, you know, how dare you do that to people, you are unjust—it went on for days. Now they only get about one a week."

So, say I, that's all of interest but what about your conversation with Mr. Brady? Allegations that I was drunk that night, habitually drunk in New York restaurants, kicked out of the Four Seasons for that reason? A torrent of words pours forth. I try to keep my end up, to make some sense out of what she is saying, but it is not easy. Her source, she says, was the Dove's manager; he'd worked at the Four Seasons years ago and said there had been a *problem*, didn't say kicked out . . . she never did tell Mr. Brady I have a reputation in New York as a drunk; "I'm smart enough as a young businessperson not to ever say that about somebody . . ." she never said my friend repudiated the story—oh, dear, now *she's* crying. Damn, but I must get to the bottom of it, so when she pauses for breath (which is not often) I interject a question. What about the Jane Porter forgeries? She says she doesn't know anything about them, so I read them out. She is shocked! She'd met Jane at work, up at Med-Den, but had no idea she could ever do such a thing. "I tell you if I even *dreamed* that she would do that I think that I would be so angry that I would bash her head against the wall."

"Rather a violent reaction," I observe mildly, "in view of the fact you did exactly the same thing in your conversation with the editor of *New York* magazine." After that, Brenda seems to run out of steam and shuts up. There is really no more to be said.

Epilogue.   Many of the cast of characters in this brief drama are no longer on stage. The manager has been fired. Jane Porter has been told her services are no longer needed. One puzzler remains: did Dr. Santo put Jane and Brenda up to their act? Both women told me no, he did not; but wishing to check further (after all, neither had been exactly candid when I had spoken with them), I called Dr. Santo to ask him directly. His secretary told me he did not wish to talk to me. It seemed almost a relief, after the verbal barrage from P.R.

CURTAIN

Note: Some names have been changed to protect those of the guilty who have already suffered enough.

COMMENT ON
TWO ''DOVE'' PIECES

I owe a debt of gratitude to Nora Ephron for getting "Checks and Balances" placed. I doubt I could have done it on my own, for I should never have dreamed that any magazine would want a full-fledged article about these events, and should have felt diffident about suggesting it to an editor.

The morning after the Dove disaster, I was frantically looking for someone who would expose that rotten enterprise. I called up Mimi Sheraton, restaurant critic for *The New York Times*, to ask if she might consider running a letter from me in her column; she was sympathetic, but explained that *Times* policy is to refrain from printing letters pro or con a restaurant unless it has previously been reviewed. Thus far she had not reviewed the Dove. She might in the future, she said; but the future was too far ahead for my liking. I tried calling Betty Furness, consumer affairs radio and TV commentator, and got a recorded announcement: "If you have a complaint, write a letter and your complaint will be investigated. . . ." As I hung up, I reflected sadly that my shabby treatment at the Sign of the Dove was hardly a matter of vital concern to the average New York consumer, beset with daily iniquities in the prices and quality of children's shoes, breakfast cereals, garage mechanics' services. Who cares if two self-indulgent old ladies, admittedly willing to splurge on a good meal, get taken? It was perhaps the least important consumer issue in New York.

Later that day I was sobbing out my tale to Nora Ephron. "Don't budge," she said. "Sit right there, I'm calling the editor of *New York*, I bet they'll love it." She did, and they did.

So far so good. But I was leaving New York the next day, which meant dashing the piece off in a matter of hours; the editor wanted no more than 750 words, always difficult of achievement. The shape of an article depends on the length, and one has to plan accordingly, as one would in cutting the pattern of a dress for a doll or a grown-up woman. In many ways the finicky work of designing the doll's dress is more demanding.

I had long since learned that you exceed the required length at your peril, particularly at the low end. If an editor asks for 6,000 words, he may allow considerable leeway, anywhere from 5,500 to 6,750 if that is what it takes to say what needs saying. But as I discovered some years ago when doing occasional reviews for *Life*, 750 words generally means an allowance of no more than twenty words either way. A *Life* review was always sandwiched snugly between two columns of advertisements, which for some reason the editors deemed less expendable than the wit and wisdom of reviewers.

I fiddled around with the Dove piece, trying to devise a 750-word "shape" for it, while the precious hours slipped by. There are few things more frustrating than working against this kind of deadline, when it begins to seem as though nothing will come right—and that perhaps, after all, the story is hardly worth telling. How to convey the bite and drama? Ah! Now I had it—a playlet, five acts and an epilogue, would at once solve the problem of condensing the narrative and obviate the need for transitions, always great space-consumers. Once I had written "Act I," "Act

II," and so forth, on separate sheets of paper, the story fell into place quite satisfactorily.

My title, "April Fool at the Sign of the Vulture" (our misadventure having occurred on April 1st) was changed by the editor, who thought "Vulture" might be defamatory, to "Checks and Balances at the Sign of the Dove." Actually this was the better title, a felicitous play on words which got the name of the restaurant right into the headline where it would catch the eye of Dove fanciers and disparagers alike.

After "Checks and Balances" was published, I began to think that, judging by the flood of letters from disgruntled Dove diners forwarded to me by *New York* magazine, maybe I had after all hit on a consumer issue of sorts. Typical was one from a man who was entertaining relatives from out of town: "Even though my wife and I are used to eating in many of the better restaurants in the city, we were quite unprepared for the astronomical bill," he wrote. He paid up with his credit card, adding 15 percent for the tip. The maître d' came over and asked loudly before the assembled company, "Do you intend to leave the rest of the tip in cash? It's customary at the Sign of the Dove to leave 20 percent." But my favorite letter was from a woman who said she had "often fantasized" writing an article like mine. "Just to add insult to injury," she wrote, "I pursued the matter further. I called the Sign of the Dove and made a reservation for six persons for dinner. Two hours after making the reservation, I called and insisted on speaking to the manager. When he got to the phone, I told him that I had made the reservation, but that after reading your piece, I wouldn't dream of subjecting myself or any of my friends to such a place. . . ."

The real drama began with the "Patti Fink" and "Anne Williams" communications. It is such unanticipated responses to an article that, in my experience, are the true reward of the writer, transcending even the pleasure of seeing one's work in print and getting paid for it. (The Dove, in fact, paid off twice and I recovered the cost of the dinner many times over.) For days after the editor of *New York* sent me the Fink/Williams communications, and told me of his conversation with Brenda Johnson, I lived in a state of concentrated excitement as clue after clue emerged: the New York Postmaster's identification of Med-Den as owner of Postage Meter No. 1147184; the discovery through "Patti Fink" of the whereabouts and occupation of "Jane Porter"; the link between Med-Den and TSOTD. . . .

Having verified the Dovish connection with the mystery postage meter, I embarked on the time-consuming job of tracking down and interviewing "Patti Fink," "Jane Porter," and Brenda Johnson. In all, I must have spent four or five hours on the telephone with those wailing ladies. "Patti" was clearly an innocent; "Jane" sounded like a sad sack, an underling ineptly trying her best in this, her first job, to curry favor with the boss, and hardly a person worth contending with. Not wishing to cause these two sufferers further misery, I gave them fictitious names in the article. But I was not about to let that self-styled "smart young businessperson" Brenda Johnson off the hook. Her name and that of her public relations agency are authentic.

While generally refusal of the principal to talk creates serious obstacles for the investigator, sometimes, as in the case of Dr. Santo, silence may prove to be golden.

The Dove saga got quite a play on television; it was discussed on the Dick Cavett and Phil Donahue shows, and on some local programs. *New York* kept the joke going for a while in their Competition page. A prize-winning entry to the competition in which readers were asked for TV pilots not likely to be seen on the air: "*The Silent Dr. Santo*. In this new adventure series, detective/gourmet Jess Mitford searches for the exclusive and mysterious Dr. Santo. Clues lead her to a once-fashionable East Side aviary." And another, in a competition asking readers for an example of bad news (such as, "Looks like ringworm to me, Farrah"): "Miss Mitford, we're calling to confirm your table reservation. . . ."

WAITING FOR O'HARA

NEW WEST / *January, 1978*

> *Is he in heaven, is he in hell,*
> *That demn'd, illusive Pimpernel?*

The Scarlet Pimpernel must have been one of the most seductive, attractive men in all literature to devotees of Baroness Orczy's novels; incomparably daring, resourceful, his motives unmixed with base desires for worldly wealth, Jack O'Hara is such a legendary figure to me. Money means little or nothing to him; he probably lives on a mere pittance. He pursues his curious path in life only for the joy of it; for sheer pleasure, not profit. And what a tightrope he walks! Dangers stare him in the face, but he never flinches. A brilliant researcher with a mind like a steel trap, he devours and analyzes facts with the rapidity of a computer.

To set the scene for this Gothic tale: It was a dark and stormy night—or, rather, it was actually a bright mid-drought November, 1977, morning in San Francisco—when attorney Dave Pesonen's secretary dashed to the courthouse and dragged her boss out of a hearing. A whispered conference ensued. There was a message, she said, from Jack O'Hara, a printer who was employed at the P. G. & E. print shop. O'Hara had just received an emergency, top-secret order from P. G. & E.'s Los Angeles investigator concerning Pesonen's client, who had a major lawsuit pending against P. G. & E. O'Hara was instructed to print up a confidential report on the client, compiled in 1972, including logs of a nine-day wiretap of his telephone plus reams of correspondence with B. B. D. & O., the advertising agency that represents P. G. & E. O'Hara could not be reached on the print shop phone—that would be too risky—but he would call Pesonen's office back from a pay phone within the hour.

Pesonen, hardly able to believe his good fortune (for this is the sort of documentation of an opponent's skulduggery that every lawyer dreams of), excused himself from the hearing and rushed back to his office to await O'Hara's call, which came through as promised. "He sounded very overwrought," Pesonen told me. "He'd worked for P. G. & E. for fifteen years; he didn't think much of my client but he did feel that this kind of unauthorized, undercover surveillance was dirty pool. I said I'd love to have a copy of the report—how could I get it? Could I bring it to my office at night Xerox it? He became even more agitated—no, that was out of the question. He could do it for me on the P. G. & E. copying machine, but there was a problem about the paper. The machine takes a special kind of roll—Kodak Triple A— which is only carried by certain suppliers. I wouldn't know where to find it, he said; he'd have to buy it himself as the paper in the shop is closely inventory-controlled. He would need two rolls, costing eighteen dollars and twenty-five cents each. It would have to be done that very day because he had been ordered to destroy the plates. He had time off that afternoon to go to the ophthalmologist, would meet me and collect the money for the paper."

They met on a street corner, and at O'Hara's suggestion went for a quick cup of coffee for which Pesonen paid. "He's a rugged-looking man with black hair, dressed in workmen's corduroy pants and a quilted windbreaker. He said, 'Excuse these,' pointing to his clothes, 'I change when I get home in the evening.'

"His whole demeanor was nervous, distraught; he had a bead of sweat on his upper lip. Over coffee he kept repeating, 'Please don't get me involved, I've never done anything like this before, I've a wife and children to consider—but you wouldn't *believe* what's in this report.' I gave him thirty-six dollars and fifty cents. We arranged to meet at 6 p.m. for him to turn over the document. I waited until 6:45, thinking of all sorts of reasons why he had been delayed—a machine breakdown? A traffic jam? He never showed.

"The next morning there was no call from him. At noon, my secretary called P. G. & E.—they'd never heard of O'Hara. I called Dave Fechheimer, a private eye who used to work for Hal Lipset [the latter-day Sam Spade who played himself in *The Conversation*], and started telling the story. David said, 'Don't go any further! I know the rest of it. He's done it to any number of lawyers, including Bob Treuhaft and Doris Walker.' "

Now for a flashback. A smoggy October, 1973, morning at San Jose State University where I am working in the unlikely capacity of Distinguished Professor of Sociology—and am locked in battle with the university authorities because of my refusal to be fingerprinted. (That, of course, is another story; see my article "My Short and Happy Life as a Distinguished Professor," *Atlantic*, October, 1974.) My husband, Bob Treuhaft, whose law firm is handling my case against the university, calls me, his voice edged with suppressed excitement. He's just had a phone call from a printer in San Francisco who has been given a rush, confidential order by the state university trustees—some five hundred pages of scurrilous information about the subversive background of Jessica Mitford! The printer makes it clear he has no sympathy for J.M.'s political outlook, on the contrary; but he does feel the trustees are dealing from the bottom of the deck. He is willing to print an extra copy of the material on his own time, but would need to buy special paper, cost thirty-six dollars.

Somebody from Hal Lipset's office is meeting him at this very minute with the thirty-six dollars, Bob tells me exultantly; by evening, we shall have this extraordinary evidence of how low the trustees have sunk in their mad determination to remove me from the campus. By next morning, their dirty dealings will be front-page news in every paper in the state! . . . But by next morning tails are between legs. The less said about this embarrassing lapse of judgment by lawyers and investigators the better, we all agree; particularly since it develops that Bob's partner, Doris Walker, had been hoist by the selfsame petard in 1971, when she was counsel for Angela Davis in the celebrated kidnap-murder case. That time, the trap had been baited in Los Angeles with the usual promise to deliver a sensational report of illegally procured wire-tap evidence.

An understandable amnesia shrouds the details of these earlier cases; Doris Walker could not remember too much about her meeting with the printer, but she does remember making every effort to find him: "When he failed to appear, I called Hal Lipset and told him to look for the man, as it was crucial for the defense to get this wiretap report. Hal took all the information and checked with every print shop in the area—nobody had heard of O'Hara. If he had produced the document," she added wistfully, "that would have been the end of the case—it would have tainted the whole prosecution, they'd have been forced to drop it."

My curiosity aroused by Pesonen's recent experience, I called Hal Lipset's erstwhile associate, Dave Fechheimer. Between them he and Lipset have been consulted about at least ten O'Hara jobs over the past several years, and have heard about others in casual conversations with lawyers. O'Hara's operation is statewide; he turns up in Salinas, Los Angeles, Fresno, San Diego, the San Joaquin Valley, the Bay Area. "But he doesn't confine his business to lawyers," Fechheimer told me. "In just one weekend I got calls from the owners of three athletic leagues—North American Soccer, the roller derby, and a hockey league—each with the same story: O'Hara had confidential documentation that others in the league were plotting against the owner. He'd say, 'I have wiretaps of your phone, showing they are trying to get evidence to push you out.' He's terribly well informed, a very shrewd guy."

Forward to Hal Lipset.

"So O'Hara's latest victim is Dave Pesonen, who met him on November 29th?" I asked.

"You're wrong!" said Lipset triumphantly. "He's struck again. Just last week I got an urgent call from the secretary of a well-known lawyer; she sounded frantic—'We've got to *find* this man!' she exclaimed. 'He's printing up some immensely important secret documents about our client, I gave him the money for the paper. . . .' I said, 'Wait a minute; did he happen to mention that he doesn't like your client but the state is doing something wrong?' She was completely flabbergasted—I was repeating his exact words."

The lawyer, Ephraim Margolin, is representing Dr. Josette Escamilla Mondanaro, former assistant director of the California Drug Abuse program, fired by Governor Brown ostensibly for using "an eleven-letter word" in a letter written on state stationery. "The governor concedes she is highly qualified," said Margolin, "and that the real reason for her dismissal is her 'sexual preferences.' At the pretrial hearing in Sacramento on December 5th, I made a strong statement accusing the governor of discrimination and political maneuvering in his firing of Dr. Mondanaro, and said I was saving detailed substantiation of these charges for the trial. This was reported in the Sacramento newspapers and on local TV.

"The next day, December 6th, I was in San Jose on another case and got a call from my secretary, Sondra Rosen, in San Francisco. She had a printer, O'Hara, on the other line; he was doing some work for the Central Committee of the Democratic Party. He had a two-hundred-and-eighty-eight-page report, much of which was censored out, leaving a hundred and thirty pages. The report dealt with Dr. Mondanaro's case; it contained letters from Tony Kline, Bert Coffey, Jerry Brown—all discussing the possible impact of my client's case on Brown's re-election and future political career. O'Hara was instructed to make five copies of the censored report and destroy the plates. He would try to make us a copy of the unexpurgated version—he couldn't guarantee anything, wanted no money, just enough to buy two reams of special paper at eighteen dollars and twenty-five cents a ream. He met Sondra that day for coffee—*she* paid for the coffee! They agreed to meet at the same place at 5:30 p.m. . . ." Margolin added, his voice shot through with pain, "The high-to-low feeling O'Hara creates for a lawyer, from highest hopes to the eventual letdown, is unconscionable. I felt *very* downcast."

Over to Sondra Rosen: "I met O'Hara at 1:30 at the entrance to Chinatown Gate. He's average height, stocky, fortyish, blue-collar type, dirty jagged fingernails, glasses, square face. He was wearing blue pants, a blue shirt with white piping, and a sports jacket. He said 'Excuse my work clothes. I change when I get home'—and come to think of it, those *are* his work clothes! He had sounded fairly nervous on the phone and was *very* nervous when I met him. His upper lip was perspiring. I could almost feel him sweating profusely. When I gave him the thirty-six dollars and fifty cents, he said he'd forgotten to ask me for the sales tax, and that he would bill us for that later!"

"Did he volunteer much information?" I asked Sondra Rosen.

"Oh, yes, lots—he had so much inside information, he named names that he couldn't have found in the newspapers. One name was not in *any* record, that's what sold us for sure."

Armed now with a fairly comprehensive picture of both O'Hara's *modus operandi* and his physical appearance, I started calling Bay Area investigators and lawyers whose cases had attracted widespread media attention. While some—including such luminaries as Melvin Belli, Sheldon Otis, Ed Merrill, and the Hallinan clan—disclaimed any knowledge of the phantom printer, I did hit pay dirt with astonishing frequency.

Lee Borden, an Oakland private eye with Central Investigations, knows of three East Bay O'Hara jobs in the past year, two pulled on lawyers and one involving a large developer. "I can't give you any details because the people who've been had don't want it known," he said; but he did vouchsafe that O'Hara had told all three victims that "he is a family man, has two children, wants no publicity, would donate his time to printing up the material in the interests of justice if money for the paper was forthcoming."

Lawyer Y of San Francisco, defending in a highly publicized murder trial, told me he requires "complete anonymity." But he was willing to confide his searing experience of December 13, 1977, when he met Jack O'Hara at 12:30 p.m. by the flower stand in front of Gump's and gave him fifty dollars.

"*Fifty dollars!*" I exclaimed. "You were overcharged; thirty-six-fifty is the standard price."

"Well, actually he asked for forty-two dollars, but I didn't have the change," said Lawyer Y somewhat sheepishly.

"Ah! So you gave him an eight-dollar tip?"

Y, now belligerent: "Hell, no, it wasn't a tip!"

Beside the sweetly scented flower stand, O'Hara had unfolded his story. He said he was a retired Marine with a wife and two children, had worked for fifteen years in the Presidio. He was printing up a clandestine wiretap report on Y's client for the Strike Force, the special Justice Department bureau that roams the country investigating organized crime.

"If he'd produced what he said he had, it would have been *extraordinary!*" said Y ruefully. "The Strike Force has been interested in my client for years. O'Hara had information going back many years that he couldn't have gotten from the newspapers, that's why he was so completely plausible."

My random check turned up half a dozen more distinguished lawyers who had waited for O'Hara: a former counsel for ACLU in Los Angeles was promised a "dossier on ACLU compiled by Evelle Younger," then district attorney; a San Francisco lawyer, under threat of disbarment, paid for a copy of "a lengthy and libelous undercover investigation of my background by the bar association"; a group of Southern California lawyers working for the California Rural Legal Assistance were offered "wiretap information about us and our cases to be printed for the Reagan administration."

While O'Hara changes employers with chameleon-like rapidity —now P. G. & E., now the Democratic Central Committee, now the bar association—his patter and demeanor remain amazingly constant. The steady type with wife and children, he has almost always worked in the same place for fifteen years. He doesn't approve of the client, *but* . . . He apologizes for his work clothes, is agitated and perspiring. The sweaty upper lip recurs in most descriptions of his appearance; does he, I wonder, hide a vial of glycerine about his person to produce the beads of sweat, much as Hollywood stars are said to use it to simulate real tears?

Had any of the victims reported their misfortune to the prosecuting authorities? It seemed unlikely, but I thought I should check with the D.A.'s office. The San Francisco deputy with whom I spoke knew of no such reports, but he would ask around and phone me back. In short order I got a call from Chandler Visher, assistant D.A. in the Consumer Frauds Division, who was boiling over with angry frustration. "I wish I could get my hands on him!" he exclaimed. "He's caused me untold grief. He pulled his routine in a case I'm involved in." This time O'Hara had contacted the business agent of a labor union in connection with an antitrust suit being investigated by Visher last October. The business agent had handed over fifty dollars for Xeroxes of reports on the potential defendants—"statements made at meetings, undercover agreements, various illegal activities. Bilking the business agent out of fifty dollars wasn't a big crime, but the reason I am chagrined is I wasted a lot of taxpayers' money trying to lay hands on O'Hara's supposedly hot information. Our people spent endless time and trouble looking for him. I sent a guy to stake out the secret meeting place where O'Hara was to turn over the documents. It's a strange M.O.—for that kind of money."

Without exception, the O'Hara victims with whom I spoke betrayed an awed if grudging admiration for the man and his methods. "He has a genius for perceiving exactly what a lawyer would like to hear," said Pesonen. "A parasite feeding on the most parasitic profession. He must research meticulously. One brilliant little touch was his mention of B. B. D. & O.—how did he *know* they handle the P. G. & E. account? And that we suspect P. G. & E. of trying to manipulate the media in this case through their public relations people? He's not only a good strategist but a marvelous actor, completely believable." So believable, in fact, that in almost every case the realization that he had been taken dawned exceedingly slowly in the victim's mind; his first impulse, after being stood up, was to try to find the man, to track him down at any cost, by his own efforts or through private investigators, and retrieve the promised booty. Some even admitted to a fleeting fear that O'Hara might have met with foul play.

Bob Treuhaft thinks he "uses the adversary system, developed to a high art, in his choice of subjects." He plays on people who rightly or wrongly believe the other side is devious and corrupt—P. G. & E., the state university trustees, the Angela Davis prosecutors—and who are therefore predisposed to accept his story at face value. Treuhaft also surmised that, in view of his geographically widespread activities, O'Hara may be more than one person: "Perhaps he's a franchise operation, like Colonel Sanders."

Estimates on O'Hara's weekly take vary wildly. Dave Fechheimer believes he makes a very good thing out of it, possibly as much as $50,000 a year. "Let's say he does five a day, that's about a hundred and ninety dollars at his going rate. Roughly nine hundred and fifty dollars for a five-day week. How many people do *you* know who take home nine hundred and fifty dollars tax-free, with no overhead?" Hal Lipset takes the opposite view, thinks he "does it for jollies." I'm with Lipset; being something of an investigator myself, I cannot conceive of anybody, even a researcher of O'Hara's stature, being able to track down and absorb the kind of detailed information needed for his line of work at the rate of five jobs a day—aside from the fact that he would soon run out of pigeons. One a *week* is more like it—yet so far my own superficial search has turned up Chandler Visher in October, 1977; Pesonen, November 29th; Margolin, December 6th; Lawyer Y, December 13th—were there others waiting for O'Hara during that time span?

Why have the lawyers failed to notify law enforcement authorities or at least to spread a word of warning throughout the legal fraternity? First, I suppose, because nobody (least of all a lawyer) likes to appear naïve and easily gulled. Thus Doris Walker, possibly wishing to avoid an unmerciful ribbing, neglected to inform her own partner of the episode. Second, nobody likes to admit to the universal weaknesses that all con men prey on: the larceny that lurks in every heart, a hankering after forbidden fruit, the hope of getting something for nothing. Third, there is the nagging matter of bar association ethics: "This is a serious question for the victim, and perhaps a reason he doesn't report it to police," said Margolin. "Is the lawyer's effort to get a copy of O'Hara's material ethical? Or is the promised document stolen property? I don't know; I've done a lot of lecturing to law students on this very subject. . . ."

Mr. O'Hara—Jack, if I may be so bold?—I feel we know each other so well, though we've never met. As you gulp down this issue of *New West* along with your usual quick cup of coffee, do not think harshly of me, for in fact you are the hero of this story. I hate to blow your cover. Yet somewhere, on the back burner of my mind, there simmers the recollection of soaring hopes and thudding downfall when you promised to deliver the trustees of San Jose State into my waiting hands—and failed me.

Dave Fechheimer says he would like to catch you at it one day, but not for the purpose of turning you over to the police. A more fitting end to your extraordinary career, he feels, would be a testimonial dinner to be tendered to you by your victims—at $36.50 a plate. Bring the wife and kids; it should be a star-studded occasion, marred only by the presence of Chandler Visher, who vows he will show up with an arrest warrant.

COMMENT

The O'Hara saga first came my way via lawyers' corridor gossip. Dave Pesonen, a partner in Charles Garry's renowned law firm, ran into my husband in court one day and related his crushing experience at O'Hara's hands. "You've joined the club!" said Bob, and told him what had happened in the San Jose fingerprint case. It just might make a jolly little piece for a magazine, I thought, if only I could find a few other O'Hara pigeons. There was delicious irony to be milked from the fact that these super-sophisticated, high-powered lawyers, whose own livelihoods depend on the myriad devious tricks of their trade, were as a class the victims selected to be tricked by O'Hara—a turning of the tables that might appeal to the reader's sense of rough and ready Western justice.

Starting with the two San Francisco private eyes, Fechheimer and Lipset, I began to accumulate case histories—but no names; private investigators are, of course, obliged to preserve the confidentiality of their clients' affairs. And, as Lipset pointed out, although lawyers are generally avid for publicity it was unlikely that they would want this ego-bruising story splashed in the public prints.

Bob and Doris, whose egos had long since been calloused by the vicissitudes of their law practice and whose O'Hara-connected cases had been fought through to victorious conclusions, were not averse to being featured in the article. Pesonen was uncertain; he was loath, while his suit against P. G. & E. was pending, to publicly concede his lusting after the illicit documents, which might be construed by the opposition as a sign of weakness. While it might be possible to write the piece giving only two names, referring to the others as Lawyer A, B, C, and so on, this would soften the impact and might even cause the reader to wonder whether the whole story was a fabrication.

A break came when Lipset consented to call the victim of December 6th and ask if he was willing to talk to me. In short order, Ephraim Margolin telephoned; he and his secretary, Sondra Rosen, unfolded their harrowing tale and gave permission for use of their names. After this it was fairly plain sailing. Pesonen decided that if Margolin had no objection, he would also go along. Both lawyers ruefully acknowledged the humor of the situation, and before turning in the piece I checked and double-checked with them each passage in which they were quoted. In the end, the only holdout was Lawyer Y.

Although the article flushed out a number of other O'Hara victims who wrote or telephoned to tell their stories, the phantom printer himself remained as elusive as ever. Has he set up shop in some other state? Left the country? Or has he reformed and decided to go straight? Having a sneaking admiration for the fellow —and even, in some recess of my nature, an affinity for him and his dreadful methods—I cannot help feeling that the last outcome would be the saddest of all.

EGYPTOMANIA:
TUT, MUT,
AND THE REST OF
THE GANG

GEO / 1979

My earliest impressions of Egypt stemmed from two main sources: the discovery of Tutankhamun's tomb in 1922, when I was quite a small child—wonderful photographs of the golden boy-king and his treasures in the *Illustrated London News* and the *Sphere*—and the fascinating sepia spreads in the film-fan magazines of the doomed Rudolph Valentino galloping across the desert in his sheik's getup or, better yet, close-ups of his kissing scenes. My older sisters, who had seen his movies (I was considered too young for such torrid entertainment), pretended to be madly in love with Rudy, so naturally I followed suit. He soon died and we greedily pored over accounts of the mob scenes at his funeral, with photos of his body decked out in formal evening clothes lying in his silvered-bronze open casket.

Thereafter Valentino and Tutankhamun merged in my childish mind. They looked amazingly alike from the photographs: so young to die! So rich and desirable! Their beautiful, if somewhat androgynous features so well preserved by the embalmer's art! Those early loves soon faded—after all they weren't too viable, to use correctly for once a commonly misused expression—to be replaced by more immediate, pressing occupations.

I gave no further thought to matters Egyptian until the summer of 1977 when I met James Manning, an archaeologist who was traveling round America with the great Tutankhamun exhibit. As he spoke of his work in Egypt, in the Luxor-Thebes area, his eyes took on the faraway look that I was to encounter time and again when I began to meet his colleagues: that of a visionary, semi-holy, not quite of this world. He is part of the Brooklyn Museum expedition financed by the Coca-Cola Company, excavating the Precinct of Mut at Luxor, he told me. (Mut who, I wondered?) Thanks to twentieth-century techniques of excavation, he said, it is now possible for the first time to think in terms of learning details of the day-to-day life of Egyptian priests, artisans, peasants. For example, a mysterious stone covered with hieroglyphs carved into tiny squares, found near the Precinct in 1817, was only recently deciphered by a modern scholar—it turned out to be a crossword-puzzle hymn to Mut! In fact, Egyptology is in its infancy; we are witnessing the sunrise of real discovery. Wouldn't I like to come along and watch? It did sound rather fascinating; perhaps a predynastic Scrabble game would turn up next. And so it was settled.

"Fancy you going to Egypt," an English friend wrote. "So hot and dusty, full of foreigners wearing long dirty nightgowns." But how to prepare for this great adventure? The very word "Egyptology" is daunting, redolent of aged antiquarians who have devoted their entire lives to this subject, of vast museums, repositories of mummies, hieroglyphic inscriptions, pottery, jewelry, and vaster libraries of tomes purporting to explain these artifacts....

Not for me the role of Instant Expert. I confined my preliminary reading to two incredibly useful books that I recommend to anybody seeking a fast introduction to Egypt: the 1929 Baedeker; and *An Alphabet of Ancient Egypt*, by Mary Chubb, recommended for ages seven to ten, which was kindly loaned to me by my youngest grandchild. I also skimmed *Death on the Nile*, a 1938 Agatha Christie murder mystery.

Thanks to Mary Chubb, I learned that the word "cartouche"

(which I had vaguely thought was French for cartridge) means the oblong lines round the hieroglyphic names of Egyptian kings, and that pylon is not only a steel tower connecting telephone wires but is also the gateway of an Egyptian temple. From Baedeker (which contains chapters with such titillating titles as "Intercourse with Orientals") I discovered that Luxor is four hundred miles south of Cairo, its mean maximum temperature in March is 85 degrees, but that "with this warmth a bracing effect is obtained from the dryness of the air." In *Death on the Nile*, an American tourist remarks (aptly, in view of my mission), "The guide says the name of one of these gods or goddesses was Mut. Can you beat it?"

TRIP NOTES

There's no easy way of getting there. The first hurdle is Cairo airport, and seasoned travelers have a name for each airline that goes that way: B.O.A.C.—Better on a Camel. P.I.A. (the Pakistani line)— Please Inform Allah. United Arab Air—Use Another Airline. It was my dubious luck to be booked on Ethiopian Airlines, for which even these jokers have as yet no pseudonym. I draw a veil. As for Cairo airport . . . it's more like a cavernous warehouse teeming with people than any airport I've ever seen. Fortunately I had been warned that progression through this mob scene is near impossible without the aid of a "courier," and now to my rescue comes Mustapha of Life Travel, located in the Nile Hilton Hotel. Life Travel is indeed the key to getting in and out of Cairo; later, Mustapha guides me and Erich Lessing, just arrived from Vienna burdened down with a ton of photographic equipment, through the maze of confusing signs to the Luxor plane.

James Manning meets us at the Old Winter Palace Hotel where I am staying, a substantial neo-Victorian maroon-colored pile on Luxor's main street overlooking the East Bank of the Nile. Compared to Erich's hotel, the Savoy, which is early-American-motel in concept, it does have a certain old world charm. Prodded forward by James (for at that point I would willingly have settled for the long sleep of the Pharaohs), we embark on a whirlwind tour of temples and tombs. We clamber into a calash, the pretty little horse-drawn open carriage that is the main means of transportation here, and proceed to Luxor temple. Its huge sandstone columns are reminiscent of the more grandiose movie palaces of the thirties—or is it the other way round? Forward to the Temple of Karnak, a majestic stone forest of soaring pillars and massive columns affording innumerable mysterious vistas and perspectives. Some say it got its name from Napoleonic soldiers who thought it looked like the huge prehistoric stones of Carnac in Brittany—one can visualize a homesick French soldier remarking to his *copain, "Tiens, mon vieux! On dirait qu'on est rentré à Carnac."*

To achieve the Valley of the Kings on the West Bank, one has a choice of ferries: the tourist ferry which costs twenty-five piasters (about thirty cents), or the regular ferry used by the locals—identical except for its price, one piaster, and its passengers. These are mostly Arab boys and men—one sees few women anywhere in Luxor—with an amazing assortment of bicycles, packages, crated chickens, containers of all sorts. On the other shore is a conclave of donkeys, camels, ponies, and a few motor taxis into one of which we pile.

The road to the tombs leads past spectacular crags, in crevices of which nestle mud-brick villages, desert-colored like their surroundings. How old are the villages? I ask. Literally as old as the hills; they date from pre-Pharaonic times, built and rebuilt with new mud brick as the old disintegrates.

Once in a while we see a house with brilliantly colored frescoes painted round the windows—one fresco, with intricate border design, covers the entire front of the house, giving it the two-dimensional look of a cutout doll's house. The frescoes, clearly derivative of the tomb paintings, indicate the householder has made a pilgrimage to Mecca and are a pictorial record of his journey; they depict men, animals, implements with the occasional up-to-date addition of a gaudy airplane or helicopter.

Arrived at the necropolis, we scramble in and out of various tombs, down dizzyingly steep stone steps, through long, low tunnels and passageways ("Mind your head!"), some dimly lit with electric light, others seen only by flashlight. The better-preserved ones, with their elaborate representations of grapevines, dancing girls, musicians, amusing monkeys, could have made rather splendid nightclubs, I reflect. Yet in view of their purpose, were they perhaps a sort of eternal nightclub for their mummified occupants?

We stand at the threshold of Tutankhamun's tomb, the selfsame spot where in 1922 Howard Carter, holding a flickering candle in a tiny opening bored into the chamber, was struck dumb by what he saw; to Lord Carnarvon's impatient inquiry "Can you see anything?" Carter replied incoherently, "Yes, wonderful things." The wonderful things, of course, have long since been removed; only a sarcophagus, a recumbent gold statue of Tutankhamun, and a few murals remain. The wonder, to me, is that these poky little chambers could have contained so much treasure.

Tomb follows tomb. Up and down, in and out we stumble; I soon lose track of the dynasties—anyway the carvings, cartouches, bas-reliefs begin to look alike. Disloyally, I inwardly echo the philistine sentiments of our former governor Ronald Reagan, who said, much to the displeasure of California conservationists bent on preserving the redwood forests, "Once you've seen one redwood, you've seen 'em all." I can't wait until tomorrow, when we shall see the latter-day Carters/Carnarvons/Petries uncovering before my eyes the stunning treasures of the Temple of the Goddess Mut.

We arrive just as the sun comes clattering up over the horizon —so sudden and spectacular is its appearance that one almost expects to hear an accompanying roar. The work crew are already at it: atop a hill the Reis, or supervisor, stands with his big stick while scores of boys and men (aged, I am told, from eight to eighty) are deployed throughout the Precinct, some whacking away with hoe-like tools, others scooping up the loose earth into baskets to be dumped out on the other side of the Reis's promontory.

My overall first impression of the Precinct of Mut is one of a desolate expanse of sand and rubble, with here and there a ruined stone gateway on which can still be seen the carved hieroglyphs, a few badly damaged sphinxes, a statue or two. To the untrained eye it all looks mostly disheartening. Is this what I have come six thousand miles to see? Yet from the occasional cries of discovery, emitted by the excavators in authentic tones of excitement, I realize I am witnessing the very process that has stirred men's souls from earliest times: the search for civilization's origins.

The precinct is divided up into large squares marked off by string barriers to enable the diggers to pinpoint the exact position of each found object. In one square James Manning is searching out a mud-brick wall, remnant of a village built atop the temple foundations in later times. Aided by one of the skilled "Kufti" workers (of whom I was to learn more later), he strokes gently away with a soft-bristled hand brush at the dirt covering the contours of the mud bricks. "It's as delicate as brain surgery," he says. The operation reminds me of a child's magic artist pad, blank paper which when lightly rubbed with a pencil reveals a picture. Sure enough, in a few hours a bit of wall does emerge, visibly separated from the surrounding earth. Mud-brick excavation was rarely done in Egypt until recently, James tells me; excavators were after inscriptions, bas-reliefs, friezes. Much of archaeological value was lost due to bulldozing through to find these treasures. As he works, James tosses an occasional shard into baskets kept handy for the purpose.

In another square Richard Fazzini, co-director of the expedition, confers excitedly with Abd El-Fattah el-Sabbahy, the young Egyptian assigned by his government's Department of Antiquities to the project. They call me over: "Look! One of the Kuftis has just found this when he was clearing up! It was lying upside down, looked like just another rock." It is a fragment of granite statue with hieroglyphs, recognized by Richard as similar to one in the Cairo Museum.

Fazzini's wife, Bobby Giella, photographer for the expedition, snaps away at the finders and their finds whilst Lisa Kuchman, a graduate student in Egyptology at Toronto University and a pottery expert, marks on each basket the date and exact spot where the shards were found.

William Peck, art historian of the Detroit Museum and an expert on ancient Egyptian drawings, meticulously maps the outlines of walls and passageways as they are uncovered by the diggers. He sports a T-shirt made for him by a friend, which bears the legend "W. F. Petrie School of Egyptology" with a heraldic design of spades around the slogan "Dig We Must!"

Our excavators are not the first to be caught up by the puzzling attraction of the Goddess Mut. They were preceded by two doughty Victorian ladies, Miss Benson, daughter of the Archbishop of Canterbury, and her friend Miss Gourlay, who had thought the area "a place to seize upon the imagination" and who dug about, apparently with no very clear idea of what they were doing, during the winters of 1895–97.

I sit on a recently unearthed granite leg, more comfortable than the surrounding rocks, reading up on these ladies in their book *The Temple of Mut at Asher,* published in 1899, whilst observing the dig in progress. Leafing through the Benson-Gourlay photographs that illustrate their book, I see that nothing much seems to have changed at the site, although there is a lovely photo of Miss Benson, tricked out and hatted as though for a croquet party in the Archbishop's garden, supervising the work from the present Reis's hill.

"We were desirous of clearing a picturesque site," writes Miss Benson. "We were frankly warned that we should make no discoveries. . . . Thus we began without any idea of publishing an account of our work. . . . We began our second season in the same mind, but unexpected discoveries demanded publication." (Their publication was by no means universally acclaimed by fellow-Egyptologists; J. Vandier, a French savant, sourly calls it *"déce-vant."*)

Besides describing their finds, the ladies seem to have swiped quite a few of them. "The authorities were very kind in letting us retain many of those objects which were not of importance for exhibition in the museum," observes Miss Benson blandly. In a letter to her mother she says, "We found a rose-granite Osiride sitting statue of Rameses II yesterday," adding in a footnote: "This statue was given to my sister, and is now at Tremans." I am told that some of the Benson loot was recently auctioned at Christie's by a collateral descendant, fetching in excess of a hundred thousand dollars. Today they would not get away with it, for the law now requires that an Egyptian representative of the Department of Antiquities be attached to oversee each foreign concession as watchdog of the treasures.

By nine o'clock the sun is already high, and a welcome breakfast break is announced. We all pile into an ancient Land-Rover, which lurches across a short stretch of rocky desert to the Canada House, built to accommodate the expedition. It is a ramshackle warren of small bedrooms, workrooms, and dining room. Near the entrance to an open-air storage area a sleepy cobra takes his siesta. "He's a bit of a bother," say Bobby Giella, "always lying about on the shards. The snake charmer was supposed to come yesterday, but was delayed." (Shades of trying to get the plumber to call at our house in California!)

Here is my first opportunity to take stock of the diggers, to discover something about their own origins, to probe their motives: what strange compulsion drives this group of young Americans to forsake hearth and home for the dubious pleasure of scrabbling in the hot Egyptian dust from sunup to sundown? And their Egyptian counterpart, Fattah, graduate of the school of Egyptology in Cairo, to choose this arduous, low-paid profession over easier, more remunerative work?

A French scholar of the last century, appalled by the systematic plunder of temples and tombs by Egyptologists of the day, described Egyptology as "a passion so violent that it is inferior to love or ambition only in the pettiness of its aims." As I listen to our excavators explain what is happening at the Temple of Mut, I recognize the violent passion—but the aims have changed radically in the past several decades.

These Egyptologists are driven souls, all right, and when you get to know them they will admit to this. Thus Fattah: "Egyptology is a kind of disease, it's in the blood of a person. Also, I warn you, it's highly contagious!" And Fazzini: "Egyptologists may be nutty, but they are harmless, except possibly to other Egyptologists."

How did they first get started? All seem to have been bitten by this bug at a very young age, five to seven is average. I think of my seven-year-old grandson, the lender of *An Alphabet of Ancient Egypt*, and the strange otherworldly glow in his eyes when he heard that his granny was going to see a dig; is he one of the predestined? If so, he will be in prime time to participate in the Mut excavation, estimated to last for at least twenty-five years.

Richard Fazzini, an ebullient thirty-five-year-old New Yorker who has been digging on and off for some fifteen years between stints as curator of Egyptian art for the Brooklyn Museum, says he does it because it's fun: "There's something new every day, and the day's not long enough to satisfy your interests. You may get engrossed in pottery and neglect your walls. Or you may come across a fragment of a statue that fits another found the year before. It's a constant challenge. Archaeologists are essentially problem-solvers. Go to any dig house and look at the bookshelf—you'll find nothing but mystery stories and science fiction. Most archaeologists are avid mystery readers, and they're also drawn to sci-fi which portrays a vision of different worlds at different times."

I asked Fattah what ultimate dream makes him toil away day after day brushing mud brick. "To see again the whole Precinct of Mut after reconstruction and restoration, with all the temples illuminated! I'll be eighty years old."

The Mut mission is one of a dozen or so international missions in the Luxor-Thebes area. During my stay in Luxor, I met Poles, Austrians, French, English, all no doubt dreaming some variant of Fattah's dream in their respective languages.

Hard by the Canada House, a short walk up the hill, is the concession of Karnak North, sponsored by the Institut Français d'Archéologie. I wander up there, but not alone; one must be accompanied by an Arab with a stout stick to ward off the savage guard dogs, one of which, I am told, chewed up the leg of an unwary tourist only last year. The concession is housed in a fairy-tale stone hut which looks ancient, but was actually built in the 1930s by the Institut. There I find a charming middle-aged couple, Jean and Hélène Jacquet, who have been digging at this site for eight seasons, collecting, surveying, working on publications.

Mme. Jacquet shows her jigsaw-puzzle pottery setup, where she is re-creating large roundish pots from myriad fragments laid out on wood trestle tables. Among these is a pretty and amusing milk jug from which large breasts protrude under the pouring lip, signifying bountifulness. About 99 percent of their finds are potshards, she says. There was once such a wealth of statues and other art objects to be found that nobody paid much attention to pots. All this has changed in the past few years; now the historical significance of stratification, the precise location of the find, and the specific technique of the potter assume great importance.

One remarkable yield at the Jacquets' dig was a loaf of bread dating from the Eighteenth Dynasty. "It smelt fresh, was still soft, you could see the broken wheat grains in the crust," says Mme. Jacquet. "We found it in an airtight layer of sand, which preserved it for some thirty centuries." She shows me a photograph of this bread next to a loaf baked last month by the local villagers; they appear to be identical. (I suppress the unworthy thought that some prankster may have planted some fresh bread at the site for the Jacquets to find.) Did the Jacquets filch a slice or two for their breakfast? "No, the loaf was sent to Paris for analysis, where they'll identify the method of baking, the ingredients, even the recipe!"

Their crowning achievement, says Mme. Jacquet, was discovery just last year of the Eighteenth Dynasty stone Treasury of Thutmose I, a unique find, as stone was generally reserved exclusively for use in temples. "No one suspected the monument was there until we found the stones, all marked 'Treasury' in the hieroglyphs of the day."

As Mme. Jacquet tells it, it all sounds most thrilling and I ask if I might see the Treasury. The Jacquets are amazed: "But you passed right by it, on your way up here!" Much abashed, I ask to have another look and they lead me to the site. I peer down into an area the size of a large paddock, covered with flagstones in which are embedded occasional round stones: the result of eight years' unremitting toil. Alas, I fear the true spirit of Egyptology will ever elude me.

Credit for the initial development of modern techniques of excavation—the careful recording of dwelling sites and artifacts of daily use as distinct from the mere plunder of tombs and temples for valuable objects—is widely bestowed on W. Flinders Petrie, the British archaeologist who, starting in 1880, dug up and down the Nile for more than forty years. It was he, I was told, who originally trained the Kuftis, those mysterious and talented villagers whose name keeps cropping up wherever two or three archaeologists are gathered together to discuss digs in progress; his methods, handed down by Kuftis from father to son, account for the esteem in which these highly skilled men are held by the Egyptologists of today.

Who trained whom? I wondered after spending a day with the Kuftis. Did they not, in fact, initiate Petrie into the techniques of discovery? In any event Petrie seems to have heartily loathed them (a sentiment fully reciprocated, as I learned): "The Kuftis proved to be the most troublesome people that I have ever worked with," he wrote. "The pertinacity with which the rascals of the place would dog our steps about our house, and at the work, was amazing." Later he grudgingly amends this harsh judgment with true British Raj condescension: "Among this rather untoward people we found however as in every place a small percentage of excellent men . . . the very best type of native, faithful, friendly and laborious. . . ."

Five of us set off for Kuft early one Friday, the Muslim holy day and day off at the dig: Richard, Bobby, Erich, Fattah, who will interpret, and I. We head for the home of Farouk, the Reis of the Mut excavation, weaving our way through labyrinthine dirt roads flanked by mud-brick dwellings.

We are ushered into the large, mud-floored living area where bronze-faced Kuftis are beginning to gather—"Our group looks so washed-out and bland compared to them!" says Bobby. Richard opens with a few words of introduction and background: "The people of this village really did a great deal of the work in all of the most important excavations. Some of them have amazing skills, the full extent of their contribution has never been told properly before." (This will shortly be corrected; Lisa Kuchman and Fattah are collaborating on the first full-length study ever to be written about the Kuftis.)

There follows an interminable wait while the rituals of hospitality are attended to. Each Kufti who enters is introduced all round, we shake hands, he offers a cigarette to each of our group. Richard quickly explains that once having accepted a cigarette, it would be bad manners to refuse subsequent offers; consequently, I soon have fifteen cigarettes ranged at my place at table. Tea is now brought, and the Kuftis leave the room while we drink, reappearing to clear off the tea things—a custom, says Richard, that obtains throughout the Middle East; the hosts traditionally serve their guests and then withdraw.

More time goes by while people go in search of the village elders, who eventually assemble. Sayed Mahmoud, immensely impressive seventy-eight-year-old patriarch, does almost all the talking, although the others join in from time to time with animated agreement, particularly when Mahmoud is describing Kufti links with the ancients. We cover considerable ground: the Kufti appraisal of Petrie, their hopes for the Mut excavation, their opinion of the various nationalities involved in the digs.

Sayed Mahmoud, first trained by his uncle from the age of thirteen, has worked in some of the major excavations of this century. What does he consider the most important find that he personally was involved in during this long labor? He thinks awhile; probably the underground rooms full of mummified people and animals at the temple in Tuna El Gebel. But he expects the excavation at Mut to transcend this in terms of historical discovery because of the care with which finds are recorded: "We'll find everything concerning the daily life of early Egyptians there; it will be one of the most productive sites because nobody has worked it before."

What about Petrie? I ask. Was he a nice man, a bad man? "Petrie was a thief!" comes the reply. "He took things that didn't belong to him. He never photographed or recorded objects he found, he just kept them." (The latter statement would be disputed by many historians of Egyptology, although Mme. Jacquet did tell me that Petrie was apt to be slapdash in his methods, "always in a hurry, had no time for adequate drawings or descriptions.") "He encouraged the workers to find things, he'd give them a tip: for beads, ten piasters; for a scarab, a pound. They liked *that*, but not him. Today, with the Egyptian Department of Antiquities overseeing the work, all that is changed, it's in safe hands; everything is being registered and photographed, and foreigners are no longer allowed to take things out of the country."

Does he discern any differences between the various nationalities working in excavating missions—any favorites? The best, he thinks, are the Egyptians. He likes the Americans because they are meticulous about recording finds. The Russians? "We were working for a Russian expedition in Nubia. The director, who had no experience, called a meeting of the workers and begged us to help him find objects that he could report back to his government." Mahmoud chuckles at the recollection: "We worked for sixteen days and found nothing. The director fell sick as a result, he pleaded with us to show him the place where objects could be found. At last we did find a few, so he was satisfied and got better. But at that expedition the Kuftis were really directing the excavation while the Russians did the heavy work, digging and carrying the baskets, because they wanted to avoid paying for the labor!"

Beyond the obvious motive of earning a living by this work, what else do the Kuftis get out of it in the way of gratification? I ask. There follows an emotional speech in which other Kuftis join, all now talking at once, their lively and expressive faces full of a passionate desire to get the point across to us. The gist is that the Kuftis feel as though each object belonged to their ancestors, that they themselves are a part of those ancient finds; that the Kuftis have a unique and special role of which they are very proud: "We have this feeling that nobody except us knows how to work in this field."

The discussion over, we are treated to a magnificent song-and-dance act put on by the score or so of Kuftis gathered in the living room. At the windows, dozens of small nut-brown children are hanging on the bars, waving, laughing, cheering on the singers. The performance begins with a chant, led by the Reis and beautifully sung in chorus by the others, in which first Richard and then the rest of us are honored in turn. Translated by Fattah, the words go something like this:

> Welcome, welcome to the one who comes,
> Welcome, welcome our director comes,

Welcome, welcome these our guests,
Welcome, welcome just arrived [they turn to me],
Welcome, welcome the Chief Inspector comes [Fattah],
Welcome, welcome the guests of foreman Farouk.
The fancy chair for this our guest
Who comes to light up this house.

Then, getting louder and faster:

With peace our bey and director,
Our guests with peace,
And our cook with peace,
And Kuftis with peace.
Just now, Director, you came
Bringing light to the desert and the house.
Just now, Madame, you came [Bobby]
Bringing light to the desert and the house. . . .

Now they break into a wild and joyous dance that reminds me of
the Highland fling, which culminates in hoisting Richard on the
shoulders of a Kufti and parading him around the room.

Nor is this all. The cook now comes into his own and we are
served a tasty feast of vegetable soup and roast duck as grand
finale to our visit.

Reflecting on this delightful encounter with the Kuftis, I felt I
had stumbled across a significant aspect of excavation that is almost entirely ignored in the voluminous writings of Egyptologists;
there is not a word about Kuftis in Howard Carter's classic account of the discovery of Tutankhamun's tomb, although they
were part of the work force that made the crucial discovery of the
first step of the staircase leading to the tomb, without which the
tomb would never have been found. It took a new wave of
archaeologists—Lisa Kuchman, the Fazzinis, and their colleagues, sensitized no doubt by their college years in the turbulent,
civil-rights-conscious sixties—to cut through the pervasive racism
exemplified by Petrie's remarks about the Kuftis and to accord

them long-overdue recognition as *primus inter pares,* first among equals of the excavation teams.

On the road to Abydos, a two-and-a-half-hour drive from Luxor, we happen upon some scenes of startling beauty that could have come straight out of the tomb paintings: a tall Egyptian farmer driving a pair of sleek oxen to which are attached a primitive one-piece plow; harvesters reaping the pale green sugar cane; a *sakieh*, or water wheel, in operation, a marvelous ox-drawn Rube Goldberg contraption of wheels-within-wheels from which dangle large earthenware pots endlessly collecting and spilling out the water over the fields. The agricultural implements seem unchanged since Pharaonic times. We stop briefly at Dendera, where in the shadow of the Ptolemaic temple a funeral procession of some two hundred mourners winds toward the cemetery—again, a tomb painting come to life. The deceased, we learn, is the young son of the mayor, killed in a shooting accident. He is uncoffined, wrapped in a winding sheet, the traditional Muslim way of preparing the dead for burial.

Our destination is the home of Um Seti (meaning Mother of Seti), a legendary seventy-three-year-old Englishwoman of whom we have heard much from the Luxor crowd. She has a considerable reputation, is said to be a magnificent copyist who has done remarkable work in many important excavations. Her real name is Dorothy Eadie, and she was written up briefly in *Life*'s 1968 series on Egypt as fancifully having come to believe she is the mother of Pharaoh Seti I.

Abydos—population 409, according to the guidebook—is a village of mud huts dominated by the vast Temple of Seti I (*c.* 1320 B.C.). I take a quick look through the temple, a massive structure built into the hillside, but avoid the guided tour, as my sights are set on the deluded English lady.

To reach her dwelling, one crosses some disused train tracks into a large dusty courtyard where village children eagerly show the way to her house: "Um Seti! Um Seti!" they cry, pointing to a wall with a small door set partway up that looks as though it might lead to a chicken house. There is a frayed pull-cord but no bell rings, just a slight thumping of wood on wood. Um Seti admits Erich and me, and we climb over the threshold into her yard.

She is small, thin, wizened, her face a crisscross of wrinkles. We sit at her table, swarming with flies; she offers bread, wine, and processed cheese and settles down to tell her life story, which I gather is a bit of a set piece that she willingly repeats to anyone who will hold still for it.

"I used to run away from my school in Dulwich, where we lived, to the British Museum. One day Dr. Wallis Budge, who was working there in the Egyptian department, asked me why I was never in school. I said, because I wanted to learn to read the hieroglyphics which was not taught at my school. He offered to teach me, and he did! I was nine years old at the time."

"Didn't your parents punish you for running away?" I asked. "Oh, yes, they punished me, but they couldn't stop me. Nobody can ever stop me from doing what I want to do"—this spoken in the self-congratulatory tones of one who knows she is a rum old bird and makes the most of it.

"I went to a horrid school, a seminary for young ladies. Dreadful place, I was bored to tears. When I was ten I was expelled for throwing a hymnbook at the teacher. The hymn we were supposed to be singing had a line in it that went 'God curse the swarth Egyptian.' Well, I refused to sing *that*."

Her first intimation as to her true Egyptian origins had occurred much earlier. "When I was three, I fell downstairs and was pronounced dead. But by the time the doctor came the corpse was quite lively. I kept saying, 'I want to go home.' Where is your home? he asked. 'I don't know, but I want to go home.' Then when I was six I saw a picture of this temple in an encyclopedia my father had given me. '*That's* my home!' I told him. 'But why is it all broken up—where's the garden?' He said 'Don't be silly, that's just an old ruined temple, thousands of years old.' But I found the garden in 1956. They were building workshops on it—I told them, 'You shouldn't be putting that in the garden,' and sure enough I found the little irrigation channels and fossilized remnants of bushes, flowers, fruit trees."

Um Seti came to Egypt at the age of twenty-eight and has never been back to England. She was married briefly to an Egyptian: "He couldn't stand my cooking. Also he liked only modern things, I only liked ancient objects. We divorced after two years." Thereafter she worked for the Department of Antiquities in the capacity of "daily paid skilled workman," excavating, cataloguing, assembling pottery fragments. "In the Department, I'm known as 'the Mad One,' " she says in her complacent way.

She has done considerable writing about antiquity but claims that most of her work was plagiarized or stolen by dishonest colleagues. This autumn, her *Story of Abydos* is scheduled to be published in the United States: "I'm relying on Tutankhamun for advance publicity in America, although I never did like that family." He died young, didn't he? I ask. "Yes, Horemheb saw to that—he gave him a good wallop in the head. Oh, Tutankhamun was thoroughly spoiled! Of course until he was eighteen he had to do what he was told, so he never was a real ruler." She gossips on about the family, Akhenaten, Nefertiti, and their children: "Akhenaten was a pacifist, of course, let the country go to pot. But Nefertiti wouldn't stand for it; she left him and who can blame her?"

Did Um Seti ever see her parents again? I ask. "My mother came out once, but we quarreled—we didn't see eye to eye about Hitler. I cried for three days when Hitler died. Recently I read *The Last 100 Days*, and I cried all over again. Oh, he may have been a little rough on some people but we could use somebody like him today."

I am getting rather fed up with Um Seti and her fly-infested hovel, so we take our leave after briefly inspecting her eternal resting place, a brick tomb that she had constructed in a corner of the yard. Erich observes that it's no wonder she admired Hitler:

"It fits right in with the authoritarian, static Egype of the Pharaohs." Her adopted son, Seti I, seems to have been a thoroughly
nasty piece of work, too; like Hitler, "an upstart with no royal
lineage behind him," according to Sir Alan Gardiner, one of his
main legacies a charter prescribing "frightful punishments" for
his political enemies.

Um Seti's delusion may be just an extreme example of the most
striking characteristic of the Egyptological mind: its total divorce-
ment from contemporary happenings, its equally total involve-
ment with the world of thirty centuries ago. Glimpses of this come
through in the writings of the early practitioners. Thus Miss Benson in a letter to her mother: "Lucy so excited on the political
situation gives me quite a turn. We try to talk politics a little, but
on the whole talk more about what happened 6,000 years ago."
And Sir Alan Gardiner, blissfully oblivious of the world about
him: "We started on our summer holiday in 1914 with the happiest hopes. . . . I was to go ahead of the others to do some work in
Berlin. . . . We met in Copenhagen, and hearing news of the
declaration of war crossed over to Sweden." The good soul adds,
"I was myself too ignorant and careless of politics to have even a
suspicion of the impending tragedy."

Time and again I bore witness to this curiously detached frame
of mind. During my stay in Luxor, the French elections, fateful
for Europe, took place; the outcome of the American coal miners'
strike hung in the balance; Israeli troops crossed into Lebanon.
Erich and I, who privately agreed we were the only sane people in
Luxor, were longing for news of these events but not a word of
any of this was breathed by our new-found Egyptologist friends.
"Doesn't anybody here ever read a newspaper, or listen to the
news on the radio?" I asked. Well, no; but the deepest passions are
stirred by politics of the Eighteenth Dynasty, furious arguments
rage over assessment of the true role of Tutankhamun, or
Akhenaten, or the goddess Mut.

Item: We are in the tomb of Rekhmire, Theban nobleman of the Eighteenth Dynasty, gazing at the magnificent wall paintings of hunting, fishing, banqueting scenes. One wall is devoted to temple workshops showing leatherworkers, carpenters, blacksmiths, brickmakers. Erich Lessing, a Bible expert, tells me that the last are believed to be the Children of Israel in slavery, making bricks without straw as per the account in Exodus. James Manning, eyes blazing, bursts out: "That's hogwash! Absolute hogwash!" Lessing, possibly fearing fisticuffs, beats a hasty retreat: "I only said *believed* to be."

Item: An Egyptologist who wishes to remain anonymous takes violent issue with the widely held assumption that Akhenaten sought to introduce monotheism into Egypt. "Bullshit!" he shouts angrily. "It was his mother, Queen Tiy, who was the genius behind that movement. Akhenaten was an epileptic idiot, a freak!" Seeing that I am writing this down, he adds hastily "For God's sake, don't quote me on that." Does he half believe, I wonder, that Akhenaten might yet spring from the nether shores into his sturdy funeral barque to bring a defamation-of-character suit in the nearest courthouse?

Item: What of the goddess Mut? A banal cipher, the unimportant, simple wife of the great god Amon? "Not a bit of it!" exclaims one of the Egyptomaniacs (as I have come to think of them). "Mark my words, although she's been terribly neglected—there's hardly a mention, not even a monograph, about her in the scholarly literature—she'll end up being recognized as one of the most complex, diversified deities in the whole Egyptian pantheon! It will be an unveiling!" Given the urgent immediacy with which these remarks were delivered, he could, I thought, be expounding on the posthumous reputation of an Indira Gandhi, a Golda Meir. . . .

TRIP NOTES

There are daily planes to Aswan but we opt for the stately train, the Cairo all-sleeping-car express which disgorges most of its passengers in Luxor and proceeds to Aswan, a three-hour run. Erich, Fattah, and I are ready for the 7 a.m. departure but the train is not; after an hour's wait, Fattah consults the stationmaster, who explains the driver overslept! At last we are on board, our compartment like one of the shabbier efforts of the British Railways but actually, Erich tells me, built by the Hungarians in the 1960s. The scenery gets lusher and more tropical as we approach Nubia. We head for the Old Cataract Hotel, its magnificent outdoor-indoor terrace with brightly painted basket chairs unchanged since Agatha Christie described it in *Death on the Nile*. One can even get Pimm's Cup there. The hotel garden is a spectacular riot of giant hollyhocks, banana plants, and brilliant flower beds; I would gladly have tarried there, but our purpose is to meet Fattah's colleague Gamal Wahbah, director of the Salvage of Philae Monuments, and to learn something of his work.

Travelers of the last century described Philae, then known as "the Pearl of Egypt," in rhapsodic terms. Amelia Edwards, who went there in 1873, wrote: "Seen from the level of a small boat, the island, with its palms, its colonnades, its pylons, seems to rise out of the river like a mirage. . . . As the boat glides nearer between glistening boulders, those sculptured towers rise higher and even higher against the sky. They show no sign of ruin or of age. All looks solid, stately, perfect."

The feathery palms, the glistening boulders, the sculptured towers have long since been submerged by the waters of the dam—to rise again, however, under the guiding hand of a remarkable twenty-eight-year-old Egyptian scholar, Gamal Wahbah.

We drive to Gamal's office near Aswan, partake of the regulation hot, sweet black tea, and depart by boat for the island of Agilkia, a granite rock on which we can already see the stunning fruits of Gamal's labors: vast colonnades and pylons, just as Amelia Edwards saw them, "solid, stately, perfect," soaring against the glaring blue Egyptian sky. Fattah is amazed; he was here on a visit with Bobby Giella only last year, when there was nothing but a concrete foundation. How is it done?

UNESCO has funded the operation to the tune of some twenty

million dollars; an Italian contracting company, Condotti Dotte-mazzi, does some of the rebuilding, but Gamal vehemently stresses time and again that responsibility for the direction of the work is in Egyptian hands: "The foreign expeditions have Egyptians attached to them, but here it's *all* Egyptian: the chief engineer, the architect, the workers—all the preparations and experience are furnished by Egyptians."

From Moustapha Naqui, chief engineer, we learn something of the magnitude and method of the operation, which began in 1972 and will be finished in '79. His first step was to build a cofferdam round Philae, pump out the water, remove the mud from monuments and pavements. The engineers made a complete plan of the temples, giving the exact position and measurements of each stone dismantled—more than forty-two thousand blocks. These were kept in a storage area while the work of preparing a foundation on Agilkia went forward. There are more dizzying statistics—heights, widths, numbers of pottery fragments found—but I don't pay much attention because I am seeing it all happen before my eyes; even as Naqui is speaking, two workmen are struggling with bits of a stone king, fitting them together to be put in place in the pylon.

We wander through the work in progress and Gamal points out the cornice, with bas-reliefs of Ptolemy giving offerings to Isis, already reconstructed from scattered blocks and erected in its original position. Along the way, Gamal and his co-workers have come upon some important discoveries: "The second pylon had lost the three upper courses, missing since before Napoleon's day. We found the scattered stones and for the first time in modern history those courses have been replaced, and the pylon is complete."

In another major discovery, during the dismantling the excavators found more than two hundred re-used blocks of a small Twenty-sixth Dynasty chapel from which they have reconstituted complete scenes, soon to be rebuilt as originally conceived. Thus Agilkia, the Cultured Pearl of Egypt, so to speak, may end up outshining its predecessor. The major reconstruction will be completed by April, 1978, after which Agilkia will be opened to tourists; nor is this all, for in another two years the inhospitable granite will be covered with imported soil to nourish plants, palm trees, grass, flower gardens, a reincarnation of Philae as the ancients knew it.

Gamal is currently working on a book about the restoration of Philae, and the new light shed by his team on the history of the island, formerly thought to contain only Ptolemaic relics: "We found work by Ramses II, also artifacts from the Twelfth Dynasty, more than a thousand years before the Ptolemys."

Again, key to success of the operation are the Kuftis, ten of whom live here in tents the year round except for an occasional visit home to their families in Kuft. "They are very, very intelligent," says Gamal with measured emphasis. "Their eyes have the experience of the antiquities, they have soft hands to clean the objects. They supervise the other workers and make sure the blocks are put in the right position, and inform us if anything goes wrong." The chief Kufti, Doctor Sha'had, is now introduced. Is Mr. Sha'had a Ph.D., then? I ask Fattah. "No, his family named him Doctor because they hoped he'd be one!"

We now take a short boat ride to Philae to watch the diving operation in which the stones outside the cofferdam are retrieved from the depths of the Nile under the joint direction of Lieutenant Commander David A. Bartlett of the British Navy and his Egyptian counterpart, Lieutenant Commander Tarik Fifaat. Twelve English lads and twelve Egyptians work in pairs from derelicts moored near the submerged island. The commanders seem like perfect specimens of their respective nationalities: Bartlett, a handsome, rugged, blue-eyed man; and Fifaat so slender and mobile, his black eyes fringed with the double-thick lashes that have been one of the most attractive features of Egyptians since the days of tomb paintings.

Bartlett shows me a 1902 photograph of Philae as it then was, part of a large collection from the British Museum which they use as a guide to reconstruction of the temples. "There are about three hundred and fifty stones to be recovered from the Temple of Augustus, two hundred and forty have been brought up so far," he says. An Egyptian and an English frogman are preparing to dive, struggling into their thick black outfits and compressed-air gear. They splash in, and guide the waiting hook and rope dangled from a crane to their quarry. There is a brief flurry when it turns out they brought up the wrong thing, a stone from a pillar, as yet unmarked—they are supposed to go only for the loose ones. "If a stone is taken from a pillar at random, once raised, there's no way of knowing its right position in the temple," Bartlett explains. "Once it's marked, and the mud cleared off it, we can look at the code years from now and see how it fits in the wall." Bartlett himself dives down to mark the blocks for the use of the archaeologists.

Bartlett may be one of those to whom, as Fattah said, Egyptology is "highly contagious." Except for occasional brief calls at Egyptian ports, he had never stayed there until this assignment came along two years ago. He immediately started reading up on Philae and became totally absorbed in the island's history. "I find it absolutely fascinating, specially to be working in the shadow of the new Philae being constructed." He goes over there about once a week to see how it's coming along, and is "amazed at it all." He hopes to come back for the official opening—"that is if I'm invited. It'll be a grand ceremony, no doubt, with boatloads of dignitaries from all over Egypt."

Curiously, the Philae reconstruction, now almost completed, has never attracted the attention of the media, Gamal Wahbah tells me. He has seven papers in the works, shortly to be published in scholarly journals; but as far as he knows, there has been no mention of the project in the popular press: "Even when an official delegation from UNESCO arrived to inspect the work, the Egyptian papers gave it only a few lines." Could Erich and I have chanced upon a journalistic scoop—a hard enough feat at the best of times and the more so when the makings of the scoop are already many centuries old—and all because Fattah was anxious to resume his friendship with a former colleague?

Returning to the Mut Precinct after several days' absence, I find our diggers have made all sorts of progress: new bits of wall and entranceways have been uncovered, William Peck's map showing these is coming along apace. "Look, we've completely cleared the forecourt, an architectural unit not known before—all previous maps ended at the pylon." Richard's mud-brick housing units are beginning to emerge as a coherent plan, now tentatively thought by the excavators to be remains of a Coptic settlement of the sixth century A.D. What's more, he has found several interesting objects, including a hoard of coins and a pair of dice; first one die was found, a week later its mate. "Fun and games in ancient Egypt!" he exclaims. Best of all, Peck has just received proofs of his forthcoming book, *Drawings from Ancient Egypt*, which will be lavishly illustrated with photographs taken by his co-author, John G. Ross. Among the hitherto unpublished offerings are "erotica and scurrilities which do not form part of the repertoire of the monumental artists, and give a glimpse of another face of Egypt beneath the veil of Isis," plus "many comic or satirical drawings—a topsy-turvy world in which cats serve mice, and the fox is the trusted guardian of the geese." I can hardly wait for the finished book, which is scheduled for publication this autumn in England, Germany, France, and the United States.

TRIP NOTES

My last night in Egypt. I have said goodbye to those dear demented diggers and am packing up my own loot; best buys in the Luxor market are polished Egyptian cotton, priced after the requisite bargaining at about six Egyptian pounds per 6½-yard length; rings of debased but pretty silver set with semiprecious (or more likely semi-demi-precious) stones, said to be nineteenth century, one to two pounds; hand-strung Nubian beads, one pound a strand; saffron, at the astonishingly low price of less than one Egyptian pound per pound of weight, although it does seem to contain a certain amount of chicken feathers and other extraneous matter. Worst buys are the horrid little fake scarabs and statues pressed upon one by vendors everywhere. "But, Madame, it's an antiquity!" said one. "Or it will be, if you keep it for a hundred years."

I think back to my first conversation with James Manning. If it is sunrise for the science of Egyptology, he said, it may well be sunset for life in Luxor as experienced by travelers over the past century. The calashes, he fears, will soon be replaced by an efficient motor-bus system; already hideous concrete hotels are sprouting along the banks of the Nile. And shall we see, in place of the ancient mud-brick village that borders the Precinct of Mut, a spanking new Mut-el?

COMMENT

In the summer of 1977 I had a letter from the editor of *Geo*, a lavishly produced West German text-and-picture magazine, asking if I would do an article about San Francisco. Regretfully (for *Geo* pays top prices) I declined. I explained to the editor that, having lived in the San Francisco area for several decades, I did not think that I could produce an original and lively piece on the subject; he would do better to find a writer for whom California would be a totally new experience and who would see it all with a fresh eye.

By one of those coincidences that disturb the even flow of life, the day after I met James Manning there came another letter from the editor: Was there *anywhere* I would like to go for *Geo?* How about Egypt, I wrote (halfway hoping he would say that was too far afield). Done, he replied. Almost immediately I began to get cold feet—or, rather, to fear hot feet, having heard dread tales of the assaulting heat in those parts—but there had now been an Offer and an Acceptance, as the law of contracts has it, so I felt committed. Why hadn't I plunged for San Francisco? Too late.

In taking on the Egyptian caper, I realized that I was violating two of my cardinal self-imposed rules about writing: never embark on a project unless you are deeply fascinated by it, and absorb all available information about your subject before approaching the target of the investigation. Obviously, since I knew nothing about Egypt I was not deeply fascinated; equally obviously, here was one case in which it would be folly to try to absorb even a fraction of the "available information." Hence the elaborate disclaimer on pages 247–48, a useful trick of the trade by which one hopes to disarm the critical reader, although actually I boned up on Egypt a good deal more than I let on.

Despite misgivings, I was looking forward to this adventure. It would be, for me, a complete departure from the abrasive, contentious, dog-eat-dog world of courtrooms, business, and bureaucracy to which I had become accustomed in my capacity of muckraker. What could be more pleasantly relaxing than to explore the quiet realms of Pharaonic life in the company of dedicated, dispassionate scholars who are unharried by worldly preoccupations and immune to the crass self-interest that motivates the rest of us, their only desire in life to contribute in some modest way to the sum total of mankind's knowledge of the Ancients?

Disillusionment was not long in coming. Muck in the archaeology world, I soon discovered, is knee-deep, there for the raking. Erich Lessing, a connoisseur of Egypt who had photographed in these same precincts twelve years earlier and had visited numerous excavation sites, clued me in: "Scratch the surface and you'll find the crudest, most vicious jockeying for position amongst these distinguished academics. . . ."

As days went on, I picked up all sorts of hints confirming Erich's diagnosis of the real malady endemic to the Egyptologist, but this story could not be told then, because it was not what *Geo* wanted, and cannot be told now—it would involve, for me, revealing too many half-whispered confidences of people who in some ways resemble the inmates of a lunatic asylum. Like those inmates, they are full of real or imagined fears, beset by notions of betrayal and perfidy, consumed by irrational jealousies. Apparently it was ever thus: in *Tutankhamun: The Untold Story*, Thomas Hoving, former head of the Metropolitan Museum, gives a devastating picture of the political intrigue, backbiting, unremitting infighting that characterized the Tutankhamun expeditions— not a word of which is breathed by Howard Carter in his account of the discovery, in which all is high-minded devotion to the science of archaeology.

It is hard to conceive of what gives rise to these quirky characteristics; surely not a lust after material wealth, for the chosen life style of the Egyptologist is austere in the extreme. Desire for power? Perhaps, in the constricted sense of power in that field of endeavor. A place in history, or at least a footnote in some archaeological journal? Who knows. Perhaps some go-ahead psychiatric institute should establish a chair for the specific purpose of finding out what makes Egyptologists tick.

Fortunately Erich Lessing, who was commissioned by *Geo* to supply the photographs for my piece, proved to be a rock of sanity in this queer ambience, and in many ways a kindred soul. Like me, he was unenthralled by mounds of ancient rubble, by the omnipresent "storage areas" filled with fragments of stones and broken bits of statues so beloved by the Egyptomaniacs, by those highly prized shards whose careful cataloguing was a major preoccupation of the diggers. (In my piece for *Geo*, mindful of the probable desire of its Teutonic readers for solid and scholarly information, I put in many paragraphs about those dismal shards, their historic importance, new developments in coding and dating them, which out of consideration for the English and American reader I have cut from the version given here.)

"Oh dear, if I never see another shard in my life it won't be too soon," I sighed to Erich as we stumbled about yet another storage area. He muttered something in German that sounded like "shard." What was that? I asked. "It's a German word, *'Schaden-*

freude, " he said. "Roughly translated, it means 'malicious joy in the misfortune of others.' " Which seemed to sum up the whole Egyptomaniacal experience.

The ending of this piece gave me trouble. Ambivalent as I was (and am) about the Egypt freaks, my original final paragraph ran as follows: "Listening to them tell of these developments, my unfortunate inborn propensity for skepticism and scoffing dissolves, and I feel most privileged to have met this attractive and dedicated group of people, to have had the rare opportunity of being in on the ground floor of some of their achievements."

This ending was greeted with shrieks of derision by those to whom I sent a draft copy of the manuscript. My daughter: "That's *really* phony, doesn't sound like you at all." Robert Gottlieb at Knopf: "What's the matter? You've gone all soft and sugary." Marge Frantz, valued helper and adviser: "Sounds like a cop-out, after all you told me about it." Pulling myself together, I rewrote the ending as in the version given here.

However, as the reader may have divined, the final-final ending was not too satisfactory to me either, for it contains no hint of my real dilemma. Going to Egypt in search of a restful vacation from my métier, I found muck up to the armpits. Had my rake been out and at the ready, I could have piled the stuff up—but *where?* There was nowhere to unload it. Restraint may not be in my nature but in this case, being for hire to *Geo*, I reluctantly hung up the rake—and although the aroma of such alluring potential muck heaps as the Coca-Cola Connection set my nostrils aquiver, I resolutely turned my back and made not the slightest inquiry as to why Coca-Cola was suddenly courting an Egyptian goddess of many millennia ago. Could it have something to do with the Arab blacklist to which the purveyors of this revolting beverage had been consigned as traders with Israel? I shall never know. "Get thee behind me, Coca-Cola" was my slogan as I staggered around the Mut excavation site. So I include "Egyptomania" here with apologies, merely as an example of one that got away.

OTHER NEW YORK REVIEW CLASSICS*

* For a complete list of titles, visit www.nyrb.com or write to:
Catalog Requests, NYRB, 435 Hudson Street, New York, NY 10014